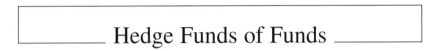

Hedge Funds of Funds

For other titles in the Wiley Finance Series
please see www.wiley.com/finance

Hedge Funds of Funds

A Guide for Investors

Chris Jones

John Wiley & Sons, Ltd

Other Wiley Editorial Offices

John Wiley & Sons Inc., 111 River Street, Hoboken, NJ 07030, USA

Jossey-Bass, 989 Market Street, San Francisco, CA 94103-1741, USA

Wiley-VCH Verlag GmbH, Boschstr. 12, D-69469 Weinheim, Germany

John Wiley & Sons Australia Ltd, 42 McDougall Street, Milton, Queensland 4064, Australia

John Wiley & Sons (Asia) Pte Ltd, 2 Clementi Loop #02-01, Jin Xing Distripark, Singapore 129809

John Wiley & Sons Canada Ltd, 6045 Freemont Blvd, Mississauga, ONT, L5R 4J3, Canada

Wiley also publishes its books in a variety of electronic formats. Some content that appears in print may not
be available in electronic books.

Anniversary Logo Design: Richard J. Pacifico

Library of Congress Cataloging-in-Publication Data
Jones, C. M. (Chris M.)
  Hedge funds of funds : a guide for investors / Chris
Jones.
      p. cm. — (Wiley finance series)
  Includes bibliographical references and index.
  ISBN 978-0-470-06205-0 (Cloth : alk. paper)
1. Hedge funds.   I. Title.
  HG4530.J664 2007
  332.64'524—dc22
                            2007041622

British Library Cataloguing in Publication Data

A catalogue record for this book is available from the British Library

ISBN 978-0-470-06205-0 (HB)

Typeset in 11/13pt Times by Thomson Digital
Printed and bound in Great Britain by TJ International Ltd, Padstow, Cornwall
This book is printed on acid-free paper responsibly manufactured from sustainable forestry
in which at least two trees are planted for each one used for paper production.

Contents

Preface

This book is aimed at those interested in understanding, working in or investing with hedge funds of funds. There are some fantastic books on underlying hedge funds (for me the best is Ridley (2006)), however, from my point of view as Chief Investment Officer of Key Asset Management – itself a hedge fund of funds – there has been nothing that I could recommend to those interested in this specific area. To redress this, I decided to write a book in this area that could be used by Key's potential investors and our trainees but also be beneficial to my students on the course I teach on this area at Cambridge; hopefully, the readership will extend a little beyond these groups also. To this end, I have sought to be as jargon-free and informal as possible whilst retaining a good degree of rigour – a bit of a tall order at times. Finally, I am not a great fan of books in this area that try to be coldly technical and dispassionate about their subject and so I have tried to be as pragmatic as possible and 'tell it like it is' even when this may not be to the benefit my 'day job'. If nothing else, this approach should give readers an inside view of the area and empower them with some tools to get to the bottom of how hedge funds of funds really work – for good and bad.

CMJ
Cambridge

Acknowledgements

I would like to thank Toby Goodworth, Igor Puljic, Philippa Owen, Emily Porter, Gideon Margo, Raj Dutta and Simon Ewart at Key Asset Management and Stuart Martin at Magdalene College Cambridge for their support, interest and encouragement with the writing of this book. Particular thanks to Toby and Gideon for their proof reading and helpful suggestions.

This book would not exist without the unconditional support and unflagging good humour of my wife, Cassie Jones, to whom I owe immeasurable gratitude.

I dedicate this book to my grandfather, William Symonds, who was rather ill during its last months of writing yet never forgot to ask about its progress:

William Henry Symonds
1917 – 2007.

Chris Jones

Part I

An Introduction to Hedge Funds and Hedge Funds of Funds

1
Introduction

1.1 ABOUT THIS BOOK

This book is about *hedge fund of funds* – funds which invest across a range of underlying hedge funds. The aim of the book is to describe what hedge funds of funds do and how they do it, and to give help and advice on assessing and investing with them. As such, it should be of use to anyone who needs to gain a deeper understanding of hedge funds of funds such as the following:

- Existing and potential hedge fund investors
- Existing and potential hedge fund of funds investors
- Hedge fund of funds personnel
- Trainee hedge fund of funds managers and analysts
- Hedge funds and their marketers
- Investment consultants
- Academics and students of the area
- Those seeking to work in the area
- Hedge fund of funds administrators
- Prime broker capital introduction personnel
- Hedge fund of funds lawyers
- Hedge fund of funds leverage providers and structurers

Given that this book describes how a hedge fund of funds assesses underlying hedge funds, those that invest directly into hedge funds themselves may also find this book of use. Also, many hedge fund managers and their marketers, especially those just setting up, tend to find the hedge fund of funds investment process somewhat opaque, and so I would hope that this book may also allow them to get a better understanding of this approach.

The book is split into four parts:

- Part I takes an introductory look at both hedge funds and hedge fund of funds.

- Part II is dedicated to understanding what a hedge fund of fund does and offers tips and advice on how to do it.
- Part III offers advice and help on selecting a suitable hedge fund of funds with which to invest.
- Part IV takes things up a notch by talking about some of the more complex ways to access hedge funds such as through structured products, portable alpha and hybrid products.

In this book, I have tried my hardest to be clear, honest, objective and concise. However, it should be noted that I work as the Chief Investment Officer of Key Asset Management – a 17 year old hedge fund of funds with USD 2bn under management – and so I obviously believe in the benefits of investing this way. In the spirit of fairness, I have indicated in the text when I believe my opinion has been a viewpoint rather than fact. Furthermore, the more rampantly opinionated of my comments have been quarantined in a section that appears throughout the book entitled 'Off The Record', which should be assumed to be subjective.

I have aimed for this book to be as pragmatic as possible, and to this end I have included two sizeable practical examples of investment reports on both a hedge fund and a hedge fund of funds at the end of Parts II and III, respectively.

As I mentioned above, the world of hedge funds is very much ridden with jargon and, given the complexity in this area, sometimes specific terminology is unavoidable, so I have included a glossary of all jargon used at the end of each chapter in Part I, with a glossary for the entire book in an Appendix.

1.2 OVERVIEW

Part I of this book is an introductory section. Here, I aim to introduce and define the concepts of hedge funds and hedge funds of funds and discuss what they do and what investment strategies they use. We will take a look at who invests in this space and why and the reasons why assets have been growing so much of late.

In Chapter 1, below, I define and describe both hedge funds and hedge funds of funds and we will take a look at the causes for recent growth. In Chapter 2 we will take a closer look at the hedge fund space by looking at the different types of strategies hedge funds practice. In Chapter 3 we will take a look at the rationale for investing in this area and take a look at the nature of returns one can expect and the reasons why different investor types chose to invest. In the final chapter of this section, I lay out the pros and cons of investing with hedge funds of funds over investing directly into hedge funds.

1.3   WHAT ARE HEDGE FUNDS?

Hedge funds are becoming hard to ignore. From the first hedge fund in 1949 until very recently, these investment vehicles have been the secret of those who are 'in the know'. But lately, hedge funds have received more and more coverage from the international press, and more and more investment from both private investors and institutions. Over the past 10 years, assets managed by hedge funds have grown exponentially, with estimates indicating that there is now over one trillion US dollars invested in this area. But what are hedge funds and why are they becoming so popular with investors?

Hedge fund is a pretty useless descriptor as it is an umbrella term that covers many different strategies which vary radically in terms of market exposure and risk. Given this breadth, I would define a hedge fund as *a fund that is incentivised and flexible enough to generate returns irrespective of the direction of core underlying markets*, although I have never seen a truly satisfying definition of the term hedge fund, including the one above. There are, however, certain characteristics that are common to most hedge funds.

True hedge funds are 'absolute return' funds, which means they do not aim to track or beat a certain benchmark or index, but instead are focused on pure return generation – they aim to make money whatever the underlying markets are doing. For example, if a traditional equity fund manager benchmarked to the FTSE 100 lost 10% in a year when the FTSE 100 lost 15%, he would be understood to have outperformed as he beat his benchmark by 5%, even though he lost 1/10 of your savings. However, a hedge fund manager investing in the same universe would consider himself to have performed badly in any other situation than making money, irrespective to the FTSE 100's loss. Anything below 0% performance (after fees) is a loss for a hedge fund manager, whatever the underlying market is doing. Of course there is a converse here: the traditional manager would be considered to have underperformed if making 20% in a year when the FTSE 100 rose by 25% whereas the hedge fund generating 20% would be compensated for this gain. Remember, hedge funds do not present a free lunch – they just have a different approach, which we will describe later in this chapter.

Characteristic of many hedge funds is their deliberate lack of insti-
tutionalisation. They are often run by small skilful teams, either within
large institutions or as breakaway groups. Even the biggest hedge funds
avoid too much peripheral support away from the investment side; for
example, I know of few hedge funds with a dedicated HR officer.

Often, hedge fund managers have previously been at the very top
of their profession in traditional investment management or trading,
and it is this expertise that has attracted them to the hedge fund world
and their investors to them. Many hedge fund managers that have
migrated from the long-only investment side have said that their skill
has been constrained by the tight mandates found in traditional funds,
i.e. long only, has to be fully invested, has to follow a benchmark.
Typically such migrants say that their skills have been wasted in
traditional investment management as they have not been able to
apply them to the full – many say it had been like working with one
hand tied behind their back – and that having the ability to take long
and short positions has allowed them to exercise their skill to the full.
Naturally, if they believe they can add more value through lessening
the constraints on their skill then this can lead to more money being
made for them also.

Hedge funds usually charge a fixed percentage 'management fee'
of somewhere between 1% and 2% per annum. Additionally, fees
based on positive investment performance (on new gains rather than
on regained loss) are usually charged at around 20% of all positive
gain per annum. This 'performance fee' alongside the fact that
hedge funds also often contain a large proportion of the personal
assets of the fund manager incentivise the hedge fund manager to
generate good positive performance. As a result, the hedge funds'
managers impose capacity constraints on assets managed to avoid
performance being 'diluted' by managing too much money, i.e. the
manager stops taking in new money to preserve the best opportunities
for the funds existing investors since this maximises the return on
his own assets and the performance fee he receives. This leads to
some of the best funds being 'closed' to new investors. This is
fantastic news if you are already invested in the fund as you don't
have to share the 'best bits' with too many others, but bad news if
you want to invest with the fund or increase your investment, as
often you can't.

Another distinguishing feature of hedge funds is the breadth of their
mandate – the manner in which they are sanctioned to manage their

funds. They are often allowed to use leverage (can borrow to invest more), invest in a multitude of financial instruments, and do many other things that a traditional fund cannot. Below, we take a look at what hedge fund managers do and how it allows them to generate absolute returns.

1.4   HOW DO HEDGE FUNDS GENERATE ABSOLUTE RETURNS?

Hedge funds aim to profit in all market conditions, even when underlying markets are falling. There are four main reasons why they can do this: by investing in areas that are obscure enough to be unaffected by falls in mainstream markets, by taking market exposure through derivative instruments such as options rather than through direct market positions, by holding cash or defensive instruments in falling markets and by taking what is known as 'short' market positions as well as traditional 'long' positions (i.e. holding stocks and bonds).

To address the last first, a short position in a stock is essentially achieved by a hedge fund borrowing stock from its owner (usually a long term investor such as a pension plan or long-only equity fund) and selling that stock into the market, leaving the hedge fund negatively exposed to the equity (since it isn't owned – just borrowed). The equity is then bought back and the debt repaid at later date. This is generally done as a single mechanism through a broker and is the most direct way of making money when the market falls. By taking short positions as well as traditional long positions hedge funds can actually profit from falling markets as well as rising ones.

This negative exposure can also be gained by buying put options and other derivative instruments. The hedge fund also has the ability to avoid loss from falling markets through moving the portfolio to cash and thus avoiding much downside, although it is notoriously difficult to 'call' markets in this way.

Many hedge funds avoid loss through the way they invest, be it by keeping neutral to the underlying markets through hedging (being short as well as long and negating the exposure) or by investing in areas that are obscure and driven by esoteric factors far removed from traditional markets. Remember, given that hedge funds are mainly rewarded by performance fees on new gains (not remade gains), they are heavily incentivised to avoid loss.

As well as the flexibility that hedge fund managers enjoy and the preponderance for skilled traditional managers to move into this area, returns exist also due to the niche nature of many of the strategies. Many such strategies are designed to exploit inefficiencies that exist in markets as a result of the rigid nature of traditional investment management. In the traditional world, the stringent mandates that govern funds and the lack of cross-disciplinary skillsets within the management of such funds means that many inefficiencies go unexploited, e.g. between equities and bonds, when complex situations occur in traditional markets such as mergers and bankruptcies, and in complex instruments such as derivatives. Some hedge funds specialise in these complexities and build cross disciplinary teams of various specialists to exploit such inefficiencies to turn them into returns.

1.5   WHO INVESTS IN HEDGE FUNDS?

In the past, hedge funds have been the preserve of wealthy individuals and endowments who were quick to recognise the benefits of the returns that hedge funds can offer. Now, more and more institutions and individual investors have money with hedge funds. This can be attributed to a number of reasons. Firstly, risk adjusted performance has been very good over the last 10 years or so and, given their lack of correlation to traditional investments, quantitative studies have shown hedge funds to be a beneficial investment class for portfolios, in terms of portfolio efficiency. Secondly, the boom/bust nature of equities over the late 1990s and early 2000s have caused many institutional investors to be wary of equity markets, instead appreciating more steady returns. Thirdly, the migration of renowned skilful fund managers to the hedge fund world has made this area difficult to ignore. Probably as a result of all three factors, the area is now viewed as a significant and established class of investment (although not an asset class since hedge funds practice strategies rather than represent a class of assets) and has been recommended by investment consultants to pension plans as a legitimate strategic investment. Similarly, more and more retail style hedge fund investment vehicles have been made available to individuals through banks and financial advisors. Interestingly, large amounts of the investment in this area have been made through hedge fund of funds, the reasons for which I address briefly below, and will discuss later in more depth in Chapters 3 and 4.

1.6   WHERE'S THE CATCH?

There isn't a catch but there are things to be wary about. Different strategies range widely in terms of risk and return. Some strategies are solid and consistent – producing positive returns almost every month. However, other strategies aim much higher in terms of returns with accordingly higher risk. There are also strategies that look consistent and involatile, but can be particularly volatile under certain conditions.

The important thing is to understand these strategies and cut through the complexity to fully assess the risks, as well as to perform rigorous analysis and monitoring on the hedge funds themselves before investing. This is one of the reasons why many investors, be they private or institutional, prefer to access hedge funds through *hedge funds of funds*.

1.7   WHAT ARE HEDGE FUNDS OF FUNDS?

A hedge fund of funds is a fund that invests in a number of hedge funds in order to give diversified investment in this area; such vehicles are also known as funds of hedge funds. Such funds of funds have been popular investments for a number of reasons. First of all, hedge funds are sometimes complex and require in-depth analysis and expertise before investing and a high frequency of monitoring once invested. Furthermore, different hedge fund strategies work better at different times and so having diversified access across the range of hedge fund strategies is desirable. Such diversification would be difficult to achieve for all but the biggest investors given that many hedge funds have minimum investments that stretch to millions of dollars. As a result, collective investment vehicles such as hedge funds of funds are particularly appealing to investors that wish to achieve informed and diversified access to a broad range of hedge funds. The main reason for the prominence of hedge funds of funds, however, has been the growth of the underlying hedge funds themselves, which has been moving at a quite dramatic pace of late.

1.8   THE GROWTH OF HEDGE FUNDS

Assets in hedge funds and hedge fund-of-funds have grown explosively over the past 10 or so years. Back in the early to mid 1990s when I started investing in the area, it was very easy to meet with practically every hedge fund manager in existence at the same conference, because there were only around 300 of them worldwide. Today there are an estimated 20 to 30 times this amount of hedge funds, with this growth being matched by inflows of assets.

Despite this recent growth, hedge funds are not a new concept. The first hedge fund was started over 50 years ago, but even by the 1980s, very few people had learned to use the term 'hedge' beyond its horticultural context. At this time, there were just a few hundred hedge funds in existence, with most of them quietly managing money for market savvy, wealthy individuals and endowments, almost exclusively in the US. Assets certainly weren't flooding in yet, and in these antediluvian days there was estimated to be less than USD 50bn in assets managed in this area, making it more of an exclusive club than an investment class all of its own. Since then, assets in this area have been estimated to have grown beyond USD 1 trillion, with some saying that this could be over USD 3 trillion when leverage is considered.

So what made this exclusive club throw open its doors to form a significant and well publicised asset class? Well, as I mentioned above, hedge fund investors in the early days were typically rich, market savvy investors. Such investors typically move in well-connected circles and sit on the boards of endowments and charities. Hedge fund investors were generally well rewarded from their investments since their hedge funds had performed well for them in the good times but also avoided loss in tough times such as the 1987 stock market crash. As a result hedge funds were seen as a highly appropriate investment for those who were rich and wanted to stay that way – an investment objective shared by wealthy individuals and the charities and endowments with which they were associated. Because of this attractive and defensive performance and word of mouth from their board members, many endowment boards and charitable trusts soon became sizeable hedge fund investors also.

This increase in assets soon rendered the hedge fund investment class big enough to catch the attention of larger institutional investors such as US pension plans, which started to notice the benefits of a steady reliable return stream that was uncorrelated with their existing equity and bond investments. Since then growth has been relentless. Now, in the US, endowments such as Harvard and Yale, and one of the world's largest pension plans, CALPERS, all invest in hedge funds. As a result, when equity markets collapsed in 2000, those that had already invested in hedge funds sighed with relief, and those that had not became very interested.

The increase in institutional investment in hedge funds has also spread to Europe. Over the past few years, European pension fund interest and actual investment in the hedge fund space has increased significantly and this is a trend that is set to continue. Mercers, the investment consultancy, report that 20% of UK pension plans have already invested in hedge funds or hedge funds of funds and, looking forward, a recent KPMG survey (Rajan *et al.*, 2006) has found that 50% of all pension plans questioned intend to invest in hedge funds of funds in the next three years.

This trend can be seen as a broader move away from equities into bonds and alternatives: the Financial Times (FTfm 6/11/06) reports that a recent Greenwich Associates survey of UK corporate pension plans estimates that the vast majority of plans intend to decrease significantly their equity exposure in favour of bonds and alternatives (roughly equally split by private equity, property and hedge funds). Such moves are certainly in line with the proposed softer stance emanating from the Alternative Investment Expert Group within the EC, that recommends an end to all arbitrary restrictions on pension plans investing in hedge funds although this is nothing new given that many major European countries allow or are about to sanction investment in this area by pension plans.

To match this growth in demand, there has been an impressive increase in supply of new funds – from 300 to over 8000 in little over a decade. Nowadays, successful traditional bond and equity managers see moving to manage a hedge fund as a natural career progression; they are well rewarded and they find their skill is less constrained. Now these managers have the power to avoid losing money when the market falls as they are no longer tied to a benchmark, and instead have the added capability to make money in such situations.

Growth in the number of new funds has been stimulated by the development of new strategies, which in turn has been stimulated by the development of new markets. For example, a recent British Bankers Association report finds that the global credit derivatives market has grown from USD 5 trillion in 2004 to USD 20 trillion in 2006 and is estimated to grow to USD 33 trillion in 2008. They also find that hedge funds were already the third biggest participants in this market in 2004 but since then their share of market volume has doubled. Not only has the emergence of the credit derivatives market allowed hedge funds to develop new strategies that profit from inefficiencies in this area, but also buy high levels of protection to further insulate their portfolios.

1.9   CONCLUSION

From obscure origins the growth of hedge funds and hedge funds of funds has been tremendous. This has been driven by the need for investments that are steady, downside controlled and uncorrelated to major asset classes – traits desirable to both institutional and individual investors. Today, hedge funds form a well-established investment class that operates in areas from liquid to illiquid, exchange traded to private and basic to complex. In the next chapter, I will explain a little about the range of hedge fund strategies in existence.

1.10   GLOSSARY FOR CHAPTER 1

Absolute Return

A fund manager seeks to generate absolute returns if he aims to generate positive returns irrespective of the movements of underlying markets or benchmarks.

Closed

A fund that is closed will not take in any new investors or investments.

Credit Derivatives

Options, swaps and other derivatives based on the credit rating of an underlying company or index.

Exchange Traded

Traded on a financial exchange such as a stock exchange as opposed to traded privately.

Fund of Hedge Funds

Another name for a hedge fund of funds.

Hedge Fund

Funds that are flexible and incentivised enough to generate absolute returns.

Hedge Fund Manager

An individual or company that manages a hedge fund.

Hedge Fund of Funds

A fund that invests solely in a number of hedge funds.

Hedge Fund Strategy

A given methodology applied to given markets that describes the approach of a hedge fund, e.g. an equity long/short hedge fund seeks to invest in equity markets with both long and short positions.

Long-Only Fund

A fund that only holds long positions (as opposed to long and short).

Long

A position in a portfolio that has been bought and is being held, e.g. long 1 equity in ABC means the portfolio holds an equity in company ABC.

Management Fee

A fixed percentage of assets that is paid to a fund for management of assets.

Mandate

A set of rules governing or restricting the management of assets issued to a fund and its manager by investors.

Negative Exposure

Having a position in a market that moves in the opposite direction to that market.

Neutral

Having no exposure to a given market (usually whilst holding positions in that market that are hedged or offset).

Performance Fee

A fixed percentage of positive returns that is paid to a fund for management of assets.

Portfolio Efficiency

The amount of return generated given the risk that is taken, e.g. portfolio efficiency is improved if more return is generated for the risk taken or, conversely, if risk is lowered whilst maintaining return.

Positive Exposure

Having a position in a market that moves in line with that market.

Risk Adjusted Returns

Returns generated scaled (divided) by the risk taken to generate them.

Short Position

Holding a position in a security that moves in the opposite direction to that security, i.e. a position that has been borrowed and sold in the market so that when the security falls, the short position gains and vice versa.

Traditional Fund

Another name for a long-only fund.

1.11   SUMMARY OF IDEAS FOR CHAPTER 1

- Hedge funds seek to generate absolute returns.
- Hedge funds are invested with for absolute returns, because they are uncorrelated with traditional asset classes and because they have shown to have good risk adjusted returns.
- For these reasons, hedge funds are popular with institutional investors and growing fast.
- Hedge funds of funds invest only in hedge funds and give diversified exposure to this area.

2
Hedge Fund Strategies

2.1 OVERVIEW

In this chapter we will take a look at the variety of hedge fund strategies in existence. Below, I split the area into four main strategy groupings: Equity Long/Short, Event Driven/Distressed, Arbitrage and Relative Value and Macro and Trading. We will take a look at each strategy area, take a look at the kind of returns to be expected, the rationale for these returns, the risks involved and cover any other points germane to each strategy.

2.2 EQUITY LONG/SHORT

This strategy is also known as Equity Hedge and is fundamentally one of the closest strategies to traditional investing. Equity Long/Short funds managers generally seek out undervalued stock to buy and over-valued stock to short and so this strategy can be thought of as the hedge fund equivalent to a traditional equity fund. There are, however, some significant differences beyond the use of shorting.

Equity Long/Short funds tend to have a higher turnover than traditional funds as they seek to manage volatility and downside on a month-by-month basis whereas traditional funds tend to have a longer time horizon. As a result, it would be commonplace for a hedge fund to take advantage of short term misevaluations in the market over shorter periods of time such as a number of days. Furthermore, some Equity Long/Short funds will take advantage of shorter term market moves where they don't even believe a misevaluation has occurred – they would just run with the market. Equity Long/Short fund managers may even take advantage of event driven situations and other anomalies that are unrelated to fundamental valuations.

Other differences between traditional funds and Equity Long/Short funds include the instruments that can be used and the exposures that can be taken. For example, an Equity Long/Short fund manager may be able to use derivatives as well as short positions to reduce market exposure in his fund (or to increase it) depending on his views. Also for example, a hedge fund manager that believes the market may fall may add more shorts to his portfolio to 'neutralise' his portfolio to market loss or even make the portfolio 'net short'; this means that there is a greater percentage of short positions in the portfolio than there are long so the hedge fund should actually generate profit in a falling market. It has to be said that usually, Equity Long/Short funds are 'net long' meaning they have a greater percentage of long positions than short in their portfolio and so they are correlated to the underlying market by the residual amount.

There is also usually nothing that forces an Equity Long/Short fund manager to invest 100% of the assets he manages; if he thinks that there are few promising positions for him he may reduce his gross exposure – the amount that is invested in both long and short positions; conversely, he may be able to increase his gross exposure to well above 100% in times when there are an abundance of positions to be placed, although this is normally limited in some way.

Different Equity Long/Short fund managers use a variety of methods to select long and short positions. Some use good old fashioned fundamental value analysis whereas some are more aware of short term market behaviour and also look at momentum of stock price or even press coverage and broker comments to gauge whether the market likes a stock or not and is just looking for any good news to buy (or hates the stock and is looking for bad news to sell on). Furthermore, the managers will often seek a catalyst (such as earnings announce-ments, board changes, etc.) which alerts the 'market at large' to these mis-valuations and hence move the stock back to fair value, realising a profit for the fund. Either way, it's generally the case that the best hedge funds execute startling depths of research to understand the companies they buy or short.

Different Equity Long/Short funds exhibit a wide range of con-straints, from funds that can invest in anything equity related with any cap size, listed in any country and with practically no limit on exposure, through to those that are limited in how much net long or short they can be and that must only invest in certain countries above a certain cap size. This variety also exists in the way short positions are placed by Equity Long/Short fund managers. Some hedge fund managers will short to generate return whereas others will only take short positions to hedge their long ones and may even use equity index futures to control exposure. In some portfolios, each short position is strongly linked to a long position for more of a 'relative value' play.

As well as more qualitative research techniques, some Equity Long/Short fund managers specialise in quantitative and/or systems-driven approaches. Here, time-series for the underlying stocks are analysed and, in addition, various models are applied to the analysis of company financials and even analysts' recommendations. Often these quantitative hedge fund managers run portfolios known as market neutral, although there are some qualitative hedge funds run in this neutral way also.

Equity Market Neutral is a specific type of Equity Long/Short investing. The long portfolio of undervalued stocks and short portfolio of overvalued stocks are designed to be equal and opposite in terms of market exposure (beta) and thereby combine to hedge out exposure to the equity market itself (beta-neutral). Often, the portfolio is constrained to be neutral by sector, cap-size and other factors also. This strategy often tends to be quantitative in nature as a quantitative capability is needed to calculate all these exposures and ensure ongoing neutrality.

Finally, there is a heavily quantitative and market neutral strategy known as Statistical Arbitrage. This strategy falls within Equity Long/Short although is slightly anomalous to other variants of the strategy. Statistical Arbitrage utilises advanced quantitative techniques to anticipate the directions (specifically the reversals of direction) of stocks within a number of carefully constructed baskets that are usually optimised to be neutral to all exogenous risk factors. Typically, this strategy accrues returns from small fluctuations in a large number of stocks, and profits especially from the overreaction of stocks that then revert back to their original level. Don't worry if the above was all meaningless to you – Statistical Arbitrage is quite a specialist strategy and not one you will encounter every day.

The typical Equity Long/Short fund manager is someone who would have learned his craft in the world of traditional investment management before extending his skills to the long/short arena. Returns in this strategy are generated as a result of hedge fund manager skill and experience but also from inefficiencies in the equity markets that result from the rigid nature of traditional fund management. Equity Long/Short fund managers generate returns from the extra flexibility they have and also from looking at areas that are less popular or less researched by the traditional asset management world, e.g. micro cap stocks.

2.2.1   Risks

The risks in Equity Long/Short are market and equity related just as in traditional fund management. However, there are extra risks that come from the extra flexibility the Equity Long/Short fund manager affords; for example illiquidity in smaller cap investments, risk from leverage or using derivative instruments to compound exposure. Also, given that an Equity Long/Short portfolio may look to generate 'double alpha' returns from both long and short positions, it could also turn into a double loss portfolio where the longs go down and the shorts go up.

2.2.2   Trade Example

The hedge fund manager's research shows that a stock A in a given sector is undervalued and company A's management plan a road show to raise awareness in a few weeks. Stock B in the same sector and with a similar beta as A is certainly not undervalued and latest broker research indicates that earnings estimates may be optimistic of late; the hedge fund manager may not fully trust this research but it reduces the chance of the stock rallying and may cause the stock to sell off before the next earnings announcement. The position would be LONG STOCK A, SHORT STOCK B with a view to unwind following the road show for A but before the next earnings announcement from B (in case the research is wrong). This results in a market hedged position with a catalyst.

2.2.3   Strategy Summary

- Equity Long/Short is an extension of traditional equity fund management but with the ability to short.
- Equity Long/Short fund managers have much more flexibility than traditional fund managers.
- The process can be based on qualitative research, quantitative screening or a mix of the two.

2.3   EVENT DRIVEN AND DISTRESSED INVESTING

Event Driven and Distressed strategies are a group of hedge fund strategies based around corporate events. Although two distinct strategies, Event Driven and Distressed investing are complimentary and require similar skill sets and so are often grouped together and practiced by the same hedge fund managers.

2.3.1   Event Driven Investing

Event Driven strategies involve a hedge fund manager taking advantage of market inefficiencies that tend to surround corporate events such as mergers, acquisitions, spin-outs etc.

For example, in the case of a corporate acquisition, as soon as the acquiring company signals intent to buy another company, the price of the company to be acquired will rise towards the acquisition price but remain at a discount to this price. This discount reflects the uncertainty in the market as to whether the acquisition will go ahead or not.

A seasoned Event Driven hedge fund manager will use his team of specialists to analyse every aspect of the potential acquisition; for example the terms of the deal, the strategic rationale, the personalities involved and the regulatory view on antitrust/monopolies. This work leads them to be able to cut through the complexity and ascertain with a high degree of accuracy whether the deal will close or not and hence generate a profit. In addition, they are often able to lock into a profit that is independent of the underlying equity market and so returns are often much less volatile than equity returns.

Event Driven investing generates returns from manager skill and depth of research but in addition there is a fundamental rationale as to why the returns exist. Generally, traditional equity managers will avoid such event driven situations as a result of the complexity surrounding the deals. Given that the 'wall of long only equity money' is absent from event driven situations, the market in this area is less efficient, leading to mispricings. Such mispricings are taken advantage of by the Event Driven hedge funds that have expertise in this area as outlined above, allowing them to generate a return from this inefficient area of the market.

In the case of an acquisition as outlined above, if a traditional manager held the stock that is to be acquired in their portfolio, he would benefit because normally the stock to be acquired would rally on news of the intended acquisition, partly as a result of the news hitting the market and partly as a result of Event Driven hedge fund managers buying in. The traditional manager, however, would have neither the time nor the expertise to analyse the complex details of the acquisition and would sell the stock prior to the deal being closed, booking a solid profit and only sacrificing the remaining upside, which in turn is locked in by the Event Driven hedge fund manager.

2.3.2 Distressed Investing

As with Event Driven investing, Distressed investing is an approach based on corporate events that has a strong economic rationale for generating returns.

Distressed investing involves investing in the debt (and sometimes equity) of companies that are 'distressed', e.g. have defaulted on debt payments or coupons, filed for Chapter 11 in the US, etc. Typically, the hedge fund manager will follow the bankruptcy process from early distress through to recovery (or otherwise) using a team of experts with legal and corporate finance expertise. Through their analysis they will estimate the 'break-up' value of the company and also its current intrinsic value, as well as estimating the chances of recovery. This information is used to make a decision whether to buy into the company or not and at what level. If the company's debt trades cheaply enough, then often the debt can be bought at a level where there is little downside. As the bonds are senior in the capital structure of the company, the bond holders will be amongst the first to be paid out from fixed assets should the company liquidate and often the value of fixed assets is sufficient to reimburse senior capital structure investors.

Often, a distressed company's debt will trade at an overly diminished price and, as with Event Driven, this is a result of market inefficiencies in the traditional investment management world.

Traditional corporate bond investors generally liquidate positions when they become distressed either due to the guidelines in their mandate or due to human nature – a traditional manager would rather get rid of a 'nightmare position' in his portfolio than have it hanging around as evidence of a bad decision. As a result of this sell off by the institutional world, the debt of distressed companies falls to irrationally low levels and at this point, Distressed hedge funds, who have no constraining rules on owning distressed debt, can take advantage of the mispricing and generate a good return.

Just as with Event Driven investing, Distressed investing produces returns from fundamental market inefficiencies caused by the constraints and objectives imposed on traditional investors. However, hedge fund managers have no such constraints and, furthermore, can specialise in such niche areas to generate steady, market independent returns.

2.3.3   Combining These Strategies

Another great benefit of these strategies is that they combine very well together. Event Driven investing generally does best when the economic outlook is either positive or neutral as this is when corporate activity is at its most widespread. Distressed performs best when economic times are tough since this is when companies tend to become distressed the most. As a result these two different strategies perform best at different times within the economic cycle and so are highly complementary. For example, Distressed has only delivered one negative year since records began (based on HFR Indices 1990 to date) which was -4% in 1998 and in this year, Event Driven delivered $+7\%$. The second weakest year in Distressed ($+3\%$ in 2000) yielded a return of $+19\%$ in Event Driven. Similar results can be found doing the analysis vice versa. In addition, adding the two strategies together (equally weighted) can be shown to give better risk adjusted returns than either of the individual strategies based on analysis of Sharpe ratio of the HFR indices, implying the strong benefits of combining investment across these strategies.

Given that the returns from these strategies have a strong fundamental rationale for their existence, it is possible to look ahead to calculate which strategy is expected to outperform, on the basis of fundamentals. For example, analysis of current bankruptcy rates, assets flows in the strategy, credit spreads, the cost of borrowing and new issuance rates allows you to gauge the expected returns for Distressed. Similarly, analysis of global deal flow, deal breaks, deal premia, corporate valuations and asset flows allows you to look forward for Event Driven returns.

2.3.4   Risks

As the Event Driven strategy has evolved, there is less of a clear cut 'arbitrage' approach as hedge fund managers look at more complex and less hedgeable situations where there may be more risks from equity market exposure. However, such exposure has always existed in this strategy when takeovers have been cash based and so there has been no need to short the acquirer's stock. Other risks in this strategy include the risk of the deal breaking and the acquisition not happening, along with the possibility of low merger and acquisition deal flow leaving little opportunity set to invest in.

In the Distressed investing strategy, the main risk is that distressed debt becomes even more distressed – in other words, that bonds that have been thought to have 'bottomed out' have fell further as more bad news hits the market. The more risk averse distressed managers avoid this by only investing after all disclosures have been made, although this tends to reduce the upside they can participate in. Distressed bonds are also only semi-liquid and sometimes difficult to price and so this is also a risk that needs consideration. Finally, distressed debt funds can lose money on the general widening of credit spreads – irrespective of the solid rationale for the specific corporate bonds owned – as sometimes the market moves all bonds in this area.

2.3.5   Trade Examples

For event driven investing, a typical position would be long an equity that is about to be acquired, and short the equity in the acquiring stock in the ratio that is being paid for the acquisition. For example, if acquiring company A is going to pay 0.5 stocks of A for every stock of a company T, the position would be LONG 1 STOCK OF T, SHORT 0.5 STOCK OF A with a view to holding this position until the deal closes or cutting it if it looks unlikely to close on the back of new information.

For Distressed, the trade would be even simpler. A simple position would be long of a corporate bond issued by a company that is now in Chapter 11 and has fallen greatly in price as a result. The hedge fund manager may want to reduce market risk by taking a short position in a credit index or proxy such as ITRAXX, but this is not always the case.

2.3.6   Strategy Summary

- There is a solid economic rationale for Event Driven and Distressed strategies to generate returns and so performance can be well understood.
- These returns are enhanced by the skill and expertise of specialist, experienced hedge fund managers.
- Such returns are particularly attractive as they tend to be independent from and less volatile than the underlying equity markets.

- Event Driven and Distressed strategies combine well together as they are counter-cyclical.
- Given the fundamental nature of the returns, it is possible to add further value by allocating between these strategies as the economic cycle evolves.

2.4 RELATIVE VALUE AND ARBITRAGE STRATEGIES

Relative Value and Arbitrage are strategies that seek to generate returns that are almost totally independent of the direction of underlying markets. The formal definition of arbitrage is *a risk free instantaneous profit from financial markets* although nowadays arbitrage refers to low (rather than no) risk and is rarely instantaneous. For example, Event Driven investing around a merger as described above is known as Merger Arbitrage although as can be seen from the previous section there are risks involved and the deal may take several months to close. Relative Value is a similar way of investing to Arbitrage since it involves a long position that is counterbalanced by a similar (but not identical) short position for example two government bonds of similar but not identical maturities.

Arbitrage and Relative Value investing involves taking advantage of anomalies or distortions in markets that are temporary and should be expected to disappear over a period of time for example the price of the same instrument on different markets. Given that markets nowadays are much more efficient than they used to be, these anomalies tend to be far from obvious and often involve taking complex positions with numerous legs to hedge out all extraneous risks. Also as a result of market efficiency, these anomalies tend to be slight and so often considerable leverage is needed to generate acceptable returns.

Why is it possible to make returns out of Arbitrage and Relative Value strategies? This is mainly due to anomalies in the market due to supply and demand, different types of investors having different time horizons and levels of flexibility and due to complexity that only niche market participants can exploit. For example, if a pension plan is buying up bonds of a given maturity, this bond may raise in price disproportionately compared to one that matures slightly later and so a relative value position of short the former bond and long the latter is placed, which should generate a near market independent return when the large buyer is done and the former bond reverts to fair value.

Many such trades are known as convergence trades as the difference in value – the spread – converges to zero as the market anomalies abate.

2.4.1 Risks

The risks in these strategies are that either the long and short positions decouple due to some event, or the spread widens to the extent that the hedge fund manager has to give up his position before it converges (the spread being the difference between long and short position and equivalent to how much the hedge fund manager can make from this trade). In the first instance, the loss is instantly crystallised since the lack of linkage going forward means that nothing will now necessarily force convergence. The second instance is only a 'mark to market' loss, i.e. not crystallised since a long as the hedge fund manager stays with the trade, the linkage that exists between the long and the short position will force convergence. In fact, if the hedge fund manager can afford to then he should add to the position if convergence is still imminent since the spread is now wider which will yield a bigger return for him on convergence. However, given the levered nature of this strategy and the need to curtail downside at some point (to stop worrying investors to the point where they run to the door), more often than not a hedge fund manager will exit the trade should the spread widen significantly, or indeed be forced out of the trade by his broker who is providing the leverage.

Given that the above has been rather abstract I will now take a look at some specific arbitrage and relative value strategies: Convertible Bond Arbitrage and Fixed Income Arbitrage and Relative Value.

2.4.2 Convertible Bond Arbitrage

Convertible bonds are hybrid instruments that can be though of as having both bond and equity tendencies; they are essentially corporate bonds with embedded call options that allow them to be converted to the equity of the same issuer. Given their complex hybrid nature they are often mispriced. Convertible Bond Arbitrageurs seek to take advantage of this situation by identifying mispricings through their superior valuation tools and experience and then buying the bond and hedging out the equity exposure (by shorting the stock) and other interest rate and credit exposures (usually through swaps) to lock in the mispricings.

As the equity moves around in price, the hedge has to be rebalanced (known as delta hedging). The trading associated with this rehedging is called gamma trading and believe it or not this actually can add to profitability. As well as profiting from mispricings, the arbitrageur can also profit from the coupon paid from the convertible bond, making the position almost self financing. Convertible Bond Arbitrage is particularly desirable as it tends to make money in volatile times and so can be though of as an insurance strategy in some markets.

This is a classic example of near arbitrage returns that exist due to complexity and the lack of flexibility held by most participants in financial markets.

2.4.2.1 Risks

There are downsides, however. Not all Convertible Bond Arbitrage hedge fund managers hedge out credit as it detracts from returns and so are susceptible to credit downgrades. In times when markets stagnate and volatility is low, this strategy can continually lose money. Also, there are few other buyers of convertible bonds and so at times when this strategy is unpopular there can be liquidity issues that compound loss.

2.4.2.2 Trade Example

Having found a convertible bond in company A of delta 0.5 and associated historic stock volatility of 50% that is undervalued, it is found out that once all risks are hedged, the misvaluation will still provide positive return of 10% p.a. provided actual volatility is greater than 45%. As this is to be expected given historic levels of volatility, the position is as follows: LONG 1 COMPANY A CONVERTIBLE BOND, SHORT 0.5 COMPANY A STOCK (equity hedge), LONG DURATION SWAP (interest rate hedge), LONG CREDIT DEFAULT SWAP ON A.

2.4.3 Fixed Income Arbitrage and Relative Value

Fixed Income Arbitrage and Relative Value fund managers seek to exploit pricing anomalies that occur in the international fixed income markets and associated foreign exchange and interest rate markets. The focus is on government bonds but some fixed income hedge fund managers also extend their remit to corporate bonds and credit. Some Fixed Income hedge fund managers also have a directional portion of the portfolio, which means the try to make money from predicting the direction of bonds and other markets.

The anomalies traded are typically between related or linked fixed income instruments such as notes, bonds, bills, rates, currencies, swaps, options, futures, forwards and other derivatives. Positions are constructed to profit from reversion to theoretically 'correct' prices and the closing of the price gap between different instruments and markets. Such positions could be based on price (outright and relative) or some other factor such as volatility and could be as basic as a long and similar short position or could be complex and multi-legged consisting of a wide variety of instruments.

Opportunities may occur due to instruments with similar exposure being traded on different markets, e.g. a bond future versus the underlying bond. Alternatively they may arise from yield curve anomalies or other short term price discrepancies. In many cases the anomalies are small but the volatility of the position is correspondingly low and so leverage is used to enhance yield.

It is possible to generate returns in this area as a result of the complexity of some of the positions needed to exploit the anomalies but also the short term mismatch of supply and demand and the rigid rules that some market participants have to follow. For example, if a pension plan enters the market to buy large amounts of bonds of a very specific duration that are needed to match liabilities within their plan, this may cause such bonds to rise in value compared to bonds with a slightly different duration, and this can only be exploited by arbitrageurs in hedge funds and bank trading desks as long only bond fund managers cannot take short positions.

2.4.3.1 Risks

For a strategy that may go through periods of very low volatility, Fixed Income Arbitrage and Relative Value can be riskier than it looks. The strategy has something of a love/hate relationship with the large market events that causes the spreads that are traded to widen. This is so in as much as investing with overly extended (widened) spreads can lead to great returns as they renarrow, but being invested with spreads as they widen causes loss, at least in the short term. The main risk is that spreads that are invested with widen and do not renarrow. This can be as a result of a market paradigm shift resulting in spreads finding a new, wider level from now on, a decoupling of the long and short positions that make up that spread or a being forced out of the spread altogether. The last point could be as a result of risk management oversight forcing the position to close, or investors voting with their feet and exiting the fund. As such, the main risks are based on spreads blowing out, but also liquidity issues.

2.4.3.2   Trade Example

Changes to the benchmark for European bond funds result in an extra country being included in this benchmark, Country C. As a result of the above, traditional fund managers will begin buying the bonds of Country C as soon as they are on the usual settlement systems. A Fixed Income Relative Value hedge fund buys the bonds of Company C ahead of this and hedges them by shorting a basket of all other European bonds until the day the bonds of Country C become clearable in Europe and are bought by the fund managers, driving up the price. The position would be LONG 1 BOND OF COUNTRY C and SHORT 1 BASKET REPRESENTING THE EXISTING EUROPEAN BENCH-MARK (e.g. through an ETF or swap).

2.4.4   Strategy Summary

- Arbitrage and Relative Value strategies involve exploiting market misevaluations in a way that is not exposed to the direction of the underlying markets.
- Typical positions consist of a long position and short position in instruments and markets that are closely linked.
- Such strategies can generate very involatile returns that are uncorrelated to the underlying equity and bond markets.
- However, there is often more risk involved than the (in)volatility would suggest.

2.5   TRADING AND MACRO STRATEGIES

These strategies are based on predicting the direction of an underlying market and successfully trading based on this prediction. The markets traded are often major ones such as global fixed income, foreign exchange and equity. The methods of prediction can range from heavily qualitative to totally quantitative.

Global Macro hedge funds tend to trade based on a 'top down' view of the world based on macro economic and political analysis. Such funds tend to have a bias towards fixed income and currency markets although may trade commodities and equities at index levels given that positions are based on a top down politico-economic view rather than micro-level analysis. Macro hedge fund managers may also trade on a short term basis, sometimes based on a 'feel' for the market and this is sometimes referred to tactical trading or discretionary trading. Global Macro hedge fund managers tend to originate from proprietary trading desks in banks although some will have evolved from being professional bank or academic economists.

Returns in this strategy are often owed to the skill of the fund manager although there is a rationale to say that given different asset classes are manned by specialists in their field, there is an advantage to be gained by a flexible and fast acting market savvy investor who is economically aware and watching all main asset classes rather than focussing on one; as such there is an additional rationale for performance although less so than in many niche strategies.

Whilst global macro and discretionary trading can be though of as a mix of qualitative and some quantitative analysis, there is a branch of trading known as systematic trading which is dominated by those know as Commodity Trading Advisors, or CTAs.

CTAs are usually systematic traders that use quantitatively based algorithms (rules) to trade futures markets. Despite their name, CTAs have evolved beyond trading just commodities and now trade the full range of futures, from metals to equity and bond futures, globally. The trading systems used by CTAs are often automated and based on the price history of each instrument and so futures markets have historically been best suited to this because of the availability of price data; also, CTAs benefit from the wide range of underlying markets that the futures exchanges cover and the ease of trading and leveraging on futures contracts.

The typical approach taken by a CTA is to use market price history and sometimes other available data from futures markets such as volume (number of contracts traded) and open interest (number of contracts outstanding) to try and identify trends. Their algorithms are often based on technical analysis techniques (which seek to identify trends based on visual inspection of market chart patterns and calculation of basic averaging indicators) but have also evolved to use advanced mathematical techniques from the disciplines of physics, engineering, mathematics and economics. Other advances range from the use of intraday high frequency price data such as tick data to building automated algorithms to interpret news flow.

2.5.1   Risks

The upside in macro and trading strategies can be excellent but the downsides can also be large. The risk is that the trader's prediction is wrong and so he gets the direction of the trade wrong and incurs loss. As such, a well thought out exit and risk process can be as important as entry point and 'stop losses' – predetermined levels (of loss) at which the trader will exit – are often used. Those with the systematic approach are particularly susceptible to market noise and sharp moves followed by reversals (called whipsaws) which can be taken as false signals. Timing is also important, as if a trader is right about direction but his position results in losses before the move occurs, then sometimes the trade is pulled and losses crystallised.

2.5.2   Trade Examples

CTA: The 15 day moving average price of the S&P 500 future moves above the measure taken over 60 days so BUY 1 S&P FUTURE FOR NEXT EXPIRY DATE.

GLOBAL MACRO: Anticipating an easing of demand and a change in interest rate policy, SHORT US TBOND.

2.5.3   Strategy Summary

- Trading and Global Macro strategies involve making predictions of the direction of financial, equity and commodity markets and taking positions accordingly
- Global Macro managers tend to be former proprietary bank traders who will make their predictions on the basis of a top-down macro-economic and/or political thesis.
- CTAs tend to take a systematic approach and trade only futures markets
- The upside can be enormous but with a corresponding downside and sizeable volatility.

2.6   SUMMARY

In this chapter I have introduced the four main strategy types in hedge funds: Equity Long/Short, Event Driven, Relative Value and Arbitrage and Macro and Trading. Of course, there are a plethora of other strategies and variations but these four make up the majority of hedge funds. Now I have gone into a reasonable amount of depth on hedge funds and hedge fund strategies, in the next chapter I will explain the benefits of investing in this area.

2.7   GLOSSARY FOR CHAPTER 2

Alpha

Return generated through skill rather than just passive market exposure.

Arbitrage

A risk free instantaneous profit from financial markets; nowadays taken to mean a low risk market independent profit.

Beta

The reliance of any return or portfolio on passive underlying market exposure.

Beta Neutral

A portfolio is beta neutral if its long and short positions are matched to leave no residual market exposure.

Convertible Bond

A corporate bond that can be converted into an equity from the same issuer.

Convertible Bond Arbitrage

A hedge fund strategy based on misevaluations and arbitrage opportunities in the convertible bond market.

Credit Spreads

The difference in yield between corporate and government bonds.

Crystallised Loss

A loss that cannot be regained from a given position (unlike a mark to market loss).

CTA

A hedge fund that uses systematic trading strategies to trade a broad range of markets (usually based on futures trading).

Delta Hedge

Hedging out the equity exposure of an option using an equity position.

Distressed Investing

A hedge fund strategy based around generating returns from companies that are in a state of stress or default.

Double Alpha

Generating alpha independently from both the long and short portfolios of a hedge fund.

Equity Long/Short

A hedge fund strategy based around buying underpriced stocks and shorting overpriced stocks.

Equity Market Neutral

An Equity Long/Short strategy where long and short positions are matched to eradicate market exposure, either with respect to beta or just invested capital on long and short sides.

Event Driven

A hedge fund strategy based on generating returns from corporate events.

Fixed Income Arbitrage and Relative Value

A hedge fund strategy that seeks to generate low risk, hedged returns from anomalies in the fixed income markets.

Fundamental Valuation

The value of an equity or bond based on analysis of balance sheet and profitability.

Gamma Trading

The trading involved in delta hedging when the delta moves around and the hedge needs to be rebalanced.

Global Macro

A broad based trading strategy with a broad geographical and asset class remit, usually based on top-down analysis.

Mark to Market Loss

A temporary loss based on short term adverse valuation; such a position has potential to become profitable again, unlike one with a crystallised loss.

Market Independent

Hedge fund strategies with returns that are notably unlinked with underlying equity and bond markets.

Net Long

A portfolio is net long if it has a greater percentage of long positions than short positions within it.

Net Short

A portfolio is net short if it has a greater percentage of short positions than long positions within it.

Relative Value

A hedge fund approach based on exploiting a temporary differential in price between similar securities by taking a long position in one and a short in the other.

Spread

The difference in price between two similar securities; usually the potential profit to be made in an arbitrage or relative value trade.

Statistical Arbitrage

A form of equity market neutral investing that seeks to capture small and short term moves in stocks.

2.8   SUMMARY OF IDEAS FOR CHAPTER 2

- Hedge funds can be broken down into four main strategies:
  - Equity Long/Short, which is the analogy to a traditional equity fund in as much as the hedge fund managers are looking to buy underpriced equities, but also to short overpriced ones.
  - Event Driven and Distressed which is based around making money from corporate events which are generally too complex for traditional managers to want to get involved in.
  - Arbitrage and Relative Value which seeks to make involatile returns from hedged positions exploiting market anomalies.
  - Trading and Macro which is based around trading a range of markets and instruments, using either quantitative bottom up or qualitative top-down analysis.

3
The Benefits and Risks of Investing in Hedge Funds

3.1 OVERVIEW

In this chapter I present the standard arguments for investing with hedge funds and both question and develop those arguments. Given that many reasons are based on the nature of past returns, I take an in-depth look at the economic rationale for the existence of such returns going forward and also take a deeper look at the nature of the drivers of returns in the hedge fund space. Investing with hedge funds also presents specific risks that are peculiar to this area and towards the end of this chapter I take a look at the risks that should be considered before investing.

3.2 THE BENEFITS OF INVESTING WITH HEDGE FUNDS

As we can see from Table 3.1, hedge funds have historically outperformed equities and bonds with volatility not too much above bonds. As a result, if this performance was anything to go by, it would

Table 3.1 Comparison of Hedge Fund Returns with Major Asset Classes.

10 YEARS: 1997–2006 Source: Datastream	CSFB Tremont Hedge Fund Index (USD, after fees)	MSCI World Equity Index (USD, total return)	JP Morgan Global Government Bond Index (USD, total return)
Average Annual Rate of Return	10.5%	8.1%	5.3%
Worst Year	−0.4%	−19.5%	−6.5%
% Negative Years	10.0%	30.0%	30.0%
Annualised Standard Deviation	7.2%	14.5%	6.6%
Correlation with HFR Index	1.00	0.52	−0.06

make sense to add hedge funds to a traditional portfolio of equities and bonds just because they seem to have better risk adjusted returns than the traditional asset classes; that is, for every percentage point of risk that is taken, greater returns are generated.

However, past outperformance is not a reason in itself to invest as there is no guarantee that these returns will continue to look so good. It isn't the magnitude of hedge fund returns as much as their steadiness and consistency that is beneficial to portfolios. Since 1997 equities, for example, have had three negative years with the worst year losing almost 20% whereas hedge funds have had only one negative year, losing less than 1%. Essentially hedge fund investors benefit from consistency and compounding rather than the magnitude of returns.

As well as consistent, hedge fund returns tend to be reasonably uncorrelated with traditional equity markets and pretty much uncorrelated with bond markets, as we can see in the table above; if we were to focus on market independent strategies, this correlation with equities would fall even further. This low correlation is a second reason for adding hedge funds, as they make the portfolio more efficient, i.e. better return for the risk taken or, to put it another way, lower risk for the return given. This uncorrelated, consistent return stream makes hedge funds a particularly effective diversifier for portfolios and even if hedge fund returns diminish going forward, there is less of a chance of them structurally changing, i.e. changing drastically in terms of volatility or correlation, which should be the argument for investing in the first place.

There have been many studies that show the benefits of investing part of an equity and bond portfolio into hedge funds based on historic returns, which make hedge funds look like a bit of a 'free lunch'. Such studies use the well established but basic quantitative methods of finance and portfolio theory that can be used to derive the best (optimal) portfolio for any given level of risk – this is known as the efficient frontier. Such studies generally tend to show that adding hedge funds to a traditional portfolio will increase returns, lower risk and increase measures of risk adjusted return such as Sharpe ratio. The resulting recommended amount to invest in hedge funds tends to blow off the positive end of the scale. These studies carry some truth but should be taken with a pinch of salt for the following two reasons:

- They are based on past returns and although hedge funds returns are unlikely to change structurally, they may diminish in magnitude.

- Such studies use basic optimisation techniques that take volatility of returns as a measure of risk; this works well for more straightforward hedge funds and traditional funds, but some complex hedge fund strategies do not show all their risk through past volatility.

The main reasons for investing in hedge funds should be that hedge fund returns are different to traditional asset classes, rather than better – one should never expect a free lunch. Hedge fund returns are different because they are of a different structure to the returns from traditional asset classes and this happens for more stable reasons than just outperformance. Hedge funds are incentivised to generate absolute returns and less volatility through their performance fee structure, absolute return targets and broader mandate and thus should be less volatile and uncorrelated with traditional asset classes.

3.3   THE RATIONALE FOR HEDGE FUND RETURNS

Although one should never invest in an area just based on past performance alone, analysis of the reasons for hedge fund outperformance shows that there is a convincing rationale for why such good returns exist, and should exist going forward. The source of hedge fund returns can be attributed to three main areas:

- The broader mandates and universes that hedge funds utilise.
  - As mentioned in Chapter 1, hedge fund managers can invest across a range of instruments and markets as well as being able to take short positions. This accompanied by absolute return objectives result in hedge fund managers incentivised and able to generate positive returns and limit loss as opposed to being tied to an equity or bond index.
- The skills and skill sets of hedge fund managers.
  - It is generally the case that hedge fund managers get compensated for their skills much more than traditional fund managers; this is because the hedge fund world offers the flexibility to use such skill to the full, accompanied by the sizeable performance fee that rewards the success of this. As a result, many of the most skilful traditional fund managers (and bank traders) have moved over to manage hedge funds. Also, given the niche but multi-asset class nature of many hedge fund strategies, cross disciplinary teams of

experts exist within hedge funds but are rare elsewhere within finance and investment management, and so such teams are rewarded for their niche skills.
- The existence of market inefficiency and the ability to take advantage of it and turn it into profit.
  - There is a considerable amount of financial market inefficiency that results from the more rigid nature of traditional fund management – the mechanism through which most assets are managed. For example, the inefficiency that surrounds corporate events in the equity markets that can be exploited to generate near-arbitrage returns, as referred to in Chapter 2. Hedge funds are one of the few market participants that have the expertise to identify such inefficiencies and the flexibility to exploit them to generate returns, and this minority position acts as a strong rationale for outperformance.

To summarise, one should never use outperformance as the only rationale for investing in any area. However, there are compelling structural reasons to invest in hedge funds based more on the characteristic low volatility and low correlation of returns than just performance based factors. This being said, past outperformance is not without a rationale for its existence, based on the flexibility and skill set of hedge funds and their managers. As long as this rationale perpetuates, outperformance may well continue.

3.4   HEDGE FUND STRATEGIES AND THE NATURE OF HEDGE FUND RETURNS

Different hedge funds and strategies have radically different levels of risk, expected return and market exposure and not all strategies suit all investors. Hedge funds work well as a diversifier because they generate steady returns and have a low correlation with traditional markets. However, some types of hedge fund seek to generate larger returns by taking considerable market exposure, rendering them less effective diversifiers but having more potential for higher return generation. For example, an investor seeking to invest in hedge funds because of their low correlation to equities should limit exposure to long-biased Equity Long/Short, which is very much correlated to underlying equity markets; however, this strategy would be perfectly suitable for those willing to take more equity risk to generate greater returns.

Arguably, the returns of any hedge fund or strategy can be attributed to two main areas: manager skill, expertise or luck (known as alpha) or long run exposures to a given market or underlying driver of return (known as beta). It is important when analysing hedge funds to consider the contributions from each of these factors to the returns of any given fund or strategy because this is how to tell where the money has been made and what risks have been taken to generate these returns. As a result, it is necessary to go beyond the basic analysis from the traditional investment world and consider hedge funds in their own broader framework.

Traditional performance analysis focuses on returns, volatility of returns and combinations of these two measurements, either outright or relative to very straightforward underlying equity and bond indices. However, given the areas hedge funds operate in, a whole range of underlying indices and factors need to be considered when assessing whether a hedge fund is generating alpha or just beta to something unusual – so called 'alternative betas'. For example, some of the driving factors of Convertible Bond Arbitrage are credit spreads and implied volatility, and so this may be a staring point when analysing a fund that invests in this strategy.

In truth, it is much easier to conduct attribution analysis of returns in some hedge fund strategies more than others. In less rigorously defined strategies such as Global Macro, the investment approach is less formula driven and there are few distinct or obvious underlying drivers of return. However, in Merger Arbitrage, say, it is clear that when deal flow is higher, when few deals are breaking, when the premia paid by acquiring companies are high relative to interest rates and when there are fewer assets in the strategy, arbitrage profits should be higher. If the conditions were the converse to those mentioned above, few merger arbitrageurs, however skilful or experienced, could make good returns, as we have seen in the past.

Generally, in arbitrage and market independent strategies where the arbitrage mandate is relatively tight, e.g. Merger Arbitrage, Convertible Arbitrage and Distressed, we should expect returns to be driven by the underlying drivers for each strategy as well as manager skill. However, in less closely defined strategies such as Global Macro, the manager has a wider mandate and so a greater opportunity to apply skill exists and so skill (or luck) has potential to make up a much greater proportion of returns.

Market inefficiency should also play a part here. For example, a small cap focussed Equity Long/Short manager should generate returns from the fact they are operating in a much less well covered area of the equity market. In essence, there is less competition and so there should be a greater payoff for conducting competent company research as this should yield an informational advantage that should in turn be converted to profit.

To summarise, not all hedge fund strategies are the same. Some strategies tend to be less correlated with traditional asset classes and some tend to be less volatile. However, these attributes cannot be assumed of all hedge fund strategies and so investors that are looking for particular qualities from hedge funds need to understand or be advised on which strategies are best suited to them. Furthermore, all hedge fund returns are not pure 'alpha' even if basic analysis may imply as much – it could just be beta to something unusual.

3.5 THE DOWNSIDES OF INVESTING IN HEDGE FUNDS

As with any investment there are upsides and downsides. In the specific instance of hedge funds, obvious downsides include high fees, a potentially 'difficult to understand' and complex investment approach, high minimum investments in the funds themselves and the possibility of not gaining access to some of the best funds, which are often at full capacity. Some of these downsides can be overcome by accessing hedge funds through a hedge fund of funds and this is this route that investment consultants often recommend and most institutional and individual investors gladly take. Despite this approach adding to fees which are already considerable, the majority of investors decide that specialist expertise and stringent monitoring and risk management is needed in this area and so delegate such responsibilities to a hedge fund of funds.

In this section, I run through some of the main risks from investing in hedge funds. Investing through a good hedge fund of funds can drastically reduce some of these risks, (but rarely eradicate them).

3.5.1 Portfolio Specific Risk

Hedge funds generally differ from traditional ('long-only') funds at portfolio level for four main reasons: hedge funds may hold short positions (a position in an instrument that has been borrowed and sold on) as well as long ones, they may use derivatives and/or other OTC instruments (securities not traded on an exchange), they may use leverage (investing in securities of total greater value than the fund's assets) and they may vary their exposure in one or more markets. Many hedge funds use only one or a few of the above techniques. Furthermore, many hedge funds use the above techniques to reduce risk rather than increase it. All the same, given the complexity resulting from the above, good risk management at a portfolio level is imperative.

When a hedge fund of funds investigates a hedge fund for potential investment, the risk from such a portfolio can be assessed by investigating how the above techniques are being used: Do short positions counterbalance long ones and hence reduce risk of exposure to market moves? Are derivatives used to hedge or to speculate? Is leverage used to add instruments that will reduce overall risk or is it used to amplify an already risky portfolio? A good hedge fund investor should ask all these questions and more. In addition, when assessing a hedge fund it is important that there is a sound risk management, monitoring and measurement function. It's not good enough just to have fantastic investment managers; there must be an equally impressive risk manager.

3.5.2   Market Specific Risk

Although many hedge funds are highly insulated from moves in the underlying markets, many carry residual market exposure due to mismatches between long and short positions and/or deliberate market bets. Furthermore, in times of market crashes and corrections, correlation structures between financial instruments change noticeably, meaning that a seemingly 'hedged' portfolio moves significantly with the market in these instances. Reliance on backward-looking risk management techniques may well underestimate market risk and so many good hedge funds use more anticipative techniques such as scenario analysis and stress-testing as a measure of the impact of varying market conditions. There is also a benefit from investing in funds with experienced managers since they would have been through tough conditions already rather than learning at your expense!

3.5.3   Strategy Specific Risk

Many hedge fund strategies are cyclical and their effectiveness varies considerably over the economic (or some other) cycle. Furthermore, some strategies diminish over time due to a withering opportunity set, or may change due to structural market changes such as, for example, changes in market behaviour due to the introduction of new classes of products, e.g. credit derivatives. It is even the case that some strategies suffer from overpopularity and returns are diminished due to vast inflows of assets. Finally, the risks in a given strategy can change drastically over time and so being invested in a strategy cannot be thought of as a static process. The best way to ensure that strategy risk is kept in check is to ensure you have a degree of diversification across strategies and their driving factors and, if possible, be sure to have (or invest through an adviser/hedge fund of funds that has) an active strategy monitoring and/or allocation process.

3.5.4   Manager/Infrastructure/Operational Risk

Risk can exist within a fund management company due to poor infrastructure. A fund management company consists not just of investment managers, but also risk managers, traders, middle office, back office and administration. It is important that all these functions exist and are well honed, otherwise it is possible for returns to be impacted for 'operational' reasons, e.g. lost trade ticket, poor portfolio monitoring, key person leaves without any written procedure to explain what they do and how they do it. The only true way to minimise operational risk is to investigate this area in considerable detail throughout the investment process from execution with the traders, risk managers, middle office, back office right through the funds accountants, administrators and brokers, and stress-testing the system by questioning procedure in worst case scenarios, e.g. disaster recovery plans, loss of computer systems, etc. Good hedge fund investors see such investigation as important as the work they would do on more investment related issues.

3.5.5   Fraud

Fraud exists in all areas of investment management and is the quickest way to lose all your money. The risk of fraud within hedge funds is concentrated in two main areas – one is theft of money from the fund and the other is overstatement of returns, thus attracting more investors and also taking an inflated performance fee. Extensive due diligence to prevent investing in fraudulent funds is imperative and requires a thorough check on infrastructure and information flows between various parties, as above, to ensure that there are suitable checks and balances in place to prevent theft. Also a thorough check on valuation procedures is needed (see below) to ensure that fund returns cannot be overstated. It is also important to gain references from counterparties (i.e. prime brokers, lawyers, auditors and administrators) and verify such counterparties to be reputable.

3.5.6   Valuation Risk

Many hedge funds trade in 'off-exchange' instruments, e.g. distressed bonds and OTC derivatives, and it is important to ensure that such instruments are being correctly valued by a third party since the valuation process of such 'difficult to price' instruments can be exploited to misvalue a fund. To lessen such a risk, it is important to confirm the existence of a pricing policy involving a third party administrator and outside price sources and regular audits from external accountants. There is always an element of discretion in pricing off-exchange instruments, but it is important to see that this is minimised.

3.5.7   Liquidity Risk

Hedge funds often trade in esoteric and off exchange instruments which can be of limited liquidity, which presents a risk to investors. It may be the case that returns that are generated from positions in illiquid securities are in fact just a premium for taking such liquidity risk, which is a risk that could materialise into a loss later down the line. Another liquidity-based risk is that the liquidity of the fund does not match the liquidity of the underlying investments, which may result in the fund not being able to pay redemptions on time.

As can be seen from above, risk is present in all types of investing, hedge funds included. Many of these risks can be reduced and managed through hard work and research, as well as through experience and proactivity. Often, specialisation is needed and specific custom-built tools can help throughout the process. As well as reducing risk through investigation and appropriate selection, diversification by hedge fund manager, strategy market and approach are all beneficial, and regular monitoring is essential. It is for these reasons that hedge funds of funds are the chosen route for many investors and, with the above risks reduced this way, the hedge fund world is capable of truly exceptional risk adjusted returns.

3.6 SUMMARY

In this chapter I have discussed the argument that it isn't the magnitude of hedge fund returns but their structural qualities of low correlation to equities and bonds and low volatility that form a compelling reason to invest. However, don't think that hedge fund returns are sure to diminish – there is a true rationale for why such returns should exist and continue to do so. I have also explained the point that not all hedge fund strategies share the same basic characteristics and some strategies may not be appropriate for some types of investors. Finally, I have run through the main risks particular to hedge funds (although commonly found elsewhere as well) and shown how a hedge fund of funds or a skilled and experienced advisor can significantly reduce these risks through expert appraisal, selection, diversification and plain hard work.

In the next chapter I will develop this argument further by taking a closer look at the nature, benefits and downsides of hedge funds of funds.

3.7 GLOSSARY FOR CHAPTER 3

Long-Biased

A portfolio is long-biased if its exposure to long positions has a tendency to be greater than its exposure to short positions.

Operational Risk

The risk of loss resulting from inadequate or failed internal or third party processes, people and systems.

OTC

Stands for 'over the counter'. Traded directly with a counterparty rather than through an exchange.

Prime Broker

The main broker for a hedge fund.

Third Party

In the contents of hedge funds, this term usually refers to a provider of services to the hedge fund and/or hedge fund manager such as broker, lawyer, administrator and auditor.

3.8 SUMMARY OF IDEAS FOR CHAPTER 3

- Hedge fund returns aren't necessarily better than that of traditional investments, just structurally different.
- Different hedge fund strategies can differ radically in terms of risk, return and market exposure taken.
- Hedge funds have risks within them that differ from those found in traditional investments and such risks need to be managed.

4

Investing in Hedge Funds Through a Hedge Fund of Funds

4.1 OVERVIEW

In this final chapter of Part I, I aim to explain what a hedge fund of funds actually does. I will take a closer look at the functions carried out by a hedge fund of funds and consider the upsides and downsides in accessing hedge funds in this way.

4.2 WHAT DO HEDGE FUNDS OF FUNDS DO?

Hedge funds of funds are widely believed to be just 'hedge fund pickers' and nothing more. Selection of outperforming hedge funds is, of course, a fundamental part of what hedge fund of funds do. However, there are many more areas that need to be covered in order to run a successful hedge fund of funds, as we see below.

- Combining the appropriate strategies to form the desired return stream
  - Before even constructing a hedge fund of funds portfolio, bespoke or otherwise, a hedge fund of funds manager needs to assess the needs and constraints of the intended investors to ensure the profile of expected returns and risk is appropriate. For example, if a particularly downside controlled portfolio is required then there would be a bias towards market independent strategies such as relative value, which tend to be involatile. However, this would not just be a matter of investing with all 'low volatility' strategies since some of the least volatile 'static return' or 'yield based' strategies have potential for significant downside. Thus the consideration of which strategies to use is far from straightforward.
- Strategy allocation
  - A hedge fund of funds needs to rebalance strategy exposures on an ongoing basis since some strategies work better at some times than

others and also sometimes risks change significantly in a strategy over time. As a result, an independent strategy allocation process is needed.

- Hedge fund selection
  - The most obvious duties of any hedge fund of funds. Less obvious is the work that needs to be done away from the hedge fund's investment process. This is based around operational risk management and anti-fraud analysis, which is as essential as any other area in this list.
- Portfolio construction
  - It isn't just good enough to pick the best hedge funds, how they are combined can make a significant difference to the resulting hedge fund of funds' return stream. Bundling all the best performing hedge funds together may look good on paper but may result in a drastic lack of diversification, concentration in certain risk factors or even a collection of strategies or funds that are past their best. All these issues need to be addressed through a rigorous portfolio construction process.
- Risk management
  - Hedge fund of funds managers are as much risk managers as they are investment managers given that the risk profile from the hedge fund of funds portfolio is important to most hedge fund of funds investors, who invest for good risk adjusted returns. Given that risks in some hedge funds are notoriously underrepresented in their track record, a probing and thorough risk measurement approach is needed. Furthermore, given the broad mandates of hedge funds, their risk levels are constantly changing and so ongoing risk analysis is essential.
- Monitoring
  - Hedge funds have a broad mandate, ever changing portfolios and assets and key person dependence and all this needs to be monitored on an ongoing basis to ensure the reasons why the hedge fund was selected are still valid. Without regular, frequent and effective monitoring, the value added from the fund selection in the hedge fund of funds portfolio may become less down to skill and more down to luck as time goes on.
- Capacity negotiation and sourcing
  - A hedge fund of funds should be a good route to otherwise closed hedge funds. To this end, a good hedge fund of funds manager needs to be very aware of when significant new hedge funds

launch, assess them and if they are desired for investment then ensure that capacity in such a fund is made available. Given that nowadays, the best new hedge funds open to new investment and then close quickly afterwards, hedge funds of funds managers can add great value through vigilance and good contacts in this area.

- Education and transparency
  - Investors in hedge funds of funds deserve to see what they are invested with and a sensible fund of funds will provide full transparency of underlying hedge fund investments so that the fund of fund can be easily assessed. It is my own personal belief that a hedge fund of funds should also seek to educate their investors as to what they do whenever possible, to facilitate fair assessment.
- Ongoing portfolio management
  - Given the ever changing nature of hedge funds portfolios and strategies, it is essential that analysis is ongoing and the portfolio reflects the outcomes of such analysis whenever possible. Furthermore, as the fund of funds experiences inflows and outflows of assets, each rebalancing opportunity should not be wasted. Hedge fund of funds management departments are sometimes referred to as 'hedge fund research' departments but a hedge fund of funds that thinks all it has to do is research is missing something big.

4.2.1   A Note on Transparency

It is always puzzling when a hedge fund of funds manager refuses to reveal the funds they are invested with. As we have seen above, much value is added through an *ongoing* set of monitoring and management processes, and so hedge fund of funds managers have little to lose from revealing the names of the funds they are invested with. Some hedge fund of funds managers say that if they reveal their underlying funds then their returns could be replicated, but surely this would only be true if they added no value through monitoring and ongoing risk management and were invested with no funds that were 'closed to new investors' – this is either unlikely or undesirable! If a hedge fund of funds manager is not willing to show every aspect of their process, systems and the funds they invest with then you have to ask yourself why this is.

As can be seen above, there is a lot of potential value added from a hedge fund of funds that transcends just picking good funds. To investigate further, next we will take a look at the role of hedge fund of funds manager.

4.3   THE ROLE OF THE HEDGE FUND OF FUNDS MANAGER

A hedge fund of funds manager has a highly varied day using both quantitative and qualitative analysis skills as well as strategy expertise and interpersonal skills. Often, time will be devoted to analysing new hedge funds that are being assessed for investment. Such funds may have been found by a quantitative screening of track records of thousands of funds, or through networks of contacts within the industry. Once a fund has been identified as a potential new investment, wide ranging analysis is performed. This could involve performing further quantitative analysis of track record, conducting due diligence on the fund's brokers and administrators, or interviewing the hedge fund manager to discuss investment process. Such analysis usually extends to site visits where the full range of employees in the hedge fund management company is interviewed – investment managers through to back office managers.

A similar amount of time is devoted to monitoring existing hedge fund investments. This can be done at a strategy level – the type of strategy that the fund practices – and at an underlying manager/fund level. Strategy level analysis typically involves looking at how drivers of risk and return in each strategy are changing over time. For example, Merger Arbitrage – a strategy that invests in companies that are merging or being acquired – should perform better if there are more mergers and acquisitions in the market at any one time. Should there be less deals of this type then the opportunity set for such funds shrinks, often meaning lower returns.

The other level of analysis is at an underlying hedge fund level. Good hedge fund of funds managers will have negotiated an appropriate level of transparency with the funds they invest with and as such they will have information that allows them to measure the full range of risk within the portfolio as well as perform portfolio attribution and a degree of style analysis. Thus, the hedge fund of funds manager is equipped to spot drifts in the underlying hedge fund's risk, style and source of returns.

Another important aspect of monitoring investments is talking to the managers of the underlying hedge funds. A good hedge fund of funds manager will invariably have regular conversations with the underlying funds' managers about their portfolio and outlook. This is another, more qualitative, way of identifying sources of risk and return and is another important source of information.

Arguably, hedge fund of funds managers are not investment managers. They select funds for investment but cannot contribute to the return of those funds. What they can do, however, is regularly search a significant proportion of the universe of hedge funds to find the best and most appropriate funds to invest with – a level of coverage beyond most non-specialist institutional investors and consultants. Once suitable candidates have been identified, a good hedge fund of funds manager will develop an in-depth understanding of how the returns are produced on a fund-by-fund basis, and then identify and measure the risks that were taken to produce such returns. This can be a valuable and important part of the investment process. Looking forward, an effective hedge fund of funds manager can estimate how those risks could change and what could happen to returns in the future. This can be done at both a hedge fund and a strategy level. As such, an effective hedge fund of funds manager is as much of a risk manager and a strategy allocator as an investment manager and this is a large part of their 'value added'.

As mentioned above, the hedge fund universe is highly populated and diverse but a good hedge fund of funds manager should have a deep understanding of all of those strategies and will cover a large part of the 8000+ strong funds that practice them. However, effective hedge fund of funds managers will spend as much time monitoring existing investments and strategies as they will selecting new ones. Pro-activity is key and true value can be added from noticing upward drifts in risk and tails-off in return. Similarly, value can be added by being quick to act when a significant change occurs in a hedge fund such as the departure of a key person or when too much new capital is raised.

In short, a good hedge fund of funds manager should be strong on risk measurement and management. They should understand the potential sources of risk and drivers of return in each hedge fund strategy and each hedge fund they invest in. Importantly, they will monitor their investments closely enough to act in a proactive and informed manner when changes occur. As a result, this combination of coverage, specialist knowledge, in-depth monitoring and proactivity has potential to add significant value.

Above we have seen the broad range of skills needed to be an effective hedge fund of funds manager, but where do they come from? Hedge fund of fund managers and analysts come from a variety of backgrounds, ranging from former hedge fund managers to former journalists. Less common are those that started in the hedge fund industry from 'day one' of their careers and instead, most hedge fund of funds managers bring skills from another area of finance or traditional investment management or trading backgrounds. My own background – academia and financial markets – is also not unusual. The job, although specialist in its need for understanding hedge fund strategies, can also require generalism given that new strategies constantly arise and need to be analysed from scratch. Similarly, a mix of quantitative competence and softer qualitative skills such as effective interviewing and building contact networks are needed. Of course there is space to specialise in certain areas and strategies, but when assessing a hedge fund all of the above skills are needed from individuals within the team. As such, a hedge fund of funds manager is something of a 'generalist specialist' and a 'qualitative quant', roles not usually found in many areas.

Above I have discussed the different areas practiced by hedge funds of funds from the point of view of a hedge fund manager. Now we have covered what hedge funds of funds do, next we will look at the benefits of investing this way, and also the downsides.

4.4 HEDGE FUND OF FUNDS VS DIRECT INVESTMENT: BENEFITS AND DOWNSIDES

Most institutional and individual investors in hedge funds choose to invest in the space through a hedge fund of funds structure. Although this adds another layer of fees, you get – or at least should get – a layer of active risk management and monitoring in exchange. In addition you should get strategies and underlying hedge funds being selected and monitored by specialists who should have a high level of expertise, understanding and experience in what is a pretty complex area. This is a good thing since restrictions on hedge fund portfolios are a lot less stringent than the 'fully invested long-only' restrictions placed on traditional funds. This added flexibility allows hedge fund managers to generate better returns, but also means that more monitoring and analysis needs to be done and this is a main source of 'value added' given by hedge funds of funds.

This isn't the only benefit, however. Many of the best hedge funds tend to be 'at capacity' which means they are closed to new investment. Investing with a suitable hedge fund of funds should give you access to a good proportion of the best, 'closed' hedge funds and should give you diversified access to funds which otherwise would be difficult to access due to their minimum investments.

Diversification is another important aspect. *Don't put your eggs in one basket* is a clichéd but wise rule in investment and most investors sleep at night knowing that through a hedge fund of funds, they get diversification by hedge fund strategy and by hedge fund manager as well as by country and industry sector. Hedge funds tend to have high minimum investments (as high as 5–10 million US dollars in some cases) and this would make even rudimentary diversification difficult for all bar the largest investors. Also, the diversification found in hedge fund of funds portfolios should be better than the basic diversification achieved from just adding more funds, since the hedge fund of funds manager should consider the complimentary nature and cyclicality of the different hedge fund strategies – not all strategies work well all the time but many strategies compliment one another exceptionally well, resulting in even smoother and steadier returns at a hedge fund of funds level.

Depending on your skill, knowledge and asset base as an investor, however, not all of the above benefits may be useful to you. It may be cheaper for the largest investors such as the bigger pension plans world-wide to hire in-house teams to select and monitor hedge funds in their portfolio and, given their size and reputation as stable investors it may be quite straight forward for them to achieve diversification, negotiate capacity and even better terms and transparency. Despite this, most of the largest pension plans have chosen to use hedge funds of funds managers as advisors, even if they don't invest in their funds.

For investors of more modest means, the main hedge fund of funds downsides boils down to the extra layer of fees payable to the hedge fund of funds manager and the fact they are one step further removed from their investments; essentially, another layer of fees and another layer of risk. This extra risk could take the form of operational risk and fraud at the hedge fund of funds level (although the latter is exceptionally rare), or through the risk of the hedge fund of funds managers messing up and detracting from value. Also, there is a need to monitor the hedge fund of funds managers themselves (albeit a significantly lesser burden than monitoring all the underlying hedge funds themselves). As a result, once having decided to invest in hedge funds, the questions to ask are: Would hedge funds still benefit my portfolio once the extra level of fees is considered? If so, can I honestly replicate or beat what the hedge fund of funds does for the fees they charge? If so, do I want to?

To summarise, there are benefits and downsides to investing with hedge funds through a hedge funds of funds:

Benefits

- Expertise
- Diversification
- Ongoing monitoring and active management
- Accessibility to otherwise closed hedge funds

Downsides

- Fees
- Another layer of risk
- Potential for negative value added
- A better deal may be possible by investing directly for the biggest investors

The above appears to be straight forward but there are hedge funds known as multi-strategy hedge funds which invest across a range of hedge fund strategies and may also allow diversified access to the hedge fund space. To close this chapter we take a look at the benefits and downsides of multi-strategy funds as an alternative to hedge fund of funds.

4.5   HEDGE FUND OF FUNDS VS MULTI-STRATEGY HEDGE FUNDS

A multi-strategy hedge fund is a fund that invests across a range of strategies, run by a single hedge fund manager. This is opposed to a hedge fund of funds, which invests across a range of hedge fund strategies each in different hedge funds run by different hedge fund managers.

Multi-strategy funds have been quite popular of late with investors looking for a one-stop shop to invest across a range of hedge fund strategies without having to pay an extra layer of fees to a hedge fund of funds.

There are benefits to investing in multi-strategy hedge funds beyond fee savings. For example, your money is closer to the portfolio, removing the extra layer of risk at hedge fund of funds level. Also, given that the hedge fund manager himself is allocating between strategies, this can be done quicker and with an ear closer to the ground since every portfolio can be seen in full.

There are downsides to investing in a multi-strategy hedge fund instead of a hedge fund of funds as well, however. Most multi-strategy funds grow from single strategy hedge funds and most multi-strategy hedge fund managers were once single strategy hedge fund managers and thus may not have a good understanding of every strategy the fund invests with. This can be dangerous since you are relying on the multi-strategy hedge fund manager to objectively monitor and allocate between strategies within his own business, which may not be within his skill set and with decisions of this type also being swayed by business considerations, e.g. new strategies may be seeded with allocations from the multi-strategy fund to get them going, before they have a live track record; there is a tendency not to divest fully from badly performing strategies just to keep the track record alive.

Another issue within multi-strategy funds is how do you know the manager of a given strategy within a multi-strategy fund is good at his job? If this specialist fund manager is one of the best there is in his area then one must question why he has chosen to work for someone else rather than run his own fund, with more autonomy and better remuneration? The advantage here is that a hedge fund of funds manager can invest with any hedge fund available to her and remove that fund if performance looks poor, but a multi-strategy fund manager is stuck with his in-house specialist alone.

Also, there is single manager risk with a multi-strategy hedge fund that does not exist with a hedge fund of funds. A single strategy blowing up within a multi-strategy hedge fund can be enough to blow up the entire fund, as we have seen with recent cases; such a blow-up in a hedge fund of funds should not directly affect the other hedge fund investments and so the hedge fund of funds would be able to carry on relatively unaffected. Recently, one multi-strategy fund lost over 60% due to a blow up in a single strategy, with corresponding fund of fund losses less than 10% of that figure.

So why do single hedge fund managers seek to move outside their area of expertise to add new strategies? Some multi-strategy funds have just evolved as a result of fund manager innovation where the manager has sought to evolve his expertise by pushing forward with innovative new strategies and has thus morphed into multi-strategy funds. However, other reasons include adding new strategies to create more capacity and hence earn more money, or to remove dependence on any given strategy, and also to generate a more resilient (and saleable) business model; neither of these intents are necessarily aligned with investor wellbeing or returns.

All in all, multi-strategy funds may be beneficial over hedge funds of funds for some investors but a degree of expertise is needed to invest with and monitor such a fund; although possibly cheaper and even better performing than a hedge fund of funds, there are risks there proportional to this benefit.

To summarise, the benefits of each way of investing are as follows:

Downsides of hedge funds of funds over multi-strategy funds

• Extra layer of expense
• Cumbersome to reallocate amongst strategies
• Further away from markets and portfolios

Upsides of hedge funds of funds over multi-strategy funds

• Total objectivity
• Can choose between the full range of hedge funds
• No hidden business agenda
• Removes single manager risk

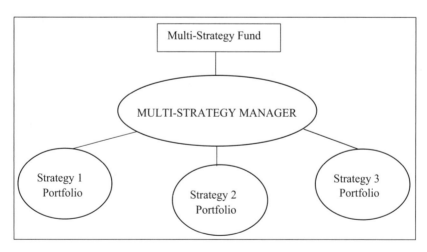

Figure 4.1   Structure of a Multi-Strategy Hedge Fund.

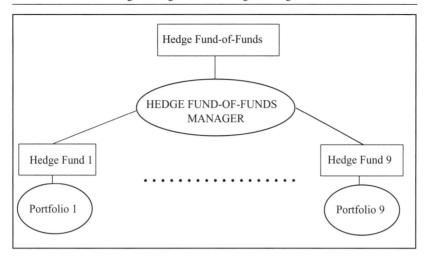

Figure 4.2   Structure of a Hedge Fund of Funds.

4.6   SUMMARY AND CONCLUSION OF PART I

In the first part of this book I have introduced hedge funds and taken a look at the range of different hedge fund strategies and return styles. I have shown that there is a rationale for the existence of these returns and how investing in the space can benefit many different types of investor. Above it can be seen that hedge funds of funds can be a beneficial way of investing in hedge funds and worthy of further analysis. Such analysis can be found in the subsequent parts if this book where I explain what hedge funds of funds do, how to select them and finally take a look at some of the advances in this area.

Should you not have the time or inclination to delve further, I will leave you with some useful tips for assessing hedge funds of funds:

- Do not be seduced by track record alone as smooth returns may hide accidents waiting to happen. Delve down beneath the surface to ensure there is adequate diversification by manager and strategy.
- Does the manager invest in strategies you may wish to consider avoiding?
- Experience of the hedge fund-of-funds manager is as important as experience of the group. Sometimes whole teams migrate, leaving the business devoid of any hedge fund expertise.

- A good hedge fund of funds can give you access to the best hedge funds, which are usually otherwise closed to new investment. Check to see if this is so, and to what extent.
- Risk management and monitoring are a great source of value added. You need to be sure that your hedge fund-of-fund manager realises he is a risk manager as well. Are they in regular contact with the managers of the underlying funds? What kind of risk monitoring do they do?
- Systems, solid processes and active management are important – get a good explanation of each. Ask potential hedge fund of funds managers who they have invested and disinvested with recently and get them to explain the rationale.

4.7   GLOSSARY FOR CHAPTER 4

At Capacity

A hedge fund that has enough assets under management to close to new investment.

Multi-strategy Hedge Fund

A hedge fund that utilises a range of hedge fund strategies.

4.8   SUMMARY OF IDEAS FOR CHAPTER 4

- Hedge funds of funds managers do more than just pick good funds, there are many other 'value added' areas.
- There is a strong argument for investing in hedge funds of funds over single hedge funds for all but the largest investors.
- Multi-strategy funds may be preferable over hedge funds of funds for some investors although the risks are bigger.

Part II
Hedge Funds of Funds in Action

5
Core Functions and Capabilities
of Hedge Funds of Funds

5.1 OVERVIEW

There are many different approaches to investing with hedge funds and hence there is a variety of different types of investment process used by different hedge funds of funds.

For example:

- Some hedge funds of funds are biased towards past performance and track record and will spend more time performing quantitative analysis of past performance and this will predominate within the investment process.
- Some funds will be more inclined to do qualitative analysis and take a forward looking view gained from analysing the investment process and finding an edge; here past track record will play a lesser role in the investment decision.
- Some hedge funds of funds may invest across a wide range of hedge funds thus diversifying away much single hedge fund manager risk from individual hedge funds.
- Some hedge funds of funds will want to give concentrated access to what they think are the best hedge funds thereby having more single hedge fund manager risk and having to spend more time on risk management.

As a result, there is a degree of subjectivity involved in assessing hedge fund of funds investment and risk processes as different potential investors in hedge funds of funds will resonate better with certain biases within the processes. However, there are core functions that need to be practiced by all good hedge funds of funds to ensure that an investment process is rigorous, effective and repeatable; and there are core capabilities that are needed to practice these functions.

In this introductory chapter I take a brief overview of these core functions and capabilities and in the subsequent two chapters in this section I will address the core functions in detail, split by *investment* and *risk management and monitoring*. Finally, this will be brought together by looking at an example of a detailed report on a hedge fund.

5.2   HEDGE FUND OF FUNDS CORE FUNCTIONS

The core functions within a hedge fund of funds can be broken down into seven main areas:

- Strategy Allocation
  - However skilled a hedge fund manager is, he will find it difficult to generate returns if the strategy he practises is doing badly. This is particularly so in the more specialised strategies such as Merger Arbitrage or Convertible Bond Arbitrage where performance is constrained by the opportunity set and the direction of underlying driving factors or markets. As a result, a good hedge fund of funds will have the capability and process in place to be able to construct an informed analysis of the outlook for the full range of hedge fund strategies in order to select those which will do well going forward.
- Sourcing Hedge Funds and Capacity Provision
  - It is important that a hedge fund of funds is linked into all the right networks to ensure that they do not miss out on good quality hedge funds that are to be launched. Similarly, for both good quality new launches and top existing hedge funds, it is important that the hedge fund of funds has capacity reserved, i.e. the promise that the hedge fund in question accepts further investment from the hedge fund of funds; this ensures that the hedge fund of funds has scalability to accept new assets without diluting its portfolio.
- Hedge Fund Selection
  - One of the main roles of hedge funds of funds is to select good hedge funds and so it is obvious that this is a core function for them. As we see below, there are particular functions within this area that one would expect good hedge funds of funds to have proficiency.
- Portfolio Construction
  - It is possible for a hedge fund of funds to select great strategies and managers but still have portfolios that do not deliver what is expected. A solid portfolio construction process ensures that this

does not occur and, as such, has to be a core skill set for any hedge fund of funds.

- Critical Analysis and Decision Process
  - A good hedge fund of funds will have an active and regular formal decision process in place to ensure that investment is not just a result of information gathering but also of in-depth critical analysis. Such a process will also continually revisit the investment decision to ensure that it is still valid.
- Risk Management
  - An advanced risk measurement and management process is the bedrock of any good hedge fund of funds. It is needed to assess and monitor the varying risks in underlying hedge funds and hence the hedge fund of funds itself to ensure that they are commensurate with what is expected. It is also necessary to check that the main risk within a hedge fund is taken in areas where the underlying hedge fund managers have expertise. Hedge fund managers taking risks in areas outside their core skillset can lead to disaster, as we have seen again and again in the hedge fund world.
- Ongoing Portfolio Management and Monitoring
  - Information has a very short lifespan in the hedge fund world given the wider mandates and broader universes that hedge funds are allowed to trade, and the greater key man dependence in this area. As a result, a regular monitoring process to assess these shifts is vitally important. Furthermore, the above processes need to be ongoing to ensure the portfolio is actively managed and represents the latest convictions of the hedge fund of funds managers and risk managers; as such ongoing portfolio management is also core.

Furthermore, within the hedge fund selection process, there must be the following processes:

- Quantitative Analysis and Filtering
  - With any good hedge fund of funds there needs to be the capability to perform informed analysis of the track record of any hedge fund up for selection and this tends to be through a quantitative approach. Similarly, there needs to be a process in place to ensure that the hedge fund universe can be quantitatively analysed and filtered to check for any outperforming hedge funds that have been missed though more qualitative measures. NB just because the hedge fund is outperforming doesn't mean that it should be automatically invested with, just that it should be investigated.

- Referencing and Operational Due Diligence
  - A good hedge fund of funds will perform in depth due diligence to ensure that a hedge fund manager has a good reputation and background and that any hedge fund up for investment has a solid infrastructure so to minimise operational risk.
- Hedge Fund Information Gathering and Interpretation
  - The hedge fund selection process involves the collection of many disparate and often complex data from many different sources. For this process to be effective it is important that it is done in a rigorous and timely manner and that all this information is draw together into a proper framework to form an investment report. The information should not be taken at face value but instead should be interpreted and assessed by the hedge fund of funds investment team in order to facilitate a proper critical analysis. As a result of the above, the capability of a hedge fund of funds to generate accurate and timely investment reports is crucial to the hedge fund selection process.

Figure 5.1 shows a detailed investment process diagram for a hedge fund of funds is outlined, allowing us to see how the functions above are integrated.

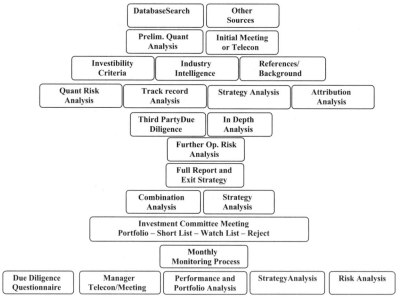

Figure 5.1   Example of a Hedge Fund of Funds Investment Process.

5.3   HEDGE FUNDS OF FUNDS CORE PERSONNEL

In order to practice the core functions, above, a certain number of skilled personnel is needed. Also, as with any business, other personnel are needed to look after operations of the business including compliance, reporting, client servicing and finance. In order to service clients and win new ones, some sales and marketing presence is needed. Finally, to ensure the company complies with good corporate governance principles, some kind of board structure should be in place.

At a minimum, a good hedge fund of funds will have the following:

- Chief Executive Officer (CEO)
  - It is important to have someone to manage the business and also ensure that there is independent oversight of the investment and risk function. CEOs are sometimes more like a COOs or CIOs in smaller hedge funds of funds but independent investment oversight is also an important function and business management skills are quite different to investment management skills.
- Chief Investment Officer (CIO) and Investment Team
  - Overseeing the team performing the majority of the core functions above; it would be difficult to effectively operate without a team of minimum of three people here. It is important to have a CIO as coordinator of the investment process to ensure process is adhered to and lead the decision process.
- Risk Manager
  - Measuring risk in underlying hedge funds and in the hedge fund of funds portfolios, an independent risk manager is essential. Also important is a methodology that allows the risk manager to report directly any risk concerns or breaches to senior non-investment staff.
- Chief Operating Officer (COO)
  - Should oversee operations including IT, compliance, finance, client reporting, etc. Many of these functions can ruin a business if not done well and so this is an important role and it is important that the team here is properly staffed. Even in the tiniest hedge fund of funds there needs to be a team of minimum two.
- Sales and Marketing
  - Unless there is at least one individual in this area it is inevitable that the investment team will be called in at an early stage and this will act as a distraction from the investment process.

- Board of Directors
  - A formal board with at least one non-executive director is necessary to ensure good corporate governance.

The core personnel, above, can be summarised in Figure 5.2:

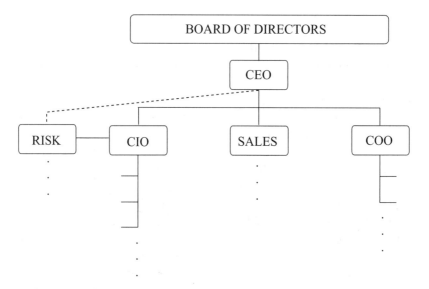

Figure 5.2   Basic Hedge Fund of Funds Management Company Structure.

Off The Record

The depth of the investment process and level of adherence to it are sometimes prone to exaggeration in sales meetings, but there are plenty of questions to ask to get a better understanding of how things are actually done, as we will see in Part III.

NB In addition to having decent processes in place for all the above functions, there must also be skilled and experienced investment professionals to run them. Also in Part III I will talk further on how to assess the investment professionals themselves.

In this chapter I have sketched out what I believe to be the core functions of a hedge fund of funds and the staff that are needed to carry them out. In the next three chapters, we take a more detailed look at each of these functions.

5.4 SUMMARY

In this introductory chapter I have defined and introduced the core functions that a good hedge fund of funds needs to perform. In addition, I have looked at the staffing levels and capabilities that are needed to perform these functions. In the subsequent two chapters in this section I will address the core functions in detail, split by *investment* and *risk management and monitoring*. In the final chapter of Part II I will attempt to bring this all together by looking at an example of a detailed hedge fund manager report.

5.5 SUMMARY OF IDEAS FOR CHAPTER 5

- Hedge fund of funds are require to practice a number of core functions including:
  - strategy analysis
  - sourcing hedge funds
  - investment and portfolio construction
  - risk management and monitoring
  - ongoing portfolio management.
- A hedge fund of funds also needs a robust infrastructure with operational as well as investment expertise.
- Skilled and experienced personnel are needed as well as a rigorous process.

6

The Hedge Funds of Funds Investment Process

6.1 OVERVIEW

In this chapter we take a detailed look at the typical investment process of a good hedge fund of funds and, for those readers who have an interest in hedge fund investing, take a look at some 'tips of the trade'. As we have already seen, this isn't just about picking good hedge fund managers but also covering a range of bases, namely:

- Strategy Analysis and Allocation
- Sourcing and Capacity Negotiation
- Quantitative Analysis
- Qualitative Analysis
- Operational Risk Assessment and Referencing
- Portfolio Construction
- Critical Analysis and Decision Process

6.2 STRATEGY ANALYSIS AND ALLOCATION

However skilled a hedge fund manager is, he will find it difficult to generate returns if the strategy he practises is doing badly and it will be tough to outperform hedge funds in better placed strategies. As a result, it's not good enough for hedge funds of funds just to 'pick good hedge funds' – they need to consider their allocations to hedge fund strategies as well.

It is important that a hedge fund of funds has considered how to allocate to strategies and that there is a formal process in place. In some hedge funds of funds there are separate teams to consider strategy allocation but this is unusual as in order to consider a strategy's outlook, one needs to be actively talking to hedge funds and so it is often the hedge fund of funds' portfolio managers and other senior investment professionals that make the strategy based decisions.

So, how can hedge funds of funds decide on strategy allocations? In general, it is a matter of considering many different attributes for any given strategies:

- What is the outlook for the opportunity set for hedge funds to generate good returns in this area?
  - The opportunity set is the set of conditions from which returns are generated. For example, in Merger Arbitrage, returns are generated from corporate mergers and acquisitions and so the opportunity set is the amount of tradable mergers at any one time. If there are no mergers and acquisitions then there can be no Merger Arbitrage. Conversely, if M&A activity is booming then, all things being equal, the strategy has a better outlook. NB not all strategies have such easy to measure opportunity sets!
- How will asset inflows or outflows constrain this opportunity set?
  - In many strategies, the greater the asset flow into a strategy, the more difficult return generation becomes as there is literally 'less of the opportunity set to go around' and so it is important to monitor asset flow in line with the opportunity set. There are various third party data providers that monitor asset flow by strategy such as Tremont. Alternately, this may be monitored in house. If the latter is the case there are benefits to this but it is important to check that the universe is well covered and it's not just a token amount of hedge funds that are monitored for asset flow in each strategy.
- Are there any legal or regulatory changes that may influence the outlook for a strategy?
  - Again, this is an area that is important to monitor as strategies can be deeply effected by even the smallest tweaks to regulation or legislation, e.g. new anti-trust protocol, reporting methodologies and the introduction of material adverse change (MAC) clauses in merger agreements may all affect the dynamics of a merger deal and hence the returns in Merger Arbitrage. It is important for hedge fund of funds managers to keep ahead of the game by monitoring for such future occurrences before they take effect.
- What is the outlook for the levels of risk and liquidity for the strategy?
  - Whatever the liquidity offered by an underlying hedge fund, this is only as valid as the underlying liquidity of the hedge fund's portfolio if everyone is heading for the door at the same time.

Therefore it is important to monitor levels and shifts in portfolio liquidity. Similarly, risks in hedge funds change over time, e.g. Convertible Bond Arbitrage evolved from a volatility based strategy to a credit based one over a period of time and it is important to be aware of these changes when investing and constructing hedge funds of funds portfolios (i.e. has the hedge fund manager got the skills to cope with the change in risk).

- What is expected of the factors that drive the returns of a strategy?
  - Many hedge fund strategies are constrained by driving factors that represent the core of returns. It is possible to take a forward looking view of hedge fund strategies based on the outlook for these factors and markets. Especially, when these factors are at extreme points then a view can be taken with greater confidence, e.g. tight credit spreads going into a period of economic turmoil may be expected to widen, adversely affecting credit exposed Convertible Bond Arbitrage and long-biased credit and high yield strategies; implied volatility (which tends to mean revert) making a new low may result in a positive outlook for Convertible Bond Arbitrage and other long-biased volatility strategies. Of course, these asymmetries may get worse before getting better but all the same this is a useful tool when considering strategy allocation.
- Is there any evidence through quantitative analysis that the structure of risks or returns has changed in a strategy?
  - There is all manner of academic and practitioner research that looks at the structure of hedge fund returns and this should be augmented with up to date in house research to scan for structural changes to the distribution of returns in each strategy.
- What are the hedge fund managers, brokers and other strategy participants saying?
  - It is important to have a practitioner's view 'on the street' as well as analysing theoretical constructs and so it is important to be linked in to a knowledgeable and widespread contact base.

Now, strategy analysis like this can be very 'hand wavy' or very rigorous, depending on the strategy in question and how tight the mandate on that strategy is. Generally, the more distinct and constrained a strategy is, the more formal and analytical the strategy analysis and the less nebulous the allocation decision can be. To illustrate this, below I give an example of each, using two different strategies – Equity Long/Short and Convertible Bond Arbitrage.

EXAMPLE 1: Typical Strategy Analysis for Equity Long/Short

In Equity Long/Short one can analyse the inflows of assets as easily as any other strategy but to be effective, the asset inflows need to be monitored by each type of Equity Long/Short sub-strategy, e.g. by geography and cap focus. Vast inflows into US Equity Long/Short will have little impact on the Japan Equity Long/Short funds. Some strategies in this area are quite specialist and, in general, the more niche the market, the more sensitive to asset flows it will be.

For Equity Long/Short, the outlook for opportunity set is difficult to predict as it is generally market related – most funds of this type have a long bias of exposure to the underlying equity markets and so should do better in up-markets than in down-markets but predicting market direction is notoriously difficult and something of a lottery. Similarly, given the simplicity of this strategy and the depth of underlying equity markets, it is less sensitive to regulatory shifts or changes to law or structure unless they are radical such as the unwinding of crossholdings in Japanese equity markets or the US change in dividend taxation policy.

The strategy, when practised in developed equity markets, is very liquid but for smaller cap managers or less developed markets, market liquidity should be monitored. Also, quantitative analysis may be used to analyse hedge funds' exposures to the markets and leverage in order to estimate the direction they think the equity market will take and their overall conviction in these positions. Further analysis of market volatility can also be used to gain an outlook for the strategy.

Overall, given the broad, liquid nature of the Equity Long/Short strategy and its imperviousness to minor changes it is a difficult strategy to predict.

EXAMPLE 2: Typical Strategy Analysis for Convertible Bond Arbitrage

In Convertible Bond Arbitrage it is possible to form an outlook on the basis of the drivers of returns, e.g. credit spreads, volatilities and market price/fair value ratios for convertible bonds. The levels of such drivers can be analysed in the context of their historic ranges. This work can be combined with analysis of inflows and the size of the opportunity set, e.g. convertibles in issuance, new issuance and assets and new assets in the strategy. Further discussions with Convertible Bond Arbitrage managers and investment bankers connected to primary convertible bond new issuance can give an estimate of the outlook for the primary issuance environment and all this work can be combined to form an outlook. Awareness of the regulatory environment for convertible bonds and equities is also of use here, e.g. when US taxation on dividends was lowered convertible bond arbitrage managers suffered due to higher dividends being paid out.

As we can see Example 2 represents a strategy that is much less difficult to predict than that in Example 1, which illustrates that strategy analysis is useful and necessary, but certainly not a science!

A good hedge fund of funds will do more that just practice the above in an ad hoc way – there will be a strategy allocation process in place with regular meetings, reviews and implementation procedures based on the above analysis. The strategy allocation process is never easy as the hedge fund of funds manager may begin to favour a strategy but cannot add to investments there as a result of risk, liquidity or capacity constraints. Furthermore in order to invest further with a given strategy, the hedge fund of funds manager would have to reduce an allocation from another strategy, which can often take some time to do and requires that strategy allocation become a relative rather than absolute discipline. Finally, given that most underlying hedge funds allow monthly investment but are now offering only quarterly liquidity or worse, the hedge fund of funds manager has to be exceptionally sure of her stance as to invest is quick but to disinvest is a slow process.

6.3 SOURCING AND CAPACITY NEGOTIATION

It is important that hedge funds of funds are proficient at sourcing new hedge fund managers. The best new hedge fund managers have no need to advertise themselves and often reach their asset targets through contacts and word of mouth and will not reopen for new investment for some time afterwards, if at all. As a result, promising new hedge funds can be often missed by hedge funds of funds without the appropriate contact base and with no 'ear to the ground'. The earlier a promising new hedge fund is discovered, the more time there is to do a thorough analysis before asset capacity is reached and so there is a clear advantage to finding new hedge funds ahead of the pack.

Useful contacts in sourcing new hedge fund managers include prime brokerage capital introduction networks, marketers and trade journalists as well as colleagues at other hedge funds of funds. However, an edge over peers can be gained by having good contacts at the trading, brokerage and asset management departments of big investment banks and investment management houses as it is these institutions that tend to be the source of the best new hedge fund managers. For these reasons the good contacts in the investment consultancy community are also useful.

On the sourcing side there is a clear advantage to the well connected but also to those hedge funds of funds that are well known and/or are well established and have been around for longer. These hedge funds of funds tend to be on all the standard call lists and so often get approached directly by the hedge funds themselves.

There are also many databases of existing hedge funds that are potentially useful for sourcing new potential investments although it is fair to say that many of the best funds are either not on such databases or are on there but closed to new investments. It is still useful to perform screens on the broader hedge fund databases compiled by the likes of Tremont and HFR, for example, as it is sometimes possible to find hedge funds that have been overlooked. Such screens tend to be based on quantitative filtering of track record and asset base for all managers within a given hedge fund strategy. It must be said, however, that the hit rate for finding new investments in this manner is low.

Once a new hedge fund is deemed worth investing with, shrewd hedge funds of funds will reserve future capacity as part of the deal associated with initial investment. Such capacity negotiation is a key duty of a hedge fund of funds as it ensures scalability of their portfolio and the ability to grow the concentration of the initial investment over time.

The process of 'scaling in' to a new investment – increasing the size of the investment over time rather than all at once – is common amongst hedge funds of funds and important for two reasons. First of all it allows the hedge fund of funds manager to build confidence with the hedge fund in question before investing too much money on day one, when the hedge fund manager is still unproven and operational risk higher. However, secondly, it is important to have that initial investment as 'day one' investors are generally treated well by hedge funds in terms of capacity and access later down the line, as it was these investors that helped get the fund off the ground.

Again longer established hedge funds of funds generally have an advantage in terms of capacity over newer arrivals, as the more established groups should have capacity with many of the outperforming well established hedge funds from the early days which are otherwise closed to new investors.

Off The Record

Some new hedge fund managers are more skilful at creating hype for themselves than managing money. In my view, the investment process should not be rushed or compromised for any fund, regardless of the hype. However, given the assets raised at open by some over-hyped hedge funds, it appears that not everybody subscribes to this point of view.

6.4   QUANTITATIVE ANALYSIS AND FILTERING

When searching for or analysing hedge funds, there is a significant amount of quantitative analysis and filtering that can be done, provided there is a track record for the fund in question. Even in funds with shorter track records, taking a quantitative look beyond the returns into the portfolio itself can add significant value.

6.4.1   Quantitative Filtering

It is common for hedge funds of funds to do a regular search on the hedge fund databases such as those provided by HFR and Tremont. Such databases consist of information such as hedge fund name and hedge fund manager name and address, strategy type, assets under management and historic monthly returns since inception. Along with the data, there is specialist software that is designed to be used for such searches and can be used to filter on most popular risk and return based measures.

The hit ratio (i.e. chance of finding a hedge fund that you end up investing with) with these databases is quite low as a good hedge funds of funds will already be aware of all the best hedge funds through their contacts and market intelligence. Also many of the best hedge funds tend not to publish their returns on such databases as they aren't looking to raise assets; even when the best hedge funds do publish their data they are often closed to new investment anyway. Although a search for the best performing hedge funds can be interesting, it's not the best of searches given that the hedge funds in the databases are taking radically different levels and types of risk so it's not comparing like with like. As a result, searches on risk adjusted return as listed below (essentially return divided by some measure of downside or volatility of returns) can be more useful.

Typical risk adjusted return measures include Sharpe, Sortino and Sterling ratios. The Sharpe ratio is the expected return over cash for a return series divided by the standard deviation of such returns. The Sortino ratio is the expected return over cash for a return series divided by the standard deviation of only negative excess returns, i.e. less than cash. The Sterling ratio is compounded annualised return for a return series divided by a measure of drawdown (biggest total loss over a period). Formulae for each of the above ratios can be found on good investment management training websites such as Investopedia (*www.investopedia.com*).

Equally effective can be a broad and simple filtering process that excludes hedge funds that have consistently lost money or have relatively enormous down months; surprisingly, once this filtration has been made and the resulting hedge funds are further divided by strategy, the resulting lists aren't that long.

Other more qualitative filtering can also be done such as excluding hedge funds with continually low assets that would not be able to deliver a suitable infrastructure. At Key Asset Management, our in house rule is that if a hedge fund management company can't (or doesn't look able to) pay out the company's fixed annual costs (salaries, bills, etc) with the fixed management fees they earn from the funds they manage, the hedge fund/manager is not investable at present. The rationale for this is that in order to stay in business, such a hedge fund will have to make a sizeable performance fee (i.e. strong positive performance) as if they don't, they can't pay the bills. This sounds like a great incentive but if that hedge fund manager isn't looking like he will make enough profit from the performance fee, he will have to take greater risks to generate greater returns to earn more fees, otherwise his company loses solvency. It would be irrelevant to such a manager whether the market environment was appropriate for taking such risk or not and so he is, essentially, out of control.

For those looking to do a quantitative search themselves, there are many different types of searches based on risk and return, but this example, below, may be of use:

1. Select the strategies for the funds you want to look at, e.g. Merger Arbitrage. Comparing different strategies is not comparing like for like and so will not lead to an effective search.
2. Select time period over which the funds would have to have been in existence, e.g. last 5 years. The longer the time period, the fewer funds will be in the search.
3. Screen out all funds that have performed less than a certain level in terms of average annual returns, e.g. 5%. This aims to filter out

hedge funds that have heavily underperformed rather than exclude all but the best performers. The return limit has to be in line with the types of return expected from the strategy in question and the broad historical returns produced by the strategy. Placing the return limit too high will create too extreme a filter.

4. Screen out all funds that have had a losing month greater than a certain large amount, e.g. -10%. This aims to filter out those with poorer risk control. Again, the threshold has to be one in line with the strategy returns.

5. Repeat again for shorter time periods, e.g. going back 3 years. This ensures that newer hedge funds aren't overlooked.

The above search represents a basic risk and return based filtering process. Note that risk and return have been addressed separately as sometimes risk return measures such as Sharpe ratios are biased towards hedge funds with low returns but negligible volatility and so doing the risk and return sections separately can allow the searcher to impose the demands he has over risk and return separately. It is also useful to save the output of each level of filtering as this allows analysis by inspection at each part of the search, to ensure threshold levels haven't been too extreme or lax, and to analyse special cases where a desirable hedge fund is filtered out too soon.

In addition to volatility and risk adjusted return based ratios, there are also other filters that can be placed, for example:

6. Screen out all funds that have had less than a certain percentage of profitable months, e.g. 70%. This is useful when consistent positive returns are desirable such as in arbitrage strategies.

7. Screen out all funds that have had less than a certain level of rolling 12 month returns, e.g. 0%. This is also a useful filter that removes the slightly arbitrary nature of (calendar-based) annual returns.

Off The Record

Overall, typical searches and filters are useful for searching for otherwise overlooked gems in the hedge fund world and reaffirming that you have what you believe are the best hedge funds in your portfolio. However, not all hidden gems are what they seem and many overlooked hedge funds with top rate performance often have other, more qualitative downsides such as poor infrastructure or lack of identifiable edge.

6.4.2   Further Quantitative Analysis

Once a potentially interesting hedge fund has been identified, there is plenty of quantitative analysis that can be done. It is not of the scope of this book to describe *how* to do this but below I list some of the useful work that can be done:

- Basic risk and return analysis of track record.
  - This involves the analysis of return and excess return (over cash) and calculating risk figures based on the standard deviation of monthly returns (volatility) and the biggest losses both monthly and over time. Simple calculations such as average annualised return, maximum and minimum monthly returns and biggest drawdown (loss over time) can be augmented with analysis of Sharpe, Sortino and Sterling ratios as outlined above.
  - In addition, analysis that considers the levels of leverage that are used by different hedge funds is also worth considering.
  - Using the return series to generate a distribution of returns is also worth doing when enough data exists. The shape and type of distribution and particularly the tail shape are useful and also the calculations that one can make of distribution type such as skew and kurtosis also help analysis.
- Peer group comparison.
  - Also of use is to analyse the hedge fund's performance in the context of peers with similar strategies and appropriate hedge fund indices based on these strategies such as HFRX or CFSB Tremont indices. This analysis can be used to compare risk, return and calculate correlation and also consider leverage and concentration deployed by the fund compared to peers.
  - Such analysis is very useful in discussion with the hedge fund managers to highlight any edge they have or any differences with other practitioners in this strategy they may exhibit.
- Attribution analysis.
  - In addition to basic statistical comparisons, the hedge fund's track record can also be used to give information on profit attribution and comparison with underlying dependent factors and markets. This helps to see whether returns are truly due to manager skill rather than just being dependent on the movements of the underlying markets and the use of leverage.

The above is of use if the hedge fund has an established track record but what can one do for hedge funds with short or no track records? In this case I would advise the analyst to try and find a track record from the hedge fund manager's former role. If the former role was a manager at another hedge fund, a bank trader or a long only equity or bond manager then the analysis may be of limited use and should not be relied on in any way but still better than nothing. Former equity managers' track records can be adjusted for market exposures and analysed and former bank traders usually have some P&L from their trading days. However, in the latter case beware as bank traders are not concerned by monthly percentage return so their way of trading will be different to some extent when they enter the hedge fund world.

6.5   QUALITATIVE ANALYSIS

Once hedge funds have been sourced and filtered, the qualitative assessment process begins. The first meeting is usually there to make an initial assessment of the hedge fund's potential as a new investment for the hedge funds of funds. The aim of this meeting is to see if, from the outset, the hedge fund is both investable and desirable. The former analysis generally assesses the suitability of infrastructure, ownership structure, risk management approach, asset base, and fund structure and is the initial step of the operational due diligence we see below. The latter analysis seeks to begin the hunt for an identifiable edge – is there anything within the hedge fund to suggest that it has an advantage over peers, e.g. experience or skill of the hedge fund manager, niche skillset or focus, first rate risk management or execution, etc. Experienced hedge fund of funds analysts will do a lot of desk-based analysis before this meeting to ensure the investability criteria is passed, allowing the meeting itself to be focussed on edge – the rationale for why the hedge fund can outperform. Edge is a somewhat nebulous concept and different investors will have different approaches to identifying it, no one way being objectively better, but good hedge fund of funds managers will be able to use their skill, context and experience to see if a hedge fund manager is worth pursuing further.

If the initial analysis is positive, further meetings are arranged and further analysis is conducted. A good hedge fund of funds will perform analysis that covers every area of the hedge fund, as we see throughout this section, with the analysis, qualitative and otherwise, written up in a structured report. The qualitative analysis should be aimed at interpreting the investment, risk and execution processes as well as operational and infrastructural areas of the hedge fund. Rather than address this qualitative analysis of investment and risk in the abstract, I will give an example of a good qualitative hedge fund report in the last chapter of Part II and describe each area of analysis with reference to this. Needless to say, such analysis must be timely as the information on which the analysis is based may become obsolete or outdated within a few months.

6.6   REFERENCING AND OPERATIONAL DUE DILIGENCE

The potential for loss in any hedge fund lies as much in the operational and 'softer' areas as it does in the investment and risk processes of that fund.

Furthermore, a bad investment process rarely if ever loses 100% but a hedge fund fraud can incur total loss; although all frauds to date total much less than 1% of the entire current hedge fund universe, the first aim of operational due diligence must be to ensure that such situations are avoided rather than leave it to luck.

The other aim of operational due diligence is to establish the likelihood for processes or business issues to break down and impinge on investment process and returns. This may happen due to weak infrastructure and operational processes, staff turnover or even reputational issues.

The assessment of operational and softer issues within a hedge fund by a hedge fund of funds manager can be split into several areas each of which requires analysis:

- back office/operations team processes;
- third party service providers' processes and portfolio valuation;
- fund structure, prospectus and fees;
- liquidity and cash management;
- staff turnover, remuneration and retention;
- business ownership, infrastructure, profitability and outlook;
- contingency plans;
- reputation and referencing.

In the following section, I address each of these areas in detail, which may be of use for those eager to see the depth that hedge funds of funds go into, or for those that seek to do operational due diligence themselves.

6.6.1 Back Office/Operations Team Processes within an Underlying Hedge Fund

A strong back office (i.e. operations and administration team) manned by experienced and long serving employees is essential for the smooth running of a hedge fund. If things go right, this function is often invisible and only comes into view when things are messed up and, as a result, the importance of back office is often underestimated. When there is not a good team and process in place, it can be a great distraction to investment professionals within the hedge fund and also could lead to missed trades resulting in unexpected loss or even the accidental mispricing of a fund. In worst cases holes in back office processes can allow unchecked fraudulent activity and so this function must be assessed in detail.

The main duties of back office are to collect information on trades executed by the investment professionals and/or trading team and ensure that these trades are noted and reflected in the portfolio monitoring software and reports. They must then reconcile these trades with the prime broker used by the fund to ensure that the trades have been placed. They will generally produce an internal estimate of fund performance with anything from weekly to daily frequency and work with the fund's administrator on its formal, independently checked monthly valuation. They may also have responsibility for cash management, currency hedging for hedge fund positions and hedge fund share classes denominated in foreign currency.

When assessing back office a good hedge fund of funds manager will realise that it is important to check the calibre and experience of personnel and that there are enough staff to get the job in hand done even, say, if one is off sick. Longevity is also important as it takes some time for operations staff to understand the full procedures in a new hedge fund, however experienced they are. Back office personnel are often underpaid and so it important to investigate turnover and staff retention and that suitably senior people are employed on difficult areas such as hedging. It is important to check through all processes to ensure that they are appropriate and robust and this can be tested by asking about failures in hedging and reconciliation failure rate. Finally, it is important to check that cash management is sensible and does not place risk with low credit counterparties.

6.6.2   Third Party Service Providers' Processes and Portfolio Valuation

By third parties I mean, mainly, the prime brokers, administrators and auditors of the fund. The prime broker is the main hub of trades for a hedge fund and almost all trades for the portfolio will end up being processed by the prime broker who almost always acts as custodian for the hedge funds' assets. The hedge fund administrator is charged with calculating a monthly independently struck price for the fund. The hedge fund auditor will perform an annual audit for the fund entity using independent sources and this should be considered the most accurate valuation of the hedge fund's assets.

Many good hedge funds of funds construct due diligence questionnaires for each of these entities to check that they are performing an adequate and independent service for the fund and its investors (and not the fund management company).

For those interested in doing third party due diligence themselves, here are some suggestions for questions to ask in such due diligence questionnaires:

Prime Broker

- Please give confirmation that you are prime broker to the fund.
- What is the start date of this relationship?
- To your knowledge, are you are the sole prime broker?
  - If there is more than one prime broker then any other prime broker needs to be questioned to ensure that the whole process is rigorous.
- Are you custodian of the fund's assets?
  - This is usually the case.
- Do you use sub-custodians?   If so, please provide further detail.
- Are fully-paid assets segregated in the name of the fund?
- Are cash balances segregated in the name of the fund?
- Does the agreement include the following: futures, options, OTCs, swaps, currencies, CFDs, structured notes, SPVs.
  - A check to see what is traded compared to what the fund manager told you.
- Do you provide all position and price information directly to the fund's administrator?
  - The most important check to be sure that the portfolio is received by the administrator independently of the fund manager.

- What is the method and frequency of data transfer for this information?
  - If not by secure electronic transfer then the information can be tampered with. This should reconcile with what the administrator tells you.
- What is the name and location (and contact details) of the fund's administrator?
  - This should match with the administrator's details.
- Do you provide any of the following services to the fund's manager: office space, office equipment, personnel, IT, systems resources. Please describe fully any additional services that you provide to the fund's manager.
- Do you have the power to close out positions without consulting the investment manager? If so, have these powers ever been invoked?
  - A test to see if the fund has been in trouble before.
- What are the fund's approximate net assets in USD million?
  - This should match with the annual financials and with what the fund manager has told you.
- Please confirm if there are any assets, liabilities or other exposures that are not typically confirmed in your periodical statements to administrators, auditors, etc. (e.g. OTC securities that are not possible to value or due to reporting difficulties)?
  - If so then the handling of these needs to be investigated.

Fund Administrator

- Please give confirmation that you are the administrator to the fund. What is the start date of this relationship?
- Do you (your company) provide the following administration services: Register of shareholders/transfer agent? Processing subscriptions? Processing redemptions? NAV calculations? A Board director to the Fund?
  - It is worthwhile checking exactly what services the administrator provides.
- With what frequency is the NAV calculated?
  - Expect monthly or better.
- Is NAV calculation independent of the investment manager? Is pricing of assets entirely independent of the investment manager? If not, please list any positions where the manager's assistance is typically required.

- ○ If not you need to know why this is and think long and hard whether this is acceptable to you or not. In all but exceptional circumstances it is dangerous to invest with a fund without a stringent independent pricing process.
- Do you provide NAV estimates? If so, are these calculated independently of the investment manager?
  - ○ Ideally, yes.
- What is the primary source of prices for listed securities?
- What is your standard process for fair valuing illiquid securities?
- Name all the sources of prices for unlisted or illiquid securities in the fund.
  - ○ Ideally, the administrator will use independent sources.
- What percentage of the portfolio is unlisted or illiquid?
  - ○ The percentage acceptable here depends on the liquidity of the fund and the strategy type.
- Are there any (or have there been any) positions which involve manual pricing or pricing which is subject to review by the manager or the fund's board? In the case of the above, describe the pricing policy.
  - ○ Again, you are looking for a rigorous process.
- Are all securities priced to bid or last traded price? Are all shorts priced to offer or last traded price? If not in either case, please state how they are priced
- Are all the assets held with the prime broker?
- Are all transaction and position statements received directly from the prime broker(s)? How often is price and position information reconciled to prime broker records? How is this information received (e.g. post, fax, email, download)?
  - ○ This should be reconciled with the answers of the prime broker and fund manager. If not by direct electronic link then there could be a way for a fraudulent investment manager to manipulate the portfolio.
- Does the fund hold positions in the following instruments; if so what is the price source? Futures, options OTCs, swaps, CFDs, structured notes, SPVs.
  - ○ This should be again reconciled with the answer from the prime broker.
- Has there previously been, or are there currently any disputes with the fund, investment manager, auditor, prime broker, regulators, exchanges, investors?

○ If the answer is yes then this needs to be looked into before investing.

• Have you ever restated any NAVs for the fund? Please confirm any differences between the year-end NAV used for trading and the annual financial statements (e.g. due to auditor adjustments, etc.).

○ Again, if yes then further analysis needed.

Auditor

• Please give confirmation that you are auditor to the fund. What is the start date of this relationship?

• What is the date of the last year end financial statements?

• It is standard audit practice to independently confirm all positions held at year-end with custodians and confirm prices against independent data providers (e.g. Bloomberg). Please confirm if this is correct for all positions in the above fund at the last year-end, the medium through which confirmations are received (e.g. post, fax, email, download) and any exceptions to this. Are all of the funds positions priced independently of the investment manager and affiliates?

○ A check on independent valuation at audit.

• Were your previous three auditors' reports standard unqualified reports, or a modified report (e.g. qualified, explanatory paragraph, etc.). If modified please provide details of the modification.

• A check on the last few audits to see if there were any non-standard issues.

Lawyer (of both fund and fund management company)

• Please confirm that you are currently the legal representatives. Please confirm the start date of this relationship?

• To the best of your knowledge is the fund/manager currently a party to any litigation or arbitration proceedings, threatened or pending. To the best of your knowledge has the fund/manager been a party to any litigation or arbitration proceedings to date?

○ A check for any past or pending legal action.

• To the best of your knowledge has the fund been the subject of any regulatory or tax investigation, inquiry or enforcement action?

○ A check for any past or pending regulatory or taxation irregularities.

The aim is to identify that the fund has the prime broker(s) it says it has and that they are in ongoing communication with the administrator for the administrator to electronically download the portfolio positions from the prime broker directly without the interference of the fund manager. As long as this is happening it is difficult for the fund manager to commit a fraud by altering the portfolio before it is sent to the administrator. The prime broker can also give you an estimated value of the portfolio which should tie in with the value that the fund manager has told you.

With the fund administrator it is important to check that they get the portfolio directly, by electronic download, from the prime broker (anybody can programme a fax heading or construct a letter heading and so mail or fax isn't good enough). It is also imperative that the administrator prices the portfolio independently using independent sources e.g. Bloomberg and specialist pricing companies and not prices from the fund manager. In some cases, the instruments traded may be esoteric and difficult to price but even in this case independent sources should be found, ideally not at the suggestion of the fund manager who may recommend brokers that think they 'owe him a favour'. In most cases, instruments with a single or no price source in the market should be very much in minority.

The fund auditor should perform an audit annually and provide a totally independent source of valuation. As well as sending them a due diligence questionnaire they should also provide current and past audits. These audits often provide portfolio details and are worth reading in full. It is also worth checking out whether an audit has been qualified in some way by the auditors – this means that there is something there that they are not entirely happy with.

In the case of all third parties it is important that they are proficient and diligent at their jobs, have solid reputations and all have the capability to pass on information to each other independently of the fund managers to ensure independence. It would be a brave investor that would invest with a hedge fund that uses relatively unknown third parties.

Off The Record

Some administrators perform what is called an 'administration lite' service for the funds, where the investment manager calculates the price and the administrator just oversees that it has been done correctly and rubber stamps it. All other things equal, this is not desirable.

6.6.3   Fund Structure, Prospectus and Fees

When assessing the hedge fund structure in depth, most hedge funds of funds managers find the hedge fund 'mem & arts' and prospectus are the best places to look. The aim is to find any hidden fees or disadvantageous conditions that are not mentioned by the fund manager (I am not saying the fund manager would hide them, just not heavily advertise them!).

For those faced with a hedge fund to assess, on the fee side, it is worth looking at any additional fees paid from the hedge fund, e.g. as directors' remuneration, expenses, administration and audit fees and whether the fund's start up fees were paid from the fund and maybe amortised. It is also worth checking that the fund is priced to a single value and there is no bid ask spread. You should check that there is a high water mark, meaning that should a fund make money, lose money then make money again, you only pay once for the positive performance. Also, you should check the frequency at which performance fees are paid to the manager – annually is usual and quarterly or monthly less straight down the line since the fee will not be calculated as a result of a full audit. Finally, it is worth checking to see if there are subscription and redemption fees and whether these are payable to the fund or the hedge fund manager (former ok, latter questionable). NB that subscription fees are almost always waivable.

As well as looking for all fees, the liquidity of the fund needs to be analysed and investors should be sure that the fund is not offering vastly different liquidity to the underlying portfolio as this could be tricky should many investors try to get their money back at the same time. Also, a lock-up may be present which means that normal liquidity may be limited or costly in the first year or so of investment; if this is so, check that the fee you would pay for early exit from the fund is paid to the fund and not the manager as then, it will compensate you if you are a remaining investor when others are leaving early.

The existence of a fund gate should also be checked; this is a limit on what percentage of the fund's assets can be withdrawn by investors in any one dealing period. For example, if a fund has quarterly liquidity with a 20% gate, should a large part – say 30% – of the fund's investor base all decide to move at the same time at quarter end then only 20% of investor's assets would be allowed out in the first quarter with the remaining 10% left in the queue to come out the following quarter.

The domicile of the hedge fund is also important – this is where the fund is established and so decides the level of oversight a fund has by the regulators and laws of that domicile. Most hedge funds are domiciled in offshore domiciles such as Cayman Islands, Bermuda, etc. as there are tax advantages to being offshore and because these are hubs of offshore investment and so there is an abundance of auditors, administrators and experienced fund directors. However there are an increasing number of funds choosing European 'offshore' domiciles such as Ireland (Dublin) and Luxembourg. Even if a fund is not domiciled in Dublin it may be listed on the Dublin Stock Exchange. The reason for this is that the fund's directors have decided to list there to be subjected to the oversight of this exchange and so give confidence to investors.

Other things of interest include the presence of an 'in specie' clause which states that you can be paid back in stock – i.e. the contents of the underlying portfolio; NB here that the clause is very common but for it to be put into practice it is very rare. Finally, the board of fund directors should be looked at to ensure experience and independence (from the fund manager).

A typical set of fund terms are as follows:

- a fee structure of 1.5%/20%;
- monthly investment with quarterly liquidity at 60 days notice;
- a hard lock up in year 1;
- a soft lock in year 2 with 3% redemption fee.

Interpreted this means the hedge fund charges a fixed management fee of 1.5% p.a. and an additional performance fee of 20% on all annual positive returns. It is possible to invest with the fund at the beginning of any month but exit is only possible at the end of any quarter and only then with 60 days' notice. A hard lock in year 1 means that you are stuck in the fund for at least a year after you invest and the soft lock up in year 2 indicates that if you want to exit the fund in your second year of investment you will have to pay 3% of your investment to do so.

6.6.4   Liquidity and Cash Management

This is an area that is easily ignored but one which could be a cause of many problems and so good hedge fund of funds managers analyse this area in depth. The most important thing to check here is that the liquidity of the underlying portfolio of the hedge fund is matched to the overall liquidity offered to investors. For example, take the extreme example of a portfolio that is virtually illiquid and would take the best part of 12 months to liquidate. If the investors are offered monthly liquidity then it is obvious that if all investors pulled their money at the same time they would not get it back for 12 months even though the liquidity they were offered was monthly.

Often, hedge funds employ what is known as a gate, as I have described above. This means that irrespective of the liquidity terms on offer, any outflows – withdrawals from investors – superseding the value of the fund gate get deferred to the next dealing period, e.g. 20% gate, 30% outflows results in 30% $-$ 20% $\div$ 10% being deferred until next time. As a result, it is important to consider gates when considering the liquidity of any underlying fund.

Finally, a diligent investor should aim to get information on any side letters. Side letters are agreements with particular investors that soften the investment terms in the prospectus in some way. Side letters, for example, may offer superior liquidity to some investors. If such side letters exist investors should be sure that they are happy with other parties being able to withdraw assets ahead of them. It is sometimes the case that the benefits of the fund outweigh negatives such as above.

Most trading and investment within hedge funds is done 'on margin', which means only a deposit is required to secure the stocks and other instruments that are bought. Similarly, when an instrument is shorted, a cash balance is also generated. As a result, hedge funds usually have significant cash balances. It is important to check that this cash is invested wisely with high credit rated cash securities or accounts to ensure that this part of the portfolio is near to risk free.

Off The Record

It is often the case that if a fund suffers significant withdrawals, other investors who would otherwise have stayed invested will also head for the door. They do this as they are worried of being the last ones in the fund and running the risk of the fund being wound down with them still invested. In such situations, remaining investors are not fully paid out until the fund liquidates its portfolio entirely, which can sometimes take a long time. As a result there is an avalanche effect that takes place as everyone runs for the door, and gets stuck!

6.6.5   Staff Turnover, Remuneration and Retention

Staff turnover in hedge funds can be very disruptive, especially when it occurs in the investment, risk and trading functions and high rates of turnover should be frowned upon. Also, turnover in the more operational areas should not be ignored. High levels of turnover are usually indicative that members of staff are not being looked after in some way, be it through remuneration structure, contractual structure or through a failure to maintain a good work environment.

When analysing this area it is important for hedge fund of fund managers to account for any abnormally high turnover rates and to look in depth at any departure of key people – how much they contributed to performance, the reasons for departure, where they are working now. In an ideal world these departed key personnel can be tracked down and interviewed separately to reconcile the reasons for their departure from both sources.

In a proactive sense it is important to check that basic remuneration is at market rate, the bonus is reflective of the effort and contribution to fund return. Also, it is important to check that the employee can't just take the bonus and leave – they must have some ongoing commitment to the fund such as deferred compensation or equity in the management company. Finally, it is important that there is a healthy and happy work environment where employees are treated with respect and not bullied – common problems in this area.

6.6.6   Business Ownership, Profitability and Outlook

When investing, it is important to look at the business ownership structure of a hedge fund management company. Normally, for independent hedge funds, the management company is owned by one or several of its principals, but sometimes strategic owners exist. If this is the case then such 'sleeping partners' should be assessed for their strategic fit, reputation and stability, terms and objective for the investment and ideally be interviewed.

Also, there are an increasing number of hedge funds run from within larger financial services companies and in these cases analysis of ownership is equally important. In some cases, recent corporate activity such as a takeover could be disruptive or there could exist conflicts within the owning group.

Sometimes it is the case that the hedge fund management company is owned by just one key individual and such an autocracy raises its own issues of stability and continuity. In many such cases other key people are aligned with the hedge fund management company's success through what is known as shadow equity, which is essentially a formula that treats these individuals financially as if they own the company but does not confer the decision making rights of an owner upon them. This is better than nothing and situations where there is just one outright owner and no equity or shadow equity are less desirable.

The profitability and business outlook of the hedge fund management company is important as it can impact on the stability and performance of the hedge funds it manages. For example, if a hedge fund manager realises that unless he generates a big return in the last two months of the year and so gets a good performance fee, he cannot afford to pay the bills and his business will shut down, he will take greater risk to do so; this is not is the best interests of investors since they want him to take greater risk only when such opportunities are in their best interests, not just his.

Also, if a hedge fund management company is losing money it will not be able to invest in the best people and infrastructure and so will diminish in its ability to manage money. As a result, it is important to assess the profitability of the business and establish where its breakeven point is in terms of assets under management, i.e. the level of assets under management where the fixed (management) fee revenue for the year pays all the bills for the year.

6.6.7 Infrastructure and Contingency Plans

It is important to check that any hedge fund management company to be invested with has a solid infrastructure. There needs to be an adequately spaced place of work with all the appropriate IT, software and systems and IT personnel to support this. There needs to be an appropriate compliance function and adequate back office personnel and financial control function. Furthermore there needs to be a working contingency plan should all this go wrong.

The best way to establish if there is a well thought out contingency plan is to ask the following unpleasant but necessary question: what would happen if a suspected terrorist explosion blew up your building at 7.00 a.m. just before anybody was in the office? How would you contact the other personnel? How soon would you be back up and running again? Where would this be and would it be far enough away? How would you retrieve the lost information? How would you trade, communicate and access market information? If the answer doesn't sound credible and well thought out, this is a serious issue.

6.6.8   Reputation and Referencing

The reputation of the key individuals in a hedge fund management company should always be assessed, especially when investing in a new fund. The best way to do this is by referencing, not just through the list of referees given by these individuals but through separate independent sources. If an investment professional is difficult to reference independently this often means that nobody prominent has heard of him and that he may not be the leading expert in his strategy that he has lead you to believe.

The best form of referencing is through well known market participants who have a good reputation themselves. Ideally these will have worked closely with the person in question but will not be on his list of provided referees, ensuring a degree of independent opinion. These references are best collected verbally and off the record to ensure honesty over diplomacy.

Another good check is by using Bloomberg or even Google to get a more general idea of what they have been up to in the past. Finally, and probably most important is to do a check on the financial regulators' websites to see if there has been any previous misdemeanours, suspensions or fines from the regulators themselves.

Off The Record

Independent referencing sounds difficult but is easier than it sounds due to the source of hedge fund managers being quite concentrated amongst the big investment banks and investment managers. A reference from the company itself will tell you little more than the dates the individual worked there – they rarely if ever express opinion.

6.7   PORTFOLIO CONSTRUCTION FOR HEDGE FUNDS OF FUNDS

Picking good hedge funds is only part of what is needed in constructing a good hedge fund of funds portfolio. Interaction between underlying hedge funds, effective diversification in different market conditions and hedge fund of fund portfolio level risk concentrations all need to be considered and, as such, good hedge funds of funds will have portfolio construction processes as well as hedge fund selection processes. Such portfolio construction processes will integrate investment and risk processes to combine underlying hedge funds to give suitable levels of risk and robustness at hedge fund of funds level. As hedge funds change and evolve their risk over time, this process needs to be ongoing instead of a one-off.

One of the main benefits of multi-strategy hedge funds of funds is diversification by manager, style, strategy and geography. However, 'naïve' diversification (through increasing the numbers of hedge funds and strategies in the portfolio) does not always work. In many situations hedge funds act as a herd and so adding more hedge funds in a given strategy may not diversify the portfolio a lot. For example, if you have a number of good hedge funds in your portfolio in a given strategy then adding a further, lower conviction manager may superficially diversify the portfolio further; however, if your conviction in your preferred hedge funds can be trusted, the addition may not diversify that effectively due to herd behaviour. Also, in general poorer funds do worse in very tough times and so this potential diversifier may worsen downside. Furthermore, the time spent on monitoring an extra hedge fund could be used to get greater depth on existing funds thus ensuring they are better covered. All in all diversification after a point is a function of courage of conviction.

Similarly, hedge fund strategies can experience contagion. Adding more strategies is certainly no guarantee of diversification since different strategies share the same factor exposures, e.g. convertible bond arbitrage, distressed, fixed income and credit strategies can all share exposure to credit spreads and all can lose money should credit spreads blow out. For these reasons it is important to understand factor exposures as well as strategy exposures, as highlighted above.

Conversely, even in single strategy portfolios it is possible to diversify by approach to a strategy. For example, in European Equity Long/Short it is possible to diversify between those managers with a value bias and those with growth focus, between medium and longer term focussed managers and those with a short term bias, between fundamental managers and traders and between those with a more event driven portfolio.

When seeking to diversify a portfolio it is also necessary to ensure that there are no hidden clusters of risk. Are underlying funds all using the same prime broker? Is there a bias towards larger funds or smaller funds? Is everybody acting with the same time scale? Also, it is important that the liquidity of the portfolio of hedge funds is matched to the liquidity of the hedge fund of funds. In a worst case scenario when all investors withdraw assets, can the fund of funds liquidate hedge funds to match the fund of funds' gate every investment period?

Off The Record

A lot of hedge fund of funds play the averages and some offer much better liquidity than their underlying portfolios would allow. In general, if a hedge fund of funds (or hedge fund for that matter) offers liquidity that looks too good to be true, don't expect to get assets back with that liquidity in a worst case scenario.

6.8   CRITICAL ANALYSIS AND THE DECISION PROCESS

Once all the information has been gathered a critical analysis needs to be formed and a decision needs to be made. In practice critical analysis is ongoing throughout the process but there needs to be a final stage of critical analysis that assesses every attribute of the hedge fund in the final context before a decision is made. Information needs to be drawn together and combined with critical analysis and a recommendation to form an investment report. I give an example of the qualitative and critical analysis part of a good investment report in the last chapter of Part II. Typically, a good hedge fund of funds investment report will consist of the following:

- qualitative analysis report;
- quantitative analysis report;
- risk analysis report;
- critical analysis report.

It is often the case that hedge fund of funds managers and analysts spend so much effort compiling the report that it is difficult to take a step back and construct a final objective critical analysis and so it is worthwhile getting somebody that has not been involved in the process to assist here.

In addition, I would recommend considering exit criteria (when to get rid of the new fund) and replacement strategy for any hedge fund invested with. Such exit or reassessment criteria for the hedge fund should be activated if performance or other parameters fall outside a pre-set critical level. It is better to impose this set of rules before investing to ensure that there is a disciplined exit strategy should the fund fail to perform in any way – it is human nature to be overly optimistic if return is drifting with small negatives and overly pessimistic in the case of a bigger single negative return, to the detriment of rationality.

The final stage is to decide whether the hedge fund is to be invested with or not and this needs to be considered in conjunction with the strategy allocation and portfolio construction process (covered above). This decision process should take the form of a formal meeting to ensure that the decision process is properly monitored, minuted, rigorous, and regular and that the role of the fund of funds as fiduciary is taken seriously. Such a meeting generally consists of the hedge fund of funds' senior investment (including risk) professionals along with a senior member of non-investment staff to ensure processes are adhered to. There needs to be a clear outcome in terms of the amount invested by each hedge fund of funds portfolio or otherwise further instructions: suggestions to resubmit after a defined amount of more work, monitor for a pre-stated amount of time or reject for clear reasons.

Off The Record

In my opinion democracy often fails in investment committees as it seems to breed mediocrity and people don't like voting against their colleagues. A challenging discussion amongst the investment committee followed by an assessment of the investment thesis and potential veto from the CIO and Head of Risk seems to work better.

6.9 SUMMARY

In this chapter I have taken a detailed look at the core functions that are needed for a good hedge fund of funds investment process, namely:

• strategy analysis and allocation;
• sourcing and capacity negotiation;
• quantitative analysis;

- qualitative analysis;
- operational risk assessment and referencing;
- portfolio construction;
- critical analysis and decision process.

As we have seen above, a good hedge fund of funds does a lot more than just 'pick good hedge funds' – the other areas above are equally important. Also of equal importance are risk measurement, management and monitoring and we will look at these areas in the next chapter.

6.10   SUMMARY OF IDEAS FOR CHAPTER 6

- On the investment side, a good hedge fund of funds will cover a range of areas including strategy analysis, sourcing, quantitative and qualitative analysis.
- The hedge fund of funds has to be forward looking when assessing hedge funds and backward looking quantitative analysis should only be used as a filter.
- A selection of good hedge funds still needs attention and a portfolio construction process is very much needed as well as a hedge fund selection process.
- There is a lot to do on the operational due diligence side to ensure that the hedge fund is a safe investment.

7

The Hedge Funds of Funds Risk, Monitoring and Portfolio Management Processes

7.1 OVERVIEW – RISK AND HEDGE FUNDS

The sources of risk vary widely from hedge fund to hedge fund. In some cases, the risk a hedge fund takes can be broadly represented in the volatility of its track record, e.g. in Equity Long/Short funds that trade stocks with larger equity caps. However, in many hedge funds, measuring the risk is not so straight forward. For example, a lot of risk may lie with the liquidity of the portfolio – less liquid instruments do not trade in a nice smooth way but they generally move in jumps when traded. As a result, should a hedge fund hold instruments of poor liquidity, this may provide a risk that is not yet reflected in the track record.

As well as hidden risk due to liquidity of a portfolio, there are some other risks that do not always reflect themselves in track record. Hedge funds may hold nonlinear instruments such as options and other derivatives which behave in ways that have less obvious impact on track records, e.g. if a hedge fund were to sell put options on the equity market this would give a steady uncorrelated return stream as long as the market didn't fall but would cause considerable loss if it did. Similarly, hedge funds that own sub-investment grade bonds will enjoy a great steady static return from the coupon the bond pays but should the issuer default, they will lose the coupon and incur losses from the decrease in the price of the bond.

Arbitrage strategies are strategies that look to make a low risk profit from inefficiencies across financial markets, with those profits being independent from the underlying markets. A practitioner of arbitrage will look for temporary mispricings in the underlying markets and then exploit them for profit. These returns are often very small and so leverage is used resulting in a smooth, market independent return steam. Remember, however, that arbitrage profits are often low risk but certainly not totally risk free and from time to time an event will cause the steady return stream to fall sharply resulting in a loss that, due to the leverage used, can be large and would not have been predicted just from the steady return stream of the track record.

As we can see above, in many cases the volatility of the track record of a hedge fund is a poor estimator of risk being taken. In this chapter we will look at the methodology for risk management used by hedge funds and hedge funds of funds in measuring hedge fund risk. Furthermore, we will see that risk measurement is not a static process and the need for ongoing monitoring of underlying hedge funds from both a risk and an investment point is crucial to the success of a hedge fund of funds.

7.2   RISK MANAGEMENT METHODOLOGY WITHIN HEDGE FUNDS

With the exception of Equity Long/Short funds, the predominant risk measurement methodology in hedge funds is based on a measurement called *value at risk* (VaR). This measurement looks at the historic volatility of the constituents in a portfolio and how they are correlated with one another, and then makes an estimate of the chances of extreme loss. For example, if a portfolio has only involatile positions then the VaR would be low; similarly if there was a portfolio of more volatile positions that offset each other because they were negatively correlated, the VaR would still be low. However, a portfolio of highly volatile and highly correlated positions would have a high VaR.

VaR is quoted as a percentage chance, a time period and a percentage loss; for example a 95% daily VaR of −2.1% means that there is a 95% probability of returning more than −2.1% in any one day, i.e. there is a 5% chance of losing more than −2.1% in any one day.

VaR is a useful overall measure but has several main faults:

(i) In some complex, new or illiquid instruments that aren't traded on exchanges, it is difficult to get a price history and so difficult to measure volatility.

(ii) VaR tends to be based on backward looking evidence of volatility and correlation so would be poor at predicting risk of portfolios where the correlation constituents would be changed by some catalyst, e.g. a corporate event.

(iii) Arbitrage managers will only put on positions where the long and short parts are correlated and, therefore, these portfolios will naturally have low VaR. However, there may be events on the horizon to cause the correlation to change adversely, thus increasing the VaR. Therefore, backward looking VaR in arbitrage portfolios will not be a good predictor of risk as it does not consider what can happen – only what has happened.

Furthermore, arbitrage managers may generate their best returns following periods when VaR is greatest. For example:

- Assume some exogenous event occurs to widen the difference between a long and short positions of an arbitrage trade (i.e. widen the spread) but the reasons for the spread to widen over the short term have no effect on the fundamental linkage between the long and short parts of the trade.
- As a result of these short term moves, VaR will most probably increase due to the market moves irrespective of whether the fundamental linkage between the long and short positions still exists or otherwise. This is because the correlation between the long and short position will have diminished even though the positions are still linked when analysed from a top down point of view. This is the difference between correlation and causality.
- However, following the market impact of the exogenous event, fundamentals once again assert themselves, the spread should renarrow and the arbitrage losses are recouped.
- Furthermore, a good arbitrageur will have added to the position when the spread has widened, knowing that the widening was driven by market noise rather than fundamentals, and made a profit when spreads renarrowed.
- In other words, when fundamentals are not broken down but spreads widen, the good arbitrageur adds to positions rather than cuts them back, even though VaR has increased.

(iv) Many VaR calculations are based on the assumptions of a roughly bell curved distribution (like the normal distribution) but given the nature of hedge fund portfolios this may not always be the case. Some distributions may have funny shaped tails or even have two central bulges (called bimodal distributions). This is a result of the non-linear instruments that hedge funds trade and the different payouts possible form arbitrage and relative value trades.

Good hedge fund managers know the limitations of basic VaR methodology if their strategy is one that is not a great fit with a VaR approach and will supplement it with other analysis.

Arbitrage and Relative Value hedge fund managers will also consider what will happen if correlation structure breaks down, i.e. historic correlations no longer hold, and will consider the outcome if all correlations went to $+/-1$ in extreme scenarios. They will also stress test portfolios and look at the impact of a large move in a given market in isolation and with corresponding moves in other markets. They will also consider historic scenarios of stressed conditions and construct future anticipated 'worst case scenarios'.

Event Driven managers will generally ignore VaR since they deal with the outcomes of corporate events that generally change the behaviour and so the correlation of the instruments and portfolio positions they hold. For example, historic correlations between the stocks of two companies will change radically when one company begins a takeover of another, as the stocks will naturally become linked together as a result. Instead of using VaR, Event Driven hedge fund managers will generally make the risk management more scenario based, and consider the outcome of the corporate event failing to go ahead as planned for their top portfolio positions.

7.3   ASSESSING THE RISK MANAGEMENT PROCESS OF HEDGE FUNDS

The risk management process of a hedge fund can be as important as the investment process. The most important thing to check is that the process adequately measures risk, that it exists in an explicit form and it is understood and adhered to. In an ideal world, there will be a separate risk manager that reports to the head of the hedge fund management company and has some power of veto in extreme circumstances, although often this is not the case. In general, the existence of independent risk managers is confined to more complex arbitrage strategies and multi-strategy funds.

If risk management systems are used, it is important to establish whether they are bought in or built and if the latter is true, there is more than one person who understands their construction in order to act as back-up. It is important to check that the weaknesses of any type of risk system are understood and that the output is not just followed blindly.

The best managers generally make augmentations to their risk systems along the lines of what we have seen in the previous section. If this is not the case and a risk system only appropriate for long only investing is being followed blindly by a hedge fund then there must be good reasons why this is so.

Another important thing to check is that risk is measured to test the impact of adding positions to the portfolio before they are actually added. In other words, the way the portfolio risk changes when a big position is added should be investigated before adding it and not come as a surprise on addition. Risk management should be an active part of the investment process and not just something that is tagged on the end. Also, in the best case there will be ex-post testing of the impact of portfolio risk on returns to gauge the accuracy of the risk system's calculations.

As well as fancy risk systems, hard portfolio limits can be very powerful. Investors should check that there are in-house limits on leverage, concentration and exposure as well as on risk statistics.

It is important that, as an investor, you get access to the risk figures and summary information on leverage, concentration and exposure on a regular basis as well as access to the risk manager himself to ensure a good job is being done. It is reasonable to ask for a detailed risk analysis on a monthly or at least quarterly basis. This is a useful monitoring tool but also will allow you to gain a good understanding of the risk manager's powers, skills and impact on the portfolio as a whole. In the section on monitoring, I will suggest what ongoing analysis that can be done on risk within the underlying hedge funds.

Off The Record

Equity Long/Short managers tend to have much less elaborate risk processes than other hedge funds. This is a result of less complexity in this space. However, it is important to find out if an Equity Long/Short fund manager understands any implicit factor bets in his portfolio such as hidden exposure to oil, gold, interest rates, value and growth factors, etc.

Also note that the risk limits in hedge fund portfolios as outlined in the hedge fund prospectus are usually deliberately chosen to be so wide that they will never ever get hit. You need to ask the hedge fund manager themselves for more realistic internal limits.

7.4 RISK MANAGEMENT WITHIN HEDGE FUNDS OF FUNDS

Just as with the underlying hedge funds, the risk management processes of hedge funds of funds vary widely with approach, philosophy and focus. However, there are a few core capabilities that lie at the heart of all good risk processes. A good risk management process for hedge funds of funds will achieve several important goals:

(i) It will take into account the fact that hedge funds can take very different risks than traditional funds and that track record volatility may be a bad indicator of future risk.

(ii) It will be consistent and accurate in approximating future downside and be able to reflect changes in risk on a timely basis.

(iii) It will be able to measure risk at a hedge fund of funds portfolio level as well as an individual constituent hedge fund level.

(iv) It will be able to approximate where the underlying hedge fund is taking risk and hence show where the risk is being taken at hedge fund portfolio level.

(v) It will be forward looking and not overly dependent on the normal distribution.

(vi) It will be transparent, easy to understand and its weaknesses will be well understood.

(vii) It will be cognizant of difficult to measure and less quantitatively based portfolio risks.

For a hedge fund of funds, such a risk process is not just a necessary tool to understand the underlying risk within hedge funds but also is an important part of the monitoring and portfolio construction processes.

Some hedge funds of funds will just reflect a consolidated version of portfolio statistics such as leverage and concentration and in portfolios of less complex strategies such as Equity Long/Short this can be a valid and adequate approach. However, when more complex strategies are added then a more universally powerful system is needed.

Some hedge funds of funds have bought or subscribed to generalist risk systems such as Riskmetrics, however given the inappropriateness of VaR covered earlier in this chapter, sometimes these approaches will not work well under certain circumstances; furthermore, a high degree of transparency is needed.

It is a difficult fact that not all hedge funds provide full transparency, although most provide enough to monitor them adequately and, as such, it is necessarily pragmatic to have a risk management system that does not require full transparency. Ideally, ongoing full transparency is available from a third party such as a prime broker or administrator. However, when a hedge fund of funds manager talks of 'full transparency' she usually refers to transparency provided each month-end by the hedge fund manager themselves. If a hedge fund manager wanted to commit a fraud then they could easily alter the constituents of the portfolio to match fraudulent returns, or could indeed physically alter the portfolio every month-end to deceive. As a result, full transparency is a little overrated although much better than nothing. Full transparency is also less useful in less concentrated portfolios (of hundreds of positions) since the work required to consolidate and measure the risk of such a portfolio can be time consuming to the detriment of other important functions. In this case, summary statistics are more pragmatically useful. It is in more concentrated and esoteric hedge fund portfolios that full transparency becomes both useable and useful.

A good hedge fund of funds risk approach will run alongside the investment process rather than occurring at the end. This allows for the investigation of risk within a hedge fund to run over time and for any information unearthed to be fed into the investment process. Another important aspect of a hedge fund of funds risk approach is that it is well understood and used by investment professionals, not just the risk management team. As a result, output need to be regular, easy to understand and explained face-to-face by risk professionals whenever needed within the investment team.

7.4.1 An Example of a Hedge Fund of Funds Risk System

Our approach at Key Asset Management is to build our own system as the ones that can be bought 'off the peg' are too generalist and not hedge fund specific. We use regression analysis and top down information to find the core factor exposures in each fund. Here we are looking for the underlying drivers of return and risk in any portfolio. Such drivers are based on a library of appropriate hedge fund factors such as markets, implied volatility, credit spreads, etc. We then use Monte Carlo simulation – a way of statistically generating the full range of potential outcomes – to consider a whole range of scenarios of what could happen looking forward. Just because there was not an adverse outcome from a hedge fund taking certain risks in the past does not mean to say it wasn't risky; taking the same risks going forward may leave the hedge fund less lucky. In other words, this risk approach is not just dependent on correlations staying as they have been historically, it also allows for things to come unstuck and for correlations to break down. Given this Monte Carlo approach, we can then look at a distribution of future risk which is, typically, far from normally distributed and we can also see which factors are driving the risk. This allows us to check if the hedge fund manager is taking risk in an area where he has expertise (desirable) or taking risk in an area where he has no expertise or edge (undesirable). Consolidating these exposures allows us to find out what exposures we are taking at hedge fund of funds level (e.g. exposures to credit spreads, interest rates, etc.). In addition, we consider historic and anticipated worst case scenarios at hedge fund and at hedge fund of funds level. Those who have interest in this area may wish to read the Cambridge University Working Paper we have written on the subject (Goodworth and Jones, 2004).

7.5   ONGOING MONITORING AND PORTFOLIO MANAGEMENT

Once a hedge fund becomes an active investment in a hedge fund of funds, it is imperative that it is monitored on an ongoing basis. Hedge funds have a broader mandate, a greater universe of instruments and more key person dependence than traditional funds and, as a result, ongoing monitoring at monthly frequency is needed to ensure that the hedge fund is still an investable and a desirable investment. Style drift, taking inappropriate risks, rapid asset growth and key people leaving are all things that could happen over a period of weeks in the hedge fund world and, without an ongoing monitoring process, the information gathered at the point of writing the investment report could be rendered obsolete. A good monitoring process flags and notes such changes and forces the question 'would we have invested in this hedge fund if it was as it is today?'.

As such, ongoing monitoring is one of the biggest 'value added' services that a hedge fund of funds can provide and yet, as a result of the simplicity of what is required, it rarely gets mentioned. A good fund of funds will monitor its underlying hedge funds on a monthly basis by reading all the output from the fund manager, by running a quantitative analysis of the fund portfolio in terms of performance and risk and by analysing any changes in terms of fund staff turnover, asset increases or decreases and changes to the infrastructure. Armed with this analysis the hedge fund of funds manager will talk with the hedge fund manager or an informed member of the hedge fund management team to ask any outstanding questions.

A good hedge fund of funds manager will have a detailed knowledge of the underlying hedge fund manager's strategy and will be able to have a more 'peer to peer' conversation with that manager than just a one sided Q&A session. As a result, she will be able to build a good relationship with the hedge fund manager over time which should be beneficial to both parties. This allows softer issues such as motivation and erosion of skill can be analysed.

The level of monitoring can be constrained by levels of portfolio transparency (as discussed above) and levels of access to the hedge fund manager. The level of transparency required varies from fund to fund, e.g. in a concentrated 15 position distressed fund it is more necessary to know the underlying positions whereas in a 400 position statistical arbitrage fund where no position is bigger than 1% it is more beneficial to know the overall portfolio exposures such as beta to the equity market, sector concentrations, leverage, etc.

In terms of access to the hedge fund manager, if a hedge fund manager is not able to commit himself or a member of his team to talk with a hedge fund of fund manager on at least a quarterly basis, one must question whether the benefits of this investment outweigh this lack of contact.

In addition to reading the underlying hedge fund's analysis and written output and talking with the hedge fund manager, there are some other quantitative and qualitative monitoring analyses that can be done on a regular basis:

Quantitative Monitoring – the work that can be done on a quantitative basis includes the following:

- analysis of changes to risk and risk distribution;
- analysis to changes in leverage, concentration and exposures;
- analysis of returns, distribution of returns, volatility and source of returns;
- peer group comparisons;

- analysis of levels of excess returns compared to market exposures;
- analysis of asset flows.

A good quantitative monitoring process will immediately flag major changes but also identify slow drifting changes that may not be easily picked up by human analysis as a result of the slowly erosive nature of style/return drift.

Qualitative Monitoring – as well as the monitoring process above, it is also worth formally (i.e. written) asking the following questions on a monthly basis:

- Have there been any staff departures, additions, promotions or demotions?
- Have there been any fundamental changes to the investment strategy?
- Have there been any changes to the group infrastructure or ownership structure?
- Has there been any legal action involving the manager or fund?
- Have there been any other changes to investments, operations, pricing or other processes?
- Have there been any changes to the fund third parties or other external service providers (e.g. addition of a new prime broker, change of lawyers)?
- Have there been any other changes that we should be made aware of?
- What are assets under management for the fund as at month end?

Off The Record

Often, within a hedge fund the investment team are much more likely to tell it like it is than the more spin-laden marketers – a quarterly call with the hedge fund manager is often worth more than a monthly conversation with the sales and marketing guy. There are some notable exceptions within the hedge fund world and these tend to be the ones that have worked on the investment side in the past.

7.5.1   Ongoing Portfolio Management

The fund of funds portfolio can never be a static entity. The ongoing monitoring risk and monitoring processes should in turn drive the investment processes to allow past decisions to be reassessed in light of any significant changes to funds or strategies. As a result, there needs to be an ongoing portfolio management process to ensure that any change to levels of conviction in constituent hedge funds and strategies is reflected in the portfolio. Furthermore, there are many more ways in which a skilled portfolio manager can add value, e.g. through adept cash management and liquidity management.

7.6   SUMMARY

In this chapter we have seen that the risk of hedge funds is not best measured by volatility of track record and, instead, more advanced methods are needed. A good hedge fund of funds takes this into account when measuring the risk in its underlying hedge funds and also when measuring the risk of its overall portfolio. Also remember, a hedge fund of funds portfolio with lots of underlying hedge funds and hedge fund strategies is not necessarily a well diversified hedge fund portfolio.

7.7   SUMMARY OF IDEAS FOR CHAPTER 7

- In many hedge fund strategies, volatility of past return underestimates risk.
- The value at risk approach to risk management is not appropriate for some hedge fund strategies and good hedge fund managers will realise this.
- It is imperative that hedge funds of funds managers realise this also.
- A good hedge fund of funds manager will understand the risks in the underlying hedge funds with her portfolio, but also the risks and exposures in the hedge funds of funds portfolio.

An Example of a Hedge Fund of Funds' Investment Report

8.1 OVERVIEW

In this chapter we will see the theory of the above three chapters put into practice as we take a look at a typical investment report. This is a report containing information and critical analysis typical of a hedge fund that has been put forward for investment by a hedge fund of funds investment professional. This is an imaginary report based on an imaginary fund and people but it is a based on a culmination of many such investment reports, and so is based on reality. In the following report I will add comments in italics to explain what is said and why.

8.2 THE REPORT

Investment Report on The XYZ Hedge Fund

8.2.1 Summary and Critical Analysis

Fund: The XYZ Hedge Fund

Manager: Jones Asset Management

Manager Contact: Martyn Johnson

Strategy: Fixed Income Arbitrage and Relative Value

Geographical Focus: United States

Fund Inception: January 2004

Manager Founded: 1982

Fund Overview

This fund invests in relative value and other non-directional fixed income strategies. The fund's investment objective is to generate absolute return through investing in an actively managed style within the world of fixed income securities. The Fund is expected to be generally market neutral. So far, turnover has been appropriate for this strategy and returns have been consistent, backing up these objectives. They say that the 'fund will be managed within a heavily risk controlled framework' and this is backed up with a very low risk target – 3.5% monthly VaR (95%)

The Fund generally expects to have multiple and diversified investment strategies in place at any time. Strategies so far have been all based around relative value and arbitrage between U.S. Treasuries, mortgage securities, corporate bonds, agency debentures, TIPS, G10 sovereign debt, and swaps, futures, options and other derivatives thereon. The fund will primarily invest in developed countries. The fund expects to maintain an average rating of A, and has limited exposure to high yield and illiquid securities and no exposure to emerging markets.

This section is just a general overview of the fund and its strategy but note that it is important to back up anything that has been claimed by the fund with hard evidence.

Reputation of Fund and Manager

Excellent international reputation as a top bond manager although unproven in the hedge fund space.

Company Overview

Jones Asset Management was founded in January 1982 by Alf Jones and his team from OldCo – the traditional bond management house, and became an SEC registered investment advisor in November of that year. In February 2000 the firm was acquired by NewCo – the financial conglomerate – of which Jones Asset Management is now an independent affiliate operating as an autonomous investment management company. In February 2001 NewCo acquired Smith Bond Management in London to broaden Jones Asset Management's non-dollar capabilities. In February 2001 Jones Asset Management established an office in Singapore to enhance its Asian research and client service capabilities. Jones Asset Management is the 10th largest fixed income only manager in the world with over $50 billion (as of end 2006) in assets under management. The portfolio management team is comprised of 50 investment professionals across the New York and London offices with an average of 12 years experience and 140 support staff. The team covers all major sectors of the global fixed income markets.

It is important to give an overview of the company as well as the fund as if either is weak then investment is unlikely. NB that time references are put in as dates since 'last year' becomes an inaccurate statement as time moves on.

3 Key Positives

Experience of professional staff
Proven track record for the firm and the fund
Depth of analysis and risk processes of a larger management company

3 Key Negatives

Potentially high level of leverage and involatile track record may mean that portfolio is yet to be tested
Manager also looks after other portfolios
Subjective bonus scheme with no lock-in

Edge/Reason for Level of Focus

This is a large traditional bond house with a good reputation that has started to prove itself in the hedge fund space. The size of infrastructure and breadth of coverage, research and risk gives an edge and the ability to attract top level people and keep them motivated in this area should maintain it.

A simple analysis of negatives versus positives, reasons for level of focus and edge cuts through ambiguity and forces the analyst cut down the analysis to 'bare bones'.

Critical Analysis

Good infrastructure and risk control. Manager seems closer to the fund than with many of the big houses and is well incentivised. He has a background in proprietary bank trading and so seems better able to manage the shorter term volatility. Relatively low levels of leverage in practice (compared to the theoretical maximum they could deploy). The only worry is that manager has yet to be seriously tested with a spell of negative returns.

Other Points

Need to keep an eye on the independence (from the manager) of the risk management function.

It's important that there is space for a summary of critical analysis, i.e. a summing up; also it is important to have space for other issues that have not been mentioned elsewhere. The critical analysis should give the opinion formed by the analyst in an objective and evidence based manner.

8.2.2   The Management Company

Management Company: Jones Asset Management

Address: 1000 Rockefeller Centre, NY, USA

Founded: 1982

Group Assets: USD 51.6 bn (as of 12/06)

Regulator: SEC (FSA in UK)

Regulator Issues: None (as of 12/06)

It's important to keep up to date info on assets and to do regular regulator due diligence (any disciplinary issues are usually listed on the regulator website.

Ownership Structure

Jones Asset Management is a wholly owned subsidiary of NewCo, a NYSE-listed, diversified financial services company based in New York State. However, Jones Asset Management operates as an autonomous investment management company, and the two firms have a revenue-sharing agreement that allows Jones Asset Management to retain control of approximately 70% of its revenues.

Group Infrastructure and Notable Changes

Jones Asset Management is managed by two high-level committees – investment and operational and sales – which oversee the firm's six major business units and three independent functional groups, each of which is responsible for a key business area such as portfolio management or finance. Each of the business units in turn contains several functional groups of its own. In total, the Firm has 14 functional groups comprised of 50 professional (28 of which are members of the investment team) and 140 support staff.

Number of People in Total: 190 (as of 12/06)

Other Offices

Offices in London, New York and Singapore. The NY office is responsible for managing US fixed-income mandates and servicing the US relationships. The London office is responsible for managing global and international fixed-income mandates, including the non-US portion of US client portfolios, and servicing most of the non-US relationships. The Singapore office is responsible for servicing all of the Asian relationships, as well as research and analysis of the regions economies and debt markets.

Notes On Any Past Or Potential Legal Action

None pending as of as of 12/06.

It is necessary to do a full analysis of ownership structure and corporate stability as well the company itself. Stability, infrastructure, atmosphere and motivation are all necessary ingredients for a good hedge fund. It is important to take a view on any issues that may cause instability in the future such as profit and loss, new expansion, takeover or acquisition, etc. Also, if the company is being sued, prosecuted or investigated by the regulator (or has been in the past) then this needs to be found out as it could obviously have future impact or tell of a past issue that could be repeated.

Company Asset and Staff Growth

Year	Assets (USD bn)	Staff
1982	1	20
1984	3	20
1986	5	25
1988	7	30
1990	8	25
1992	10	35
1994	15	50

1996	20	50
1998	25	80
2000	30	90
2001	40	120
2002	35	170
2003	37	170
2004	46	170
2005	48	190
2006 to date	50	190

Future Growth Strategy and Vision

Aim to grow business and will move into bigger premises in 2007. Expect to grow fund to USD 1bn and then consider a credit fund and a macro fixed income/fx/rates fund.

Analysis of growth should include the growth in assets and staff at a company level. Here I would ask for a breakdown of investment and non-investment staff over time and turnover rates. I would also question them about drops in numbers of assets and staff, e.g. above staff dropped by five in 1988 and it would be interesting to see what happened there and also when staff rocketed post takeover in 2001; assets dropped post takeover and didn't recover until 2004 – I would be interested to see why this was.

8.2.3   Portfolio Management Team

Portfolio Managers

Martyn Johnson, one of Jones Asset Management's senior portfolio managers and a member of the firm's strategy setting committee is lead portfolio manager.

Who Else is Involved

John Smith spends three quarters of his time on the risk and analytics for the fund. Alf Jones is the Chief Investment Officer of the group and is involved at a top down strategy level. There is much information sharing throughout the group.

Time Commitment

MJ and JS spend 80% and 75% (resp.) of their time, AJ a lot less.

Other Responsibilities

MJ manages some other client accounts and JS does some other analytics work.

Financial Participation, Remuneration and Lock-Ins

MJ not locked in. Bonuses are subjective and 'compensate those that have contributed ideas'. Key (MJ but not JS) professionals are paid incentives in recognition of outstanding performance, which include NewCo stock options.

Staff Turnover

Nobody who works on this fund has left.

Key Person Turnover

Nobody who works on this fund has left.

Key People

MJ only. They say 'The firm's fixed-income discipline emphasises a team approach that unites groups of specialists dedicated to different market sectors. The investment responsibilities of each sector group are distinct, yet success is derived from the constant interaction that unites the specialty groups into a cohesive investment management team. The sector teams are comprised of senior portfolio managers, research analysts, and an in-house economist who are highly skilled and experienced in all major areas of the fixed-income market. They exchange views on a daily basis and meet more formally twice each week to review the firm's economic outlook and investment strategy.' Despite this, we see MJ as the focus for this team effort and we feel that the fund would not be desirable without his expertise and focus.

The above section looks at who manages the fund, who else is involved and what is the time commitment of each participant. It is important, especially in big groups, to check that one of the portfolio managers devotes most of his time to the fund in question and 'feels pain' if the fund does badly and is well remunerated if the fund does well, otherwise the fund is almost 'run by committee' and generally doesn't prosper. Key people (i.e. those without which the fund would lose its edge) need to be identified. Also, turnover is an important issue and stability is desirable; if a key person has left the fund then more work needs to be done to check if the fund is still viable without them.

8.2.4   Investment Process

Investment Universe

US Treasuries and TIPS, Government agency debentures, G10 sovereign debt, mortgage backed securities, futures and options (OTC and listed), swaps and swaptions and investment grade credit. The fund will generally invest in large liquid issues.

The fund may also invest in money market instruments, repos, reverse repos, dollar rolls, CMOs, and asset backed securities.

The fund cannot own emerging market securities.

Equities: No			
Large Cap: No	Mid Cap: No	Small Cap: No	Micro Cap:No
Bonds: Yes			
Government: Yes	Corporate: Yes	High Yield: Yes	
Distressed: No	Convertibles: No		
MBS: Yes	Commodities: No	Currencies: Yes	
Basic Securities: Yes	Futures: Yes	Forwards: Yes	Swaps: Yes
CFDs: No	Options: Yes	OTCs: Yes	Exotics: Yes
FX:Yes			

Other Instruments: Swaptions

It is important to establish exactly what markets and instruments the fund will invest with before you make an investment decision. Work must be done to confirm what they don't invest with as well as what they do invest with. Establishing this information up-front will confirm that the fund avoids areas that are undesirable to their investors and also can be used as a future check for style drift, i.e. if this fund suddenly started trading equities having previously confirmed that they would not, there would be an issue.

Investment Strategy

In majority (around 70%) non-directional fixed income, i.e. relative value. The rest is more macro driven. Vast majority (over 90%) of the portfolio is invested in investment grade securities.

The strategy is relative value/arbitrage with a macro economic overlay. The fund generally expects to have a range of diversified investment strategies in place at any one time. Strategies are focused on relative value arbitrage between US Treasuries, mortgage securities, corporate bonds, agency debentures, TIPS, G10 sovereign debt, swaps, futures, options and other derivatives. The fund is expected to be generally market neutral.

Some sample strategies are: basis trading on treasury and agency futures, inter-market spread trades, yield curve arbitrage, directional market positioning, relative value options trades and some relative value volatility trades.

Historically, the Funds largest positions have been basis trades, volatility trades, and relative value trades.

The aim of this section is to get a general overview of the fund's approach to investing whereas the Investment Process section aims to find out how it is done.

Investment Process

MJ acts as gatekeeper to the ideas of the different teams from the traditional side and turns these ideas into portfolio positions if he likes them and also adds his own (he is an ex prop. trader). He sits next to AJ (CIO) and they swap ideas, having known one another from bank proprietary trading days. JS is a 75% hedge fund dedicated quantitative analyst who sits next to MJ also and provides quantitative analysis and risk analysis ex ante when adding or investigating potential positions.

MJ also benefits from the outlook of the Investment Strategy Committee. This committee comprises of senior professionals throughout the group. These senior professionals are sector specialists with total expertise that pretty much spans the fixed-income market and there are no notable exceptions. They interact on a daily basis to evaluate developments in the market and the economy, and meet formally at least every month to review the macro and investment outlook (across the board rather than for this fund). In addition there are weekly meetings between London and NY offices and weekly Yield Curve and Credit meetings.

The sector specialists, who are grouped by issue type (i.e. corporate, mortgage-backed, federal agencies and G10 sovereign debt), concentrate on research and identifying inefficiencies and price dislocations in the market that can be exploited to add incremental value.

The Research Group at Jones is sizeable and its members appear to have considerable experience in this area (average 10+ years). They have immediate access to current market, security, and issuer information through up-to-date data retrieval technology. Daily monitoring of issuer information and market news is conducted using a combination of direct contact, Bloomberg systems, and external services (e.g. SEC Filings). Direct contact with issuing company's senior management is also a regular occurrence. Wall Street analysts, both credit and equity, are used for input, although outside research is used primarily as a supplement to internal research or for investment idea generation. The Research Group combines qualitative judgment with in-house developed quantitative tools to analyse credit valuations, market and sector movements and micro and macro economic trends, and how portfolios are positioned to take advantage of these trends. The research effort focuses on the non-government sectors such as corporate, mortgage-backed, and asset-backed securities that might provide better relative value opportunities (G10 sovereign research is done by sector specialists outside this group). Of equal importance in the analysis of specific issues is liquidity.

The foundation of the investment approach is based around MJ's own ideas and his interpretation of the output from the Investment Strategy Committee, the research Group and from talking directly with the specialist teams and other sector specialists. Also, the analytics/risk management team are heavy users of quantitative tools that can be utilised ex-ante. Fundamental and technical analysis tends to be used in equal proportion. MJ is resolute that he does not take any quantitative work at face value and tends to apply common sense to any quant output. Jones Asset Management say they are fundamentally value managers but MJ seems to be less driven by this doctrine and more opportunistic on shorter term trades.

MJ has sign-off on all positions and there are written guidelines to this effect.

The aim here is to find out how the portfolio manager makes his decisions, what thought processes, tools and information flows he uses, and the quality of this output. It is important to interpret this information rather than just report what the portfolio manager or firm has told you and to independently question rigor of the process and the strength and quality of output used in the decision process.

Portfolio Construction

MJ expects the fund to maintain an average rating of A within the portfolio, with minority exposure to high yield/sub investment grade and illiquid securities (max 30%). No exposure to emerging markets. Investment in unrated securities is limited to 20%. OTCs have made up as much as 25% in the past and there is no official limit other than when there is a sub-investment grade, illiquid or unrated underlying, as above.

The size of individual positions and strategies are determined by their perceived risk and their contribution to overall portfolio risk budget rather than basic % size. There are typically 10 to 20 strategies (each with several positions) that are aimed to be uncorrelated, ranging 1 day to 1 year time to fruition.

Quantitative position sizing and portfolio optimisation techniques are used but these are for information only – qualitative discretion from MJ is used as a frequent override and this is a matter of policy.

Options are used mainly to hedge securities such as TIPS, MBS and other areas that are difficult to hedge through shorting. Options are also used in volatility plays. The fund will sometimes take an outright position on an in-the-money option to implement a directional trade.

The Portfolio Construction section is important as this function can effect returns and risk as much as investment process. In this section a hedge fund investor should aim to understand how positions are sized and combined in terms of absolute size, risk budget, correlation (quantitatively and qualitatively assessed) and maturity. There should be evidence of a rigorous, well thought out process that ensures limits on risk and investment are adhered to and the portfolio reflects the intentions of the portfolio manager.

Portfolio Averages

Typical Portfolio: 40% US Treasury, 25% Mortgage, 10% G10 Sovereign Debt, 25% Options/Derivatives/Swaps

Average Number Of Positions:	10–20 strategies, 25–50 positions
Average Long-Side Leverage:	200%

Average Gross Exposure:	390%
Average Net Exposure:	10%
Average Holding Period:	6 months
Average Position Size:	20% of risk budget
Average Cap Size:	>$2bn on corporate issuers

Targeted duration is +/− 3 years.

Planned Changes to Processes Going Forward

No changes planned

Finding out average portfolio characteristics will give you a feel for the portfolio and how past returns have been made. Also, this information provides a good anchor point to check for style drift going forward. Finally, it is always worth asking about planned changes to any of the above going forward given that the firm may not think to mention this if they see you are close to investing anyway.

8.2.5   Portfolio Risk Management

Named Risk Manager:	Rob James – Head of Risk
Monitoring Frequency by Portfolio Manager:	Intra-day
Monitoring Frequency by Risk Manager:	Daily

Risk Management Policy and Processes

Scale in trades and strategies and assume no diversification benefit between strategies. Disciplined stop-loss limits to reduce risk. Currency risk will generally be fully hedged.

The guidelines to control and limit risk are well defined and written up. The idea is to take risk commensurate with the goal of not losing more than 3.5% of NAV in any month. MJ augments his subjective judgment with quantitative analysis from JS to be sure positions, strategies and the portfolio as a whole are within risk guidelines. A variety of trading and quantitative tools are used. Quantitative measurements include VAR, scenario analysis, and stress testing with specific market outcomes assessed.

They can calculate the duration and dollar value of a basis point (duration times the price times the position size) of each position in real time. They then aggregate the risk of each strategy, adjust for expected volatility, and monitor this position's total expected dollar risk as a percent of the risk budget. The general target maximum dollar risk is 10–20% of the total risk budget for any strategy. To calculate the size of any position in a strategy, they work backwards from this approach. The position's unit risk is calculated and then they can calculate the size of the position consistent with the limits specified in the risk budget.

If the portfolio is down −1.5% then they start reducing risk and aim to be completely hedged or liquidated by −3.5% with −5% as a worst case scenario.

NB although RJ (the group head of risk) is the named risk manager, the day-to-day work is done by JS with the aid of the risk management group. Comfort can be taken by RJ being the named risk manager, however, as he would have the power to intervene and override if MJ was ignoring JS's risk advice to the level where risk parameters were breached.

Risk Measurement

The risk management team, specifically JS, uses a variety of measurements:

They perform stress tests that assume spreads and interest rates move by one standard deviation against the portfolio at the same time. They also perform balance sheet stress tests that assume a loss of two thirds of repo + credit lines.

In the worst case scenario analysis MJ determines the realistic market outcomes that would cause a given strategy worst loss and evaluates worst case scenarios based on historical market levels. Further scenario analysis uses arbitrage-free interest rate models to run parallel and non-parallel interest rate shifts to test risk estimates. Worst case scenarios such as corporate default are also analysed.

They use a bespoke version of the Riskmetrics approach. The system is well programmed and backed up as one would expect from a group of this standing. The approach is well integrated throughout the different offices and takes a very visual approach to displaying output. The VaR calculation uses historical variance and covariance estimates from CovCo – the accepted third party provider of this data. VaR is based on simulation as well as historical return distribution.

Securities are fully modelled and curve scenarios are generated using a two-factor curve model. On a factor basis, they also perform sensitivity analysis on both a fund level as well as for individual strategies for changes in various market factors.

The approach is very thorough and model risk is minimised through the multi-faceted approach. The only worry above would be the dependence on MJ's subjective scenario analysis but as this is one of many approaches to risk, the issue is mitigated.

It is important that you have a good understanding of the way risk is measured and managed. A thorough assessment of risk measurement software and the way it is applied, with what frequency and by whom is essential. Different measures of risk are better suited to different strategies and so the risk process has to be appropriate. Ideally, there is a separate risk manager with a reporting line into someone with power of veto as all too often the risk process is more cosmetic than effective. The risk philosophy of the team, especially the portfolio manager, is important also; you are looking for a portfolio manager that really buys into the benefits of risk measurement rather than just sees it as a necessary evil.

Portfolio Monitoring

The portfolio system tracks profit/loss and risk by individual strategy and overall, allowing MJ to evaluate any strategy in real time. MJ quickly (intraday) reduces or adjusts the hedges on positions that breach the risk guidelines.

Also, throughout the trading day, all trades are reviewed by the compliance team stationed in the trading room, and the account's assigned compliance officer screens the portfolio to ensure that no activity has inadvertently caused the portfolio to breach its guidelines. At the end of each day, all portfolio activities are reconciled with the custodian. Finally, compliance officers receive exceptions reports each morning that cover all statistics specified by the guidelines. These reports highlight not only actual violations, but also variables that are nearing their limits.

Further monitoring occurs monthly, with a formal review of the portfolio by MJ with risk and compliance representatives. The portfolio is also reviewed for adherence to its current investment strategies by MJ and AJ. In addition, monthly reconciliations versus the custodian are performed and any account exceptions reports are reviewed by the firm's Operating Committee.

The next level of monitoring occurs at quarter end. At this time, a meeting of the entire portfolio-related, client service and compliance staff is held to provide both an overall and detailed review of all accounts including this portfolio, while assessing client needs and objectives. The compliance staff rotates accounts so that no compliance officer reviews the same accounts they are responsible for on a daily basis. This provides a check on the work of each compliance officer and also helps familiarise all compliance staff with each account. The quarterly meeting focuses all portfolio management, research, compliance, and client service staff on the fund's objectives and guidelines.

Finally, compliance officers are authorised to initiate reviews any time it appears necessary, such as on the occurrence of significant economic, financial, or other events, which might impact investment strategy although this has never happened for this fund.

If any of these steps reveal that an account is out of compliance with its guidelines or strategy, the compliance officers work with the investment staff to ensure that appropriate action is taken in a timely manner. Again, this has never happened for this fund.

Ideally, the portfolio manager can check the profitability, risk and other characteristics of the portfolio in real time, and is automatically alerted to any intraday breaches, large changes in the portfolio or movements therein. Also, it is important to check that the portfolios are well monitored by compliance staff as well as by the portfolio manager and risk team to ensure that breaches are dealt with quickly and there is no room for fraud.

Risk Limits

Maximum Long Side Leverage:	2000% – soft limit
Maximum Position:	20% of the fund's risk budget – soft limit
Maximum Sector Exposure:	n/a
Maximum Gross Exposure:	n/a
Maximum % Of Cap Size:	n/a
Maximum Country Exposure:	n/a
Maximum Net Exposure:	n/a
Minimum Cap Size:	n/a
Maximum Strategy Exposure:	n/a

95% VaR limited to -3.5%

Targeted duration of $+/-3$ years

High yield/sub investment grade and illiquid securities max 30%.

No exposure to emerging markets.

Investment in unrated securities is limited to 20%.

The currency risk will generally be fully hedged.

Diversification, Concentration and Other Limit-Based Issues

Only 10–20 strategies but with multiple instruments and exposures in each strategy and with historic low levels of correlation between strategies.

There are no pre-set stop losses for individual positions but stop losses are considered on a position by position basis. Stop losses for individual positions are determined by several factors, such as position size, historic trading levels, and volatility. The overall portfolio does not have rigid stop loss limits. However, positions are (risk) reduced in line with experienced losses and perceived volatility. Each individual strategy will have stop/loss limits set prior to entering the trade.

It is important to know all risk limits be they internal guidelines or limits that are listed in the prospectus. It is a bad sign if even softer internal limits are breached as this shows a lack of discipline by the portfolio manager. Above, notice that there are few limits with this fund – this is common with fixed income funds as they tend to limit concentration through percentage of risk budget rather than through outright position limits; in this space it is possible to have large positions that are very low risk and vice versa.

Liquidity Analysis

Liquidity risk is addressed by focussing on larger, heavily traded issues, i.e. publicly traded securities that have an issue size of USD500 million or greater, that are supported by multiple underwriters, and have a number of bids and offers in the market. They may purchase illiquid securities if the risk/reward analysis is compelling although historically this has been less than 5% (max combined limit of 30% with high yield). Even if they buy illiquid securities they say they must be of sufficient size and traded actively enough to be able to easily mark to market and trade. This is a highly liquid portfolio and the only issues would arise if the illiquid/high yield portfolio would approach its limit, so will monitor this sector and discuss again should the total amount of illiquid/HY get beyond 20%.

Estimated Efficient Liquidation Time: 2–3 days
Estimated Extreme Liquidation Time: 1 week

The liquidity of the portfolio needs to be examined to ensure that it is appropriate for the strategy employed and that the liquidity offered to investors broadly matches the liquidity of the underlying. If the fund is more liquid than the underlying portfolio then this could spell trouble if investors try to get out en masse; if a fund is unnecessarily illiquid then this may be purely due to fund manager greed, also not a good sign. The quickest time to liquidate the portfolio and the price impact of doing this, and also the time it would take to liquidate the portfolio with no price impact needs to be estimated. It is important to do your own liquidity analysis and not rely solely on what you are told by the portfolio manager.

8.2.6 Qualitative Risk And Infrastructure

Infrastructure and Organisation

The firm employs 10 full-time portfolio managers, 10 portfolio manager/ research analysts and 15 research analysts – along with risk and other investment roles there are 50 investment professionals in total. There are 140 support staff (sales, back office, admin etc). Offices in NY (HQ), London and Singapore (mainly sales).

Improvements and Changes

No key improvements or major changes but have invested heavily in IT and systems development.

Support

There are 2 dedicated back office personnel for this fund but wider support from the operations team. This team consists of specialist units for fund accounting (including cash management, hedging and custodian liaison), reconciliation and settlements, performance analysis and pricing (which covers the daily pricing of all assets held in the fund). The team consists of 70 personnel group wide.

Systems Audit

Jones Asset Management uses a mix of off the shelf, in-house bespoke and third party provided solutions. Off the shelf includes the likes of Microsoft Word and Tradar, third party includes Barra and Bloomberg, i.e. systems where ongoing data is supplied, and the bespoke would have been built or commissioned by the 40 person IT team. Bespoke software would be custom solutions which address specific needs that cannot be met by existing products, and include products developed both externally and in-house, such as Jones Asset Management's risk system.

Their quantitative systems are: BARRA, Bloomberg, JonesStress (macro generated scenario generator), JonesForecast (internally designed interest rate model), J.P. Morgan Analytics software and some internally designed pricing software.

Portfolio Management Systems

The two portfolio accounting systems are 123 Portfolio Accounting and Management system and 345 Portfolio Management Information System. The former is used for US dollar-denominated investments, and the latter is used for non-dollar exposure as it is a stronger tool for dealing with currency exposure and hedging. Both systems were designed for institutional fixed income investment organisations, and provide real-time trade date and portfolio summary reporting and also interface with all major trustee and custodian banks, allowing for electronic download of settlement activity and facilitating daily cash reconciliation. The systems are consolidated through a bespoke system built internally. From this internal system, one consolidated holdings report can be generated along with attribution analysis; also bespoke reports can be prepared.

The compliance monitoring system is called Compliex and is fully automated so that specific account guidelines, regulatory requirements, and risk exposure limits are monitored for violation.

It is important to check that the infrastructure is sizeable and robust enough to support the fund. Even in bigger companies, it is important to ensure that there are operations people dedicated to the fund. Systems should be audited to ensure they are appropriate and, in the case of bespoke systems, that they are well documented and backed up.

Dealing

No dedicated traders for this fund as MJ oversees execution of his trades and farms them out to the trading team of five dedicated generalist traders (dedicated to the group not just this fund). All of Jones Asset Management's full-time portfolio managers and portfolio manager/ research analysts are authorised to trade for any of Jones Asset Management's accounts provided they have PM approval for that account and are specialist in that given area. MJ may also utilise this capability if niche expertise is required.

Good execution can be as important as good investment process and the robustness of the dealing process needs to be checked.

Information Flow to Prime Broker

The prime broker acts as custodian for 90% to 100% of the funds assets. The exceptions are usually collateral, repurchase/reverse repurchase agreements, and OTC derivatives contracts that are not executed through the prime broker. Both portfolio monitoring systems track collateral that has been transferred out of the prime broker's custody, and reconciles these positions daily with the prime broker, along with all other positions. Also, see below.

Information Flow to Administrator

After a portfolio manager writes a trade ticket, this individual is no longer involved in the trade unless they need to provide information for a trade dispute. Both the prime broker and the administrator receive trade information from the settlements team at Jones Asset Management. The prime broker also sends trade information to the administrator by secure electronic transfer.

Jones Asset Management's Settlements team receives the trade confirmation from the executing broker and reconciles with this entity. If the executing broker inquires, the prime broker will also confirm with the executing broker. In order for the trade to settle, both the prime broker and the administrator need to agree with Jones Asset Management and the executing broker on the details.

On the night before settlement, Jones Asset Management's Operations group reviews the reports from both the prime broker and the administrator to make sure that all parties have all information and all trades are accounted for. If there are any problems, they contact the administrator, the prime broker, and Jones Asset Management's Settlement team.

If a trade is not properly captured, the prime broker settles the trade internally and negotiates the fail with the executing broker (contractual settle). The administrator then processes the trade as if it settles normally.

The investment staff have no access to accounting, settlements, pricing, and compliance systems. Furthermore, there are double checks on all trading activity through direct communications with counterparties by back office staff. The multiple personnel from within the Operations team review and monitor each account; and Compliance reviews all portfolios and trading activity. Jones Asset Management also performs regular checks on both the prime broker and administrator.

In addition, we have checked with the prime broker and administrator and they have confirmed in writing that they swap information by regular encrypted electronic download independently of Jones Asset Management and have a regular quarterly conference call before fund board meetings.

One of the most important pieces of operational due diligence is to check that the fund administrator and prime broker are in direct contact with each other and that portfolio information is transferred by secure, electronic download independently of the fund management company. This is the only way to ensure that a fraudulent fund manager cannot manipulate portfolio data and hence commit fraud.

NAV Calculation Process

NAV is independently calculated by the administrator, PPP, using its own independent pricing sources and purchased independent third party pricing sources through data feeds to value the securities held in the fund. When no pricing sources are available, no less than three brokers are found to give indicative quotes and the median is taken as the price.

In addition, Jones Asset Management employs an internal team of three individuals dedicated to the investment accounting of the fund as another set of eyes. This team also reviews the NAV calculation and security pricing, and challenges prices if it is thought to differ significantly from the market in either direction. Price challenges must be accompanied by documentation of at least three brokers' prices (just like the administrator) supporting the challenge. OTCs would be included in both procedures if held.

QQQ – the prime broker acts as custodian to 90% + of assets (ex repos and OTCs). Pricing is performed according to the offering document which requires that bid prices are used for debt securities held long, except for short term investments valued at amortised cost. Options are valued at the last sale price or last bid price in the absence of a sale on a given day. Swap contracts are valued using Bloomberg's swap pricing screen with the appropriate data.

Other Pricing and Position Information

The positions are valued daily in three places: Jones Asset Management's proprietary trading book, its accounting system, and the fund administrator. Jones Asset Management checks with dealers at least monthly to verify marks. As mentioned above, the official monthly pricing is performed by the fund administrator, PPP. PPP prices easy-to-price securities daily for an independent internal daily estimate also but only prices independently the difficult to price securities at month-end. For reconciliation and monitoring purposes, Jones Asset Management also prices all securities in the fund daily. The vast majority of its securities (all those included on regular price sources such as Bloomberg) are priced daily, with the remaining securities priced once a week by obtaining three quotes from broker-dealers representing the market trend and taking the median to obtain a final price.

Pricing Issues

Jones Asset Management reviews security pricing and NAV and challenges prices as necessary. All pricing issues must be considered by Jones Asset Management's Pricing Committee with representatives from various areas of the firm, including compliance. This has not yet happened yet – currently, all positions have been determined by PPP without challenge. The NAV has never been restated.

It is important to pay attention to pricing, especially in 'difficult to price' securities such as those with few or no quotes in the market. The pricing should be totally independent from the fund manager in an ideal world, since even if he recommends brokers to quote for a difficult to price security, they will probably be the brokers he uses regularly and so will be biased in his favour. Also be wary of positions that are part priced using brokers' indicative prices as these may be far away from the prices they would trade at.

Margin, Financing and Brokerage Agreements

It costs $3 per transaction for futures trades. Fixed-income trades are done on a net basis. They are aware of the impact that trading has on the market levels of the firm's portfolio holdings and use a variety of trading strategies to mitigate any negative impact of turnover on performance and to limit cost to the portfolio. Trading costs are monitored by generating internal trading reports, which detail all trading activity by broker, portfolio and instrument.

We have performed an analysis of brokerage agreements and Jones Asset Management have managed to use their size to negotiate stable long term agreements which would make it extraordinarily difficult for the broker to force a liquidation in all bar the most extreme circumstances and so the fund can be thought to be at advantage here.

Soft Dollar and Commission Recapture Policy

'The Fund does not participate in any soft dollar trades.'

Changes to Third Parties

'There have been no changes to third parties associated with the fund.'

Cash Management

They assess the market opportunities for financing securities and lending cash on a daily basis and dynamically manage any cash to optimise the income earned from financing the positions long internally or with a dealer and investing the cash.

They have a cash forecasting system which summarises available cash for the fund on a daily basis and recommends the best cash management strategy.

Good margining and cash management can be used to add value on a daily basis. However, some funds put their cash in higher risk investments, thus adding to portfolio risk and this should be assessed. Stable agreements with brokers are fundamentally important, especially in 'deep pockets' strategies such as Fixed Income Arbitrage, where the need to be able to ride out severe short term losses is beneficial; here, the last funds standing (not liquidated or hindered with margin calls) will survive to make the most money should spreads re-narrow once a crisis averts.

Note also the need to seek out any changes in third parties and if there have been changes there needs to be legitimate reasons why – fraud is easier if the administrator is constantly changed, for example. Finally note the importance of putting 'quotation marks' around quotes to differentiate between what they say and what you say.

Contingency Plans

The above IT infrastructure is operated out of Jones Asset Management's IT Group which has an onsite presence in each of the offices but is headquartered in a secure building within the offsite premises in New Jersey. In the NY office they have an uninterruptible power supply system capable of six hours of emergency server room support, and a backup generator capable of providing emergency power to the entire building, fire-retardant construction with heat and smoke detection and fire suppression equipment, and drip detection equipment with rack-mounted servers and raised flooring. Wide Area Networks connect Jones Asset Management offices with its offsite HQ. The LAN consists of over 200 Microsoft Windows NT Server file servers running on Intel-based hardware from Dell and 20 Sun Solaris servers running on Sun computing platforms.

The primary off-site location is in NJ but there are also hired alternatives throughout the United States. This agreement includes a 24-hour quick-ship requirement for computers and phones, fax machines, and other necessary office equipment are available at the facility allowing any office to be operational within 24 hours, accessing critical systems in NJ via internet connectivity.

Jones Asset Management's London and Singapore offices have three options for backup contingencies. First, critical staff can be flown to either the NY office or one of the US offsites. Second, critical staff can access applications utilising their laptops and secure remote access VPN. Thirdly, they have offsite offices in both cities 10–15 miles away. These preparations would allow the office to be operational within 24 hours, again accessing critical systems via internet connectivity.

The contingency plan is tested regularly every quarter and a full simulated disaster recovery including 20% of all staff is tested annually. The most recent tests included a full simulation with the firm's Incident Management Team and third party recovery specialists, conducted in October 2006.

In the event of disaster call:

		London: Bob Smith	Singapore: Al Smith
MJ	AJ		
Office: ########	Office: ########	Office: ########	Office: ########
Mobile: ########	Mobile: ########	Mobile: ########	Mobile: ########
Home: ########	Home: ########	Home: ########	Home: ########
Offsite: ########	Offsite: ########	Offsite: ########	Offsite: ########

If one of the other offsite offices have been used then call ####### or email #####@####.com for more information.

It is important to know whether the management company could carry on whatever the event (natural disaster, terrorist attack, power cut, etc.) so it is important to know that a full back-up plan has been considered and well practiced. It is also important to know where to contact the managers themselves in the case of emergency. I would not recommend calling managers in market hours in such circumstances as they will need their time to concentrate on trading the portfolio; instead a client services operative would be the one to contact in the first instance.

8.2.7   Qualitative Performance Analysis

Sources/Driving Factors of Returns

Shocked / temporarily widened spreads

Volatility

Supply-demand inefficiencies

Inter-market discrepancies.

If there was a quiet, thin market then the opportunity set and returns would diminish

Estimated Value Added Due to Edge

Fixed income is such a well-covered market there are few natural inefficiencies that can make large returns. Much value added coming from the coverage and skill base that such a large company as Jones Asset Management has, and its skilled application to the relative value space by a seasoned prop trader such as MJ.

Qualitative Return Analysis

Best Monthly Return: 2.0%   Date: January 2005   Correct as of 12/06

Explanation: All strategies made money that month for different reasons. One interest rate based strategy that had previously lost money (see below) generated an outsized return. This return is within expectations given the skew to the return distribution and the expected volatility.

Worst Monthly Return: −1.1%   *Date: September 2004   Correct as of 12/06*

Explanation: More losing strategies than positive. One strategy lost more than expected as markets unexpectedly switched their interest rate outlook based on spurious comments from the Fed. This return is within expectations given the volatility target of the fund.

Worst Drawdown: −1.1%   *Date: September 2004   Correct as of 12/06*

Explanation: This was the only negative month to-date. See above.

Worst Expected Monthly Return: −5%

Best Expected Monthly Return: Unless there is an exceptional market event then expect maximum monthly return to be no more than 2.5–3%

Rationale for Expectations: The greatest risk to the portfolio would be a poor judgement call by management, such as a bad trading decision or chasing less profitable trades because of a dearth of opportunity in the market. An example (had the fund existed back then) might have been 1997 and 1998, where spreads were very tight and market volatility very low. Losses could also incur due to the models breaking down and failing to describe the market environment although this is less likely as MJ is always questioning the models as a matter of course.

Actions in Event of Worst Expected Return

The fund seeks to limit the worst-case loss in any one month to 3.5% although in fast moving markets, the worst case scenario is expected to be −5%. The fund uses a stop-loss based approach to manage this risk. If losses reach 1.5%, the portfolio managers start to scale back on risk. If the losses continue, the fund reduces the risk in the portfolio further. Risk reduction continues until all positions are liquidated or completely hedged before the fund experiences a 3.5% loss. There are no preset stop losses for individual positions. Stop losses for individual positions are determined by several factors, such as position size, historic trading levels, and volatility. In the event of the risk reduction process taking place, risk would be increased again in the following month if opportunities existed to do so. However, if the portfolio maxed loss at 5% then MJ says he would very slowly start increasing risk again unless the loss was purely mark-to-market and was due to an independent exogenous event, e.g. 9/11 when the situation would be analysed and risk possibly built straight back up the following month to ensure that widened spreads were recaptured.

Peer Group/Competition: Big houses with similar types of hedge funds leveraging off the larger long only fixed income business.

This section facilitates the discussion of the track record of the fund in a more qualitative manner. It can be informative to analyse what drives the returns and when the fund will do well and do poorly. It is important to perform an attribution analysis on extreme past returns and assess what would most likely cause extreme returns going forward; this way a good feeling for what drives risk and returns can be acquired. It is also of interest to see what the portfolio manager thinks about this and how they would envisage responding to tough times. NB the returns above are date stamped to ensure they are kept up-to-date.

8.2.8   Fund Asset Growth And Investors

Assets

Fund Assets:	$1.2 billion	Last Updated December 06
Capacity Limit:	$2bn	Last Updated December 06

Asset Growth

Q1/04 USD 200m

Q2/04 USD 250m

Q3/04 USD 250m

Q4/04 USD 300m

Q1/05 USD 600m

Q2/05 USD 600m

Q3/05 USD 600m

Q4/05 USD 750m

Q1/06 USD 900m

Q2/06 USD 1.0bn

Q3/06 USD 1.1bn

Q4/06 USD 1.2bn

Just as I analysed company assets at the start of this report, it is even more important to analyse the movement in fund assets. As we see above, performance doubled in Q1 05, most probably once a year-long track record had been generated. Assets were then flat in 2005 – why was that? Also, is the performance as good now with USD 1bn as it was at lower asset levels? All these questions need to be asked.

Investor Base

Number of Investors: 55   Last Updated December 06

3 Largest Investors: 21%   Last Updated December 06

Hedge funds of funds make up 80% of assets; the majority of the remnant is pension plan money.

There needs to be a suitable number of investors in the fund (e.g. more than 10) with no one owning too large a percentage of the fund (e.g. more than 20%) since if an outsized investor were to remove their assets then this could impact the portfolio. Ideally there will be good diversification of investor type; here it would be better if the percentage invested by hedge funds of funds was less, but this is often the case.

8.2.9   Fund Structure and Reporting

Fund Structure and Fees

Domicile	Dublin
Currency	USD
Management Fee	1%
Performance Fee	20%
High Watermark	Yes
Minimum Investment	$1m
Minimum Top Up	USD 100,000
Subscription Frequency	Monthly
Subscription Fee	No
Redemption Frequency	Quarterly
Redemption Fee	2% if redeemed before 12 months invested
Notice Period	1 calendar month
Lockups or Other Clauses	20% gate
Changes to Fund Structure	None
Return of Funds	10 business days
Initial %	95%, rest after next audit
Possible Payment in specie?	Yes

Methodology for Manager's Collection of Fees
Management fee quarterly in arrears, performance fee annually

Side Letters, Fee Deals and Equity Stakes Held by investors
None

In this section you need to perform an independent analysis of fees and terms within the fund – investigating these directly through the prospectus rather relying on what the fund management company tells you. Here we see fees are a standard 1% management and 20% performance fees that are collected in the usual manner. Liquidity terms allow you to remove money at every quarter end with 30 days, notice but NB there is a 20% gate and a fee if you have been invested for less than a year. Also note that they could elect to pay you 'in specie' which means they give you a portion of portfolio holdings rather than cash – this is a common clause but a rare occurrence in reality. Finally, it is a good sign that no other investors have negotiated better terms than you through side letters, which can be dangerous when funds go bad as others otherwise may be able to run for the door quicker, leaving you amongst the last ones there.

Reporting

Final NAV Reporting	15 business days after month end
Estimated Monthly NAV	3 business days after month end
Source	Administrator
Intra-monthly estimates	Weekly
Source	Manager

Discrepancies, Restatements and Suspensions
None

Manager Reporting
Full transparency with monthly commentary and risk analysis. Very good level of depth.

Accounting

Date of Last Audit	y/e 2005
On File?	Yes
Audit Transparency	Full transparency
Qualifications	None

Comments on Financials
No problems given the good standing of the manager, no qualifications, known auditor and level of detail.

For this section, the accuracy and frequency of NAV calculations are investigated. Estimated returns on a weekly basis are usual. Estimated month end returns should be a close estimate of final NAVs, which should also be timely and accurate. If not, you must question why this is. Also, any restatements or suspensions of NAV need to be investigated as these suggest serious issues with pricing. Finally, the last several sets of audited financials need to be analysed for any qualifications or unusual notes, which should be investigated and discussed with fund manager and, if at all possible, auditor. If there is not full transparency in the financials you should ask the manager and auditor why. The audited financials are a good source of information on the level of assets in the fund – they should correspond with the estimates of assets from all other sources.

8.2.10   Contacts

Investment Manager Contacts

Samples:

Name	Bob Smith
Title	Director, Client Service, London
Telephone	#######
Fax	#######
E Mail	####@####.com
Has Left	No
Interviewed	Yes (see file)
Responsibilities	Head of International Client Service
Principal of Company?	No
Key Person?	No
CV	
1999 – present	Director, Client Service (London) Jones Asset Mgt
1990 – 1999	Client Services manager, GGG Asset Mgt

1989 – 1990	Year out (spent travelling and finding job)
1986 – 1989	BSc (IIi) Law, Leeds Uni (unverified)
Born	1968

No references carried out

Name	Martyn Johnson
Title	Portfolio Manager
Telephone	#######
Fax	#######
E Mail	####@####.com

Has Left	No
Interviewed	Yes (see file)
Responsibilities	Portfolio manager for the XYZ hedge fund (80% of role)
Principal of Company?	No
Key Person?	Yes

CV

2003 – present	Portfolio Manager, Jones Asset Mgt
1994 – 2003	Vice President, XXXX Asset Management
1993 – 1994	MBA, Harvard Business School (verified)
1990 – 1993	BSc Finance, Princeton University (verified)
Born	1972

Comment

MJ joined XXXX as an Associate following business school and was quickly promoted to VP with his own proprietary trading book in fixed income, where he reported to AJ. When AJ joined Jones Asset Management as CIO, he took MJ with him to establish and manage the hedge fund. There is no return data available for MJ at XXXX but we have seen 8 years of P&Ls and MJ was consistently profitable, backed up by references (see file)

Full references carried out – five on file.

Other Contacts

Sample

Name	Edgar Evans
Role	VP; Head of account for the XYZ fund
Company	PPP Inc
Company Type	Administrator
Telephone	########
Fax	########
E Mail	####@####.com

The contacts section should contain all people connected with the fund (including relevant non-investment personnel). Those closest to the fund should be independently referenced to ensure their background was as described in their resume (as you can see above, we verify the qualifications of some individuals as well). Note that we have past jobs in chronological order to ensure that any gaps are accounted for.

8.2.11   Meetings and Updates

A sample of a meeting (abridged)

CJ teleconference with MJ   1 Nov 2004 – 16:00
October was a decent month and they are up around 1%. They were very cautious following their loss in September as they couldn't understand the logic the market was using but positions have steadied and risk is back to regular levels. Most strategies did well in October. The strongest performer in the fund was MBS area which contributed about 50bps to the overall performance (this rationale for this trade was discussed in the meeting for Aug 04). Global Relative Value (long Sterling rates versus Eurodollar) also performed well and contributed around 25bps. Various credit plays added around 25bps also. Around USD 50m of inflows for October as investors buy the dip in performance from September. No changes to the portfolio going forward as yet but MJ is waiting for a predicted widening in credit spreads and so is taking profit on credit and expects to add once again after the widening.

Due Diligence Update   **Nov 2004**

1. Have there been any staff departures, additions, promotions or demotions?
   No changes.
2. Have there been any fundamental changes to the investment strategy?
   No changes.
3. Have there been any changes to the group infrastructure or ownership structure?
   No changes.
4. Has there been any legal action involving the manager or fund?
   No changes.
5. Have there been any other changes to investments, operations, pricing or other processes?
   No changes.
6. Have there been any changes to the fund third parties or other external service providers (e.g. addition of a new prime broker, change of lawyers)?
   No changes.
7. Have there been any other changes that we should be made aware of?
   No, there have been no other changes.
8. What are assets under management for the fund as at month end?
   AUM = USD 289m (est.), making an inflow of USD 39m on the month.

Above we can see sample records of past meetings (abridged) and updates. It is important to keep notes in this way as meetings with the portfolio manager should be as much about what he intends to add to the portfolio as what he has done to it. The regular written updates also ensure that the records are up to date and we would be quick to find out if there were any infrastructural changes.

END

8.3 SUMMARY

Above we see the qualitative analysis that should be carried out on a hedge fund by a hedge fund of funds manager that is considering investment. As we have seen in this and all the chapters in Part II, a hedge fund of funds' analysis needs to be thorough, critical and independent and also needs to cover not just investment management but a wide range of other investment and operational areas. The same applies to those seeking to invest in a hedge fund of funds. In the next section we will see how to evaluate a hedge fund of funds' ability to execute the above effectively and successfully.

8.4   SUMMARY OF IDEAS FOR CHAPTER 8

- When investing with a hedge fund, a thorough qualitative analysis needs to be carried out for every aspect of the fund, its manager and its third parties; this includes analysis of back office and systems.
- Such an appraisal must be based around interpreting what the hedge fund manager tells you rather than taking this for granted and just quoting his answers.
- Performing critical analysis and forming opinion is essential – appraising a hedge fund is not a box ticking exercise.

Part III

Evaluating, Selecting and Investing in Hedge Funds of Funds

9
Assessing Hedge Funds of Funds

9.1 OVERVIEW

In this section, I aim to give a fairly in-depth description of how one could assess, select, invest with and monitor a hedge fund of funds. This chapter – the largest in Part III, aims to help with the actual selection of a hedge fund of funds. The second chapter in Part III deals with designing such a selection process. The third chapter deals with the actual process of investing with a hedge fund of funds and the necessary monitoring and benchmarking processes that follow. Finally, I will give a sample report on a hedge fund of funds as an illustration of the theory in Chapter 9.

In this chapter I aim to give an overview of how I would go about selecting a hedge fund of funds to invest my own institution's money in. In this role I am a something of a 'poacher turned gamekeeper' since my main job is as a Chief Investment Officer of a hedge fund of funds – Key Asset Management. As such, I have tried to use my specialist knowledge of how hedge funds of funds are managed to provide some tips and pointers on how a good hedge fund of funds can be identified.

Just as when assessing a hedge fund, there is a range of issues to consider – namely the strength of the investment process, risk process, infrastructure and operations. However, given the 'one step removed' nature of hedge funds of funds there will be differences also, as we will see below.

As you may remember from the last section, I identified the core functions of a hedge fund of funds as follows:

- Strategy Allocation
- Sourcing and Capacity Provision
- Hedge Fund Selection
- Portfolio Construction
- Decision Process
- Risk Management
- Portfolio Management and Monitoring

Just as in the last section, I address each of these core functions, split into two areas: Investment Process (covering strategy allocation, sourcing and capacity provision, hedge fund selection, portfolio construction and decision process) and Risk Management, Portfolio Management and Monitoring covering the remnant. However, for the hedge fund of funds to be assessed, three further areas need to be looked at:

- Track Record – does the track record show that the hedge fund of funds has an edge?
- Team – is the hedge fund of funds' team up to the job?
- Operational – is the hedge fund of funds operationally sound?

Below, for each of these core areas, I describe the parts that are critically important to the overall process and then arm you with some questions to ask, accompanied by some help interpreting the answers you receive. The questions below are supplementary and assume that you have already had the processes described to you by the hedge fund of funds manager. The answers and their interpretation can then be used to form an investment report, an example of which is given in the last chapter of this section. The questions are split into Key questions and Killer questions. The Key questions are aimed at gathering information that you can analyse to form a better understanding of the processes and strategy whereas the Killer questions are aimed more at testing the limits of the hedge fund of funds and finding the true range of the manager's abilities and edge. Depending on the amount you have to invest and the amount of time you and the hedge fund of funds' management company have to give, there may not be a chance to cover all the questions. In this instance, I would at least ask the Key question marked with an asterisk[*] and then use the Killer questions where you think the process may be weak.

Off The Record

The aim of this section of the book is to give you practical help in selecting the best hedge funds of funds. Part of this process will involve empowering you to 'hold your own' in a meeting with hedge funds of funds managers and marketers. This may sound flippant but believe me it is important; if you are assessing a hedge fund of funds and they sense that they can get away with making bolder statements about their prowess and remain unchallenged, they often will. Similarly, if you are using a consultant, they will work harder for you if they see you have taken the time to understand what's going on.

9.2   INVESTMENT PROCESS

As I have said in the previous section, a good hedge fund of funds will have a well thought out, well explained and well adhered to investment process to ensure they generate returns through strategy allocation, hedge fund selection and portfolio construction. Almost all hedge funds of funds have a smart investment process diagram but this does not demonstrate that the process is effective or even properly applied so further investigation is needed. To this end, this section focuses on assessing the effectiveness of the main investment processes of a hedge fund of funds, namely strategy allocation, sourcing and capacity provision, hedge fund selection, portfolio construction and decision processes.

9.2.1   Strategy Allocation

My own view is that a strategy allocation process is a necessary part of a modern hedge fund of funds and that it adds a great deal of value to the investment process. This is a subjective view that is difficult to prove or disprove. However, if a hedge fund of funds claims to have a strategy allocation process then it should be tested.

Key question:

- What is the current strategy outlook and how has it been established?
  - This answer should illustrate the strategy allocation process in action.
- Is there a formal strategy allocation meeting? With what frequency? How does it work? Are there any formal strategy reports written? Please provide examples.
  - Further evidence that the strategy allocation approach is an active and rigorous process.

Killer question:

- How is the current strategy outlook reflected in the portfolio construction? Give evidence.
  - To check that the strategy process is well integrated into the portfolio construction process as opposed to being a purely cosmetic exercise.

9.2.2   Sourcing and Capacity

This set of questions aims to establish how a hedge fund of funds manager would source their hedge funds and maintain capacity in them. It is easy to buy databases of quantitative information on the universe but this normally doesn't provide information on many of the best hedge funds, who choose to stay 'off database'; furthermore such databases would not have information on hedge funds yet to launch. Many hedge funds of funds rely on the capital introduction services offered by prime brokers along with databases for their primary sources, but the best hedge funds of funds have a much wider contact base that can be called upon.

Key questions on sourcing:

- How do you source new hedge funds?[*]
  - You should expect an answer saying that databases and prime broker capital introduction services are used. A better answer will also refer to 'other sources' based on market contacts. This question is a check to ensure that the hedge fund of funds uses all standard sourcing techniques.
- Which databases do you subscribe to?
  - Generally, standard 'off the shelf' databases provided by the likes of HFR and Tremont, for example, are used. A better answer will also refer to internal databases that are constructed in-house. This is a check to ensure that at least one database exists for filtering and screening out new and existing hedge funds.
- What are the 'other sources' you refer to?
  - This question allows you to dig deeper at the contact base of the hedge fund of funds to see if they have any edge from that.
- Are there any hedge funds that you have 'missed' through not getting information in time? Were any improvements made as a result?
  - Honesty should be appreciated here but ideally, there will be evidence that the hedge fund of funds managers learn from their mistakes and evolve the process so that mistakes are unlikely to be made twice.

Killer questions on sourcing:

- Provide a list of all hedge funds you have invested with over the past 12 months and for each tell us how you found them?
  - If there is time and willingness to do this 'case study' then it can give a good insight to whether the process that has been described is beneficially applied.

- Have any of the hedge funds sourced in the last 12 months been found through sources other than databases or prime broker capital introduction processes?
  - ○ This should show whether the hedge fund of funds really does source through their contact base as well as through the standard sources.

Key questions on capacity:

- What is your strategy on reserving capacity with hedge funds?
  - ○ This establishes whether a hedge fund of funds is actively thinking about and securing capacity or not.
- What is your strategy in growing the assets of the hedge funds of funds?
  - ○ Here you are looking for evidence that the hedge fund of funds you may be invested with will not grow so fast as to diminish returns by diluting the best underlying hedge funds too much.
- To what asset level could each of your hedge funds of funds grow without diluting holdings in all closed hedge funds? Without diluting holdings in the majority of closed funds?*
  - ○ This question is the main test for how much capacity is in each of the funds. It would be fair to expect moderate dilution but not to expect the majority of otherwise closed constituent hedge funds to be diluted due to lack of capacity provision.

Killer question on capacity:

- For a chosen hedge fund of funds, identify which hedge funds are closed and of those funds, how much capacity is available?
  - ○ This case study should give greater insight into the levels of capacity available.

What you are trying to do here is to check that the sourcing process is finding good hedge funds using the standard sources of prime broker capital introduction services and off the shelf hedge fund databases. In addition, better hedge funds of funds will also have developed an edge through building a range of other sources and contacts; hence, if there is a good hedge fund out there launching or otherwise doing well but keeping relatively low key, the hedge fund of funds will hear about it sooner rather than later and keep ahead of the pack. Finally, you are checking to see if the hedge fund of funds is sustainable to asset growth through ongoing capacity in otherwise closed managers.

9.2.3   A Note on Screening

There is an overwhelming number of hedge funds nowadays – a figure in excess of 8000 has been suggested. Although a large proportion of these funds are not worthy of investment, it is still important that there is a reliable screening process in place to deal with the volume of funds that present themselves on the databases used in the sourcing process.

Key question:

• Can you give details of the last database screening and outline any actions as a result?[*]

The main thing that needs to be checked here is that the screening/-database search is done rigorously, regularly and with appropriate frequency (e.g. once a year at least although quarterly is better). It is also important to check that the screening process is not geared only to picking those with the best performance but also has a risk component. Selecting hedge funds on performance alone usually results in selecting the riskiest hedge funds with the downside yet to come.

9.2.4   Hedge Fund Selection

Once a hedge fund has been sourced for potential investment, both quantitative and qualitative analysis comes next. It is important here to ensure that the process goes beyond information gathering and that the information gathered from the hedge fund in question is interpreted (and not just relayed) and challenged, and that critical analysis is performed. Also, it is important that there is some uniformity of approach and subsequent write-up to facilitate 'like with like' comparison, i.e. each hedge fund's investment report is similar in structure. The whole basis of the investment report is to identify independently the hedge fund/hedge fund manager's edge or comparative advantage and similarly identify areas of existing or potential weakness in a timely and accurate manner, and hence make an investment decision.

Key questions:

• How much information gathering is done by questionnaire? When performing analysis on a hedge fund, how much is desk based and how much time do you spend face to face, via teleconference and on email?[*]

○ A good process will have a significant face to face portion otherwise it would be difficult to find out where the areas of strength and weakness lie.

• How much time does it take to write an investment report?

○ This question is here to check that investment reports are not rushed out but also to check that they are done in a timely manner as information in this area changes quickly and is time sensitive. Anything shorter than two weeks is too short, anything longer than three months means that some of the information gathered and analysis done may be out of date.

• How is the investment report split by concentration on investment, risk and operational analysis and is that reflective of the time spent on each area?[*]

○ A check to ensure that risk and operational analysis isn't neglected – in my view these topics should represent at least half of the report.

• How much of the investment report is based on analysis and how much on information received directly from the hedge fund manager?

○ All information should be analysed and interpreted rather than just blindly added to the report.

• Give an example of a great looking hedge fund that ended up not getting invested with.

○ A question to find out more about the process and to get an idea how disciplined it is.

• What are the three most important issues on the operational side? Risk side? Investment side?

○ A check to see how deeply the individual concerned has thought about the process she practices. On the operational side you must ensure that valuation issues, liquidity and anti-fraud are well covered.

• How do you avoid fraudulent hedge funds?[*]

○ A check to see if this part of the process is well thought out. Ideally, there will be reference to independent valuation of the portfolio. There should also be a good third party referencing process where prime brokers, administrators and auditors are checked out.

• How do you reference key personnel?[*]

○ A check to see if there is a proper referencing process in place. Ideally, there will be independent referencing in addition to checking references from the referees provided by the hedge fund manager himself. Checking key personnel with regulators such as the FSA is also important.

- How do you identify 'edge'?[*]
  - ○ It is important that the investment professionals at a hedge fund of funds understand this is what they are supposed to do, i.e. find hedge funds that have a strong rationale for why returns are generated. Often the process of writing a hedge fund investment report is so long and varied that it is sometimes difficult to see the wood for the trees and hence critical analysis is diminished. There is no 'right answer' here but an answer that demonstrates they have thought deeply about edge should be regarded as promising.

Killer questions:

- Please show us a report on a hedge fund you invest with, of our choice. Why was this fund selected? Has the fund made money? Were there any parts of the process not covered for this hedge fund? How much of this report is interpretation and critical analysis and how much is straight from the hedge fund manager? Who was referenced in this report and what did they say?
  - ○ The main point here is that you see a true example of an investment report rather than one that has been specially prepared for the presentation, and thus assess the process in its true rather than idealised form.

The hedge fund selection process is one of the most important parts of the investment process. Once given a description of the process, asking the questions above should give you a good idea of how this process really works at a given hedge fund of funds. You should then be able to assess the depth of information gathered, how well it is analysed and hence how effective this part of the investment process is.

9.2.5   Portfolio Construction

This section suggests some questions that should reveal whether the portfolio construction process within a hedge fund of funds is a distinct process or just based on adding good funds with no top-down or risk processes embedded. A well thought out and effective portfolio construction process will integrate the strategy allocation and risk processes and have an element of ongoing management.

Key questions:

- Describe the portfolio construction process. How do you build portfolios from scratch? How is the portfolio construction process used to add managers to existing portfolios?[*]
  - ○ Portfolio construction is often not referred to in standard hedge fund of funds presentations and so you may need to ask specifically for an overview of the process in their own words.
- How is correlation analysis used?
  - ○ Correlation analysis works well over a long run but can break down especially in times of market stress and this should be acknowledged and discussed in the answer.
- How is diversification achieved? How many hedge funds in a typical multi-strategy portfolio?[*]
  - ○ This is an opportunity to discuss how diversification is achieved and to check that diversification is not just a function of adding more hedge funds but also considers the correlation between the positions and exposures within different hedge funds and strategies.
- What risk work is done before adding a new hedge fund to the portfolio?
  - ○ A good portfolio construction process integrates the risk process in its operation and ideally there should be evidence of risk analysis being done on the proposed portfolio *before* adding a new hedge fund.
- Are any strategies, hedge funds or instruments used solely for portfolio insurance purposes?[*]
  - ○ Get a feel for whether the hedge fund of funds manager is willing to sacrifice returns to lessen downside. Whether this is good or bad depends on how much downside control is needed.

Killer questions:

- What deliberate risks/overweights/underweights are currently being taken in the hedge funds of funds and what is the rationale for this?
  - ○ A check to see if the portfolio is constructed deliberately to encompass top down views. If so, one must assess the hedge fund of funds manager's skill at forming these views.
- What event would cause the most contagion in the portfolio and what would be your expected outcome? Has any action been taken to reduce this outcome?

○ Contagion is when all hedge funds act in a similar manner, usually at times of market stress. The answer will give an idea of how much the 'worst case scenario' has been considered and if any action has been taken to manage risk in the toughest times.

The answers to the above questions should give you a good feeling for the way portfolios are constructed within the hedge fund of funds. After this analysis you should feel confident that the approach is both rigorous and pragmatic and have a good feeling about the interaction of the risk and investment functions within the portfolio construction process.

9.2.6   Decision Process

It is important that there is a regular forum for investment reports to be discussed, proposed hedge funds to be considered and investment decisions to be made. The aim of a potential investor in a hedge fund of funds should be to understand this mechanism and check that it is effective.

Key questions:

- With what regularity is the investment meeting held and how long does it last?[*]
  ○ Ideally looking for a regular meeting of some substance, e.g. monthly three hour meeting.
- Who attends? Who chairs?[*]
  ○ Ideally you would want all senior investment professionals present and definitely the people who did the analysis on any given hedge fund should be there. There should also be some operations/ compliance representation to ensure that due process is adhered to and operational aspects are represented.
- What happens if the senior person is off sick? Has the investment meeting ever been missed?
  ○ The aim of this question is to check that a continuity plan exists and that the process isn't totally reliant on one individual. Also, this checks that the meetings are held regularly and that nothing allows the decision process to go untended for a period of time.
- Are the meetings minuted? What happens to minutes after the meeting?
  ○ A check that the decision process is documented and monitored and can be back-checked if necessary. It's not a bad thing if the minutes are read over by someone outside the meeting as a failsafe for errors or abuse of process.

- How is information conveyed to meeting attendees?
  - A check to see if everybody has time before the meeting to read the investment reports and form opinion rather than hedge funds being 'steam rollered' through for approval on the day.
- What happens in the meeting?*
  - It is necessary to check the style of the meeting, be it a 'challenge environment' or a more passive approach. The important point is that everybody gets a chance to express opinion and that opinion is taken on board. Particularly of importance is the need for those who have done the work on the hedge fund in question to be present and allowed to express opinion.
- What happens as a result of the meeting?*
  - A necessary question to ensure that the outcome of the meeting is implemented in a timely and well monitored manner.

Killer questions:

- How are decisions made? Who outside the investment team is part of this process?
  - It is important to check that the decision process is well defined and adhered to, be it by vote, veto or consensus. It is also important to check that the decision is biased towards investment professionals and cannot be overridden by those whose day-to-day job is not investment based, e.g. CEO rather than CIO.
- How many hedge funds are rejected typically?
  - A check to see that the process actually works and isn't just a 'wave through'.
- What happens when a difference of opinion/deadlock occurs?
  - The answer should give a good insight into the structure of the process.
- Who retains right of veto and how often are vetoes used?
  - It is good if there are vetoes in existence at least on risk and on operational structure, however if vetoes are used regularly, e.g. monthly then the whole investment process isn't working.

The decision process should also be ongoing, constantly reassessing existing constituent hedge funds but we defer discussion of this to the section below on monitoring and portfolio management.

To summarise, asking the above questions during or following a presentation of investment process should truly test the claims of a hedge fund of funds and result in a much deeper insight into what they do in this area. Next, we provide a similar approach for the more ongoing aspects of managing a hedge fund of funds.

Off The Record

Some hedge funds of funds have great investment processes but leave the decision in the hands of senior people who do not go near hedge funds on regular basis and so are not best placed to make such decisions. It's therefore of paramount importance to check that the decision process does not create this trap.

Also, democracy sometimes is not the best method for decision making in an investment meeting. It tends to favour the established mediocre over that with a better outlook, and removes power from the hands of those with best experience and knowledge of the hedge fund in question.

9.3   RISK MANAGEMENT, PORTFOLIO MANAGEMENT AND MONITORING

In this section I suggest some questions aimed at getting to the heart of the risk management approach of a hedge fund of funds to check that this process is appropriate for the type of funds invested with, well understood and adhered to. Furthermore, I suggest some questions to check that the hedge fund of funds is actively managed with ongoing assessment and monitoring of the underlying hedge funds, which is also very important.

9.3.1   Risk Process

A solid, well thought out risk process is as important as a good investment process. The risk system doesn't necessarily have to be complex (although an approach that has some depth is necessary for more complex hedge fund strategies such as arbitrage) but what is important is that the hedge fund of funds manager has a rigorous and regular process for her to fully understand what the potential risks are in every hedge fund in the portfolio (or to be added to the portfolio), where those risks are taken and how they change over time.

Key questions:

- Please describe the approach to risk and all risk systems used. Please show us a risk report for a hedge fund of funds portfolio and an underlying hedge fund.*
  - The risk reports should not look overly complex otherwise the hedge fund of funds managers may find them difficult to interpret. Similarly, the risk reports should not be more than a few pages otherwise you can bet they will not be read in full by other members of the investment team.
- Is there a dedicated risk manager? If so, what is her reporting line?
  - It is very difficult to switch mindset between being a hedge fund of funds manager and a hedge fund of funds risk manager and so there should be a dedicated risk professional separate from the fund managers themselves. Ideally the risk manager will have a dual reporting line to a CIO and to a non-investment professional such as the COO or CEO as this will allow any risk breaches to be visible even if the CIO tries to cover them up!
- How often does the risk manager meet with underlying hedge fund managers?
  - Ideally the risk manager will have regular meetings with hedge fund managers and hedge fund risk managers to discuss the risks in the underlying hedge funds.
- Is the risk system bespoke or off-the-peg?*
  - Neither answer is better here but if bespoke, there should be good evidence that the system does something beyond the off-the-peg solutions rather than being just a cheap imitation. Similarly, if the system is off the peg then it must be appropriate at measuring the risk in the strategies used; also the risk manager must show a good knowledge of how the system works rather than just using it as a black box.
- Is the risk system specifically built for hedge funds/hedge funds of funds?*
  - If not, you must investigate further to check the risk system is appropriate as hedge funds and hedge funds of funds do a lot of complex and esoteric things compared to the traditional investment world.
- If off-the-peg, has the risk system been augmented or added to in any way to make it more appropriate for hedge funds/hedge funds of funds?

- ○ Personally, I would say there are many ways that off-the-peg systems can be expanded to make them more useful but this is a viewpoint only.
- Give a layman's overview of any complex mathematics the risk system uses.
  - ○ The better they explain the above, the better they themselves understand how it works, irrespective of whether you are a maths professor or outright innumerate!
- Is the risk system dependent on a statistical distribution such as the normal distribution? How does the risk system handle the nonlinear nature of hedge fund portfolios and the resulting non-standard distributions hedge funds sometimes exhibit?
  - ○ Again, a test of how well they understand how the system works. Hedge funds are generally non-normal and different strategies have different distributions so any system that relies fully on the normal distribution or indeed any single distribution may be a poor estimator of risk, especially at the extremes.
- Is the system in any way forward looking or is it totally dependent on past track records and price histories?
  - ○ Many risk systems rely purely on what has happened whereas in an ideal world, the risk approach will have a broader consideration and be in some way forward looking instead of being purely reliant on the past.
- How reliant is the approach on transparency of underlying hedge fund portfolios and how does that effect the way you select hedge funds and manage the hedge fund of funds portfolio?
  - ○ The system should be developed enough to handle partial transparency. Not all hedge funds give full transparency on a monthly basis and the system should be able to cope with this. Those hedge funds of funds that limit themselves to the need for full transparency on a monthly basis dramatically reduce the number of hedge funds open to them. Given that hedge funds generally have quite high turnover anyway, the benefit of full monthly transparency is a little bit overrated since the portfolio may look totally different by the next day anyway.
- With what frequency are risk reports compiled?
  - ○ Given that a hedge fund of funds should be considered for rebalancing every month, the risk assessment for a hedge fund of funds portfolio should also be no less frequent than monthly. Similarly, risk reports on the underlying hedge funds should be compiled ideally monthly or at least quarterly.

- How is information passed on to other investment professionals in the team?
  - ○ The risk manager should work closely with the rest of the investment team to ensure that they understand the analysis that has been done and the resulting output. A report based relationship alone may lead to a lack of appreciation of subtleties in the risk report.
- When does the risk analysis of a prospective hedge fund investment begin?
  - ○ Ideally risk analysis begins at the same time as investment analysis rather than just tagged on the end as an afterthought to the investment process. This way, the risk manager can get a full understanding of the hedge fund in question prior to an investment decision being made.

Killer questions:

- Please provide a risk report for a relevant hedge fund of funds. Please show us the risk report/assessment for a hedge fund of our choosing within this hedge fund of funds.
  - ○ This way you can check that the risk process is genuinely all encompassing rather than selective for presentation purposes.
- Please can you explain where the risks lie within this hedge fund of funds and how they have changed over time?
  - ○ Ideally this is answered by the manager of the hedge fund of funds. This should demonstrate that the risk approach plays a pragmatic role to the identifying and tracking of risk in the portfolio and that this is understood by the managers of the hedge fund of funds as well as just the risk manager.
- Please can you explain where the risks lie within our chosen underlying hedge fund and how they have changed over time?
  - ○ As above but at a deeper level.
- What is the beta to equity markets in this hedge fund of funds? What is the beta to credit spreads?
  - ○ A good risk approach will be able to give answers to these crucial questions and allow the hedge fund of funds manager to understand the risks they are running to conventional markets.
- Suggest some worst case scenarios in this hedge fund of funds, the likely outcomes for such scenarios and any action that has been taken to avoid them or reduce impact.
  - ○ Aimed at testing how much they consider worst case scenarios and whether there is any activity to this end.

- How is liquidity and operational risk measured and managed?
  - A fundamentally important part of risk management although difficult to measure and hence usually dealt with in the investment process. However, a question worth asking as it is important that the risk manager has a good understanding of the existence and importance of these risks.
- What are the weaknesses of this approach to risk? Which hedge fund strategies does this approach work best/worst with and has anything been done to improve on the process for strategies where this approach is worst?
  - All risk management systems have weaknesses in some areas and these are better to be known and well understood than ignored. If a risk manager assumes that this approach is the holy grail of risk systems then there will be over reliance on the output of the system, itself a risk. A pragmatic risk manager will understand the weaknesses of the approach and make those weaknesses well understood. Also, different risk approaches work better for different hedge fund strategies and it is equally important that this is recognised by the risk manager.

9.3.2   Monitoring and Portfolio Management Processes

It is important that the investment process extends beyond the one-off assessment of hedge funds and the construction of a hedge fund of funds portfolio. Ongoing monitoring, assessment and rebalancing are necessary in keeping the portfolio in good shape and weakness in this area is as bad as weakness in the investment process itself.

Key questions:

- With what frequency are investment reports on any given manager updated, e.g. assets under management, staff turnover?
  - A good check to see that there is some sort of basic ongoing monitoring in action and information is not allowed to go stale. Ideally the updates would be done monthly.
- How often do you talk with the hedge fund management company and the manager himself? How often are meetings face-to-face? Onsite?*
  - In an ideal world there would be monthly talks with the hedge fund manager or another senior investment professional and

face-to-face meetings a few times a year with an onsite visit at least once a year.

- How soon before the investment decision meeting do you have accurate information on inflows and outflows in the fund?
  - Fund of funds portfolio managers should have good time to consider putting new money to work or making forced liquidations well before the investment meeting.
- How much is a typical cash balance in the portfolio? What is the largest the cash balance has been? How is cash managed?
  - An ongoing cash balance of more than 5% is worth noting and an ongoing cash balance of more than 10% is a significant issue as cash may be being held for liquidity purposes or maybe capacity with existing hedge funds has run out and there are no new funds lined up to invest with.
- How do you switch between hedge funds, i.e. redeeming from one and then adding another? Is any leverage used at hedge fund of funds portfolio level?
  - It is useful to use leverage to make new investments whilst other divestments are being returned but long term leverage is not good in anything but an overtly leveraged hedge fund of funds.
- How is liquidity managed?[*]
  - There is a need to ensure that the liquidity of the underlying hedge fund portfolio is managed in line with the liquidity of the hedge fund of funds itself.
- What are the concentration limits for the fund? What if a fund grows to be more than this limit?[*]
  - There should be concentration limits in place at hedge fund, hedge fund management company and strategy level. For multi-strategy hedge funds of funds, expect a limit of around 10% per fund or even lower and ensure that if this limit is surpassed there is a policy to trim back the position. Ensure that there are strategy concentration limits but that they are broad enough to allow the portfolio manager to allocate between strategies but tight enough to ensure diversifications, e.g. no more than 50% in any one strategy.
- Are positions rebalanced in a way that corresponds to fund of funds inflows and outflows?
  - A check to ensure that position size is deliberate rather than dependent on exogenous factors. A general check for discipline in the process.

Killer questions:

- Please show meeting/monitoring notes for the past 12 months for a hedge fund I select.
  - To ensure that the reality of the monitoring process matches the theory.
- Would you be able to provide liquidity should 25% of assets flow out of the fund of funds? 50%? 100%?
  - A check that liquidity is being well managed. NB it is usual for there to be a gate in place that restricts too much outflow in any one trading period.
- Please reconcile the current strategy allocations in the hedge fund of funds with your top-down strategy view.
  - A check to ensure that strategy conviction is actually being reflected in the portfolio management process and not just cosmetic.
- Are there any structured products based on the portfolio and has that altered concentration or liquidity limits in any way?
  - Sometimes, structured products are based around hedge funds of funds and that imposes more stringent limits on liquidity and concentration, thus potentially impacting the returns of non-structured product investors in the hedge fund of funds in question.
- Are there any side letters with investors?
  - A check to ensure nobody has any better liquidity terms than you. Inevitably, different investors will be paying different fees.

Portfolio monitoring and management tend to get less attention than other parts of the investment process due to the slightly more straightforward nature of what needs to be done. These questions should reveal whether the hedge fund of funds has a disciplined approach to monitoring and managing portfolios. If it doesn't, I would avoid it.

9.4   TRACK RECORD ANALYSIS

Analysis of track record is a good way of measuring the impact of investment and risk processes on returns. If a hedge fund of funds is generating far from adequate returns then obviously, few will invest. However, it is also important not to exclude one hedge fund of funds for marginally underperforming another until the level of risk taken by the two funds of funds is also considered. There is little standardisation within the hedge fund of funds universe and different funds may take different levels of concentration, diversification, market and strategy exposure and risk at underlying hedge fund level.

As a result of the above, it is important that hedge fund of funds track records are risk adjusted, i.e. returns are scaled by the levels of risk taken. To construct truly risk adjusted returns is not as straight forward in the hedge fund world as the traditional world where volatility of returns is a proxy for risk. This is because hedge funds (and hence hedge funds of funds) do not display all their risk through volatility alone. However, there are some rudimentary measures that can be taken and some questions to ask which may shed further light on what risks are being taken.

Basic risk adjusted returns are returns that are scaled (divided) by the volatility (standard deviation) of those returns. Given that this is a quick and simple measure, it should certainly be analysed. However, as well as considering volatility as a measure for risk, other risk measures can be used as well, such as concentration levels, the risk manager's estimate of Value at Risk, estimated market exposure, worst down months and maximum drawdown.

Given the imperfection of volatility as a measure of risk in this area, it is worth noting that the least volatile hedge fund of funds track record isn't necessarily the one with the lowest risk. Complex strategies that generally have smooth track records but can be prone to big one-off risks, such as mortgage backed securities arbitrage and asset based lending strategies may make up big positions. This would give an exceptionally smooth track record that appeared to be low risk but may blow up in future, so beware.

If there is a need to compare performance to an underlying index then any of the investable hedge fund indices will suffice (e.g. CSFB Tremont, HFRX). Investable indices should be used as the returns of the general (un-investable) indices cannot be replicated or accessed in practice. Similarly of interest are hedge fund of funds peer group rankings as published in journals such as Investhedge. However, these rankings are based on returns alone and so are of limited value when analysing risk adjusted returns.

Key questions:

• What are the top three monthly returns and bottom three monthly returns – what happened then? How was the portfolio constructed in the best and worst months? Give an attribution analysis.[*]

- ○ Look for a good understanding of why these returns occurred and the risks that were taken to achieve them.
- What caused the worst drawdown?
  - ○ Drawdowns can be a result of cumulative small negative returns rather than sharp shocks and are worthy of investigation in case the portfolio has gone off the boil or is being overly influenced by one hedge fund or strategy.
- What is the best performing and worst performing hedge fund over the past 12 months? Best/worst performing strategy?
  - ○ Again, getting this attribution will show what has been driving the track record and if it is overly reliant on any one area.
- Is any leverage used at hedge fund of funds level?*
  - ○ A check to see if performance is being boosted through borrowing.

Killer questions:

- What are the worst three performing hedge funds you have been invested with? What happened?
  - ○ This allows any 'blow-ups' to be identified and gives a good feel for how the hedge fund of funds manager acts in a crisis and learns from mistakes.
- Are you invested with Asset Based Lending, Mortgage Backed Securities or any other strategy that have overly smooth track records? What are the hedge funds and hedge fund strategies you invest with that do not reflect the true risks in their existing track records?
  - ○ This should give an idea of how much the track record is being smoothed through access to these strategies and how aware of future risk from these areas the hedge fund of funds manager is. It is not necessarily bad to be invested in such strategies as long as there is awareness of the risks.
- What is the hedge fund that you are invested with that has the highest percentage of positive returns in their track record? Can this continue and why?
  - ○ As above.

The above questions should yield information on how reliant the returns are on any one hedge fund or strategy and whether volatility is being suppressed in a way that underestimates future risk. When coupled with a basic quantitative (return, volatility and downside) analysis of track record, this should give a good insight into how successful the hedge fund of funds really is.

9.5   THE HEDGE FUND OF FUNDS TEAM

When investing in a hedge fund of funds, it's not just the investment and risk process you are buying but the skilled operation of such processes. As a result, it is important to assess the full range of investment professionals within a hedge fund of funds.

It is important that a hedge fund of funds management company employs an investment and risk team of suitable levels of experience and skill and keeps this team motivated and stable. Furthermore it is important that the team is big enough to practice the investment process with suitable levels of detail and that the team is well supported by operations, administration, sales, marketing and client servicing professionals.

These questions should help with assessing the strength of the hedge fund of funds team.

Key questions:

- Run through the backgrounds of each member of the investment and risk team. How many are full time on the investment side?[*]
  - This question should give you a general introduction to the team. It is interesting to see if they include people who aren't full time on the investment side but are considered investment professionals as this may imply they are added just to bump up the numbers.
- Who leads the team?[*]
  - Ideally the team will be led by an investment professional within the investment team, i.e. a CIO not a CEO. Sometimes, investment teams are run by an individual from outside the team which may result in a reporting line to somebody who does not fully appreciate the subtleties of the job. Needless to say, whoever leads the team must have suitable experience and ability to gain the team's respect.
- Is there a dedicated risk manager and what is her reporting line?[*]
  - My own view is that risk cannot be managed impartially by somebody who is also involved in selecting managers, and so a separate risk manager is essential.
- Describe the typical day of an investment professional.
  - An attempt to see if they are honest about how much non-investment related tasks are done, e.g. meeting with investors. Different hedge funds of funds have different approaches – some have more people in the investment team but also have greater non-investment expectations of the team members.

- How is time split between seeing/talking to new managers and existing managers, monitoring, travelling, report writing and desk-based research?
  - A good example to see if there are any weak spots or comparative advantages compared to other hedge funds of funds, in terms of the time spent on different areas. Ideally you should be looking for an equal balance between all areas.
- Are other continents covered by investment professionals travelling from this office, overseas offices or both?
  - It is worth getting formal details on research travel and overseas offices to check that there are no geographical weak spots. Overseas offices need to be checked out in detail to be sure they have enough staff to cover the universe in that area and to be sure that communication lines with head office are strong and regular.
- Are investment professionals well supported with secretarial help?
  - In many instances this is not the case and too much of investment professionals' time is spent on administrative issues rather than investment issues.
- How many conferences are covered a year? How much time is dedicated to ongoing education and development?
  - It is important that investment professionals attend industry conferences and have some structure for ongoing education to be sure they are up to date with industry developments and new markets. The hedge fund world is a rapidly evolving area of finance and it is necessary for hedge fund investors such as hedge fund of funds to have the knowledge to analyse new areas objectively, rather than just learning about new areas from hedge fund managers. Underlying hedge fund managers are not incentivised to give away the 'killer questions' that they themselves would be scrutinised by!
- What professional qualifications are necessary or encouraged?
  - Some formal training is important for those training in this area. In my own view the CFA qualification is much more testing than the current industry qualification CAIA. Despite the latter being more specialised, the CFA is an in-depth three stage course and so requires more effort and has greater overall depth.
- Are all investment professionals generalists or do some specialise in certain areas?
  - Given the complexity in some hedge fund strategies I would be looking for a degree of specialisation here although would also be wary of information silos – ideally individuals would not be so specialised as to prevent information flowing within the team.

- Are there separate portfolio managers and analysts?
  - There are many ways to structure a hedge fund of funds investment team either with the dual role of portfolio manager/analyst or with the portfolio manager role being a separate role to that of analyst. That is, the people who manage the funds of funds are different to those that investigate and analyse the hedge funds. Both ways have merits, but if the latter is used then there needs to be a check on how information flows between both roles.
- How does information flow between members of the investment team and what regular meetings occur?
  - Here you should be looking for a degree of regularity and a conscious effort to ensure information flows well. Without this it would be inevitable that errors will be made. NB be wary of 'overly process driven' information flows based on memos and emails – there needs to be ongoing face-to-face interaction as well.

Killer questions:

- How much time is spent on marketing, investor meetings and other non-investment related tasks?
  - Seemingly large teams may actually spend as much time on meeting with investors and potential investors as on investment issues and so an investment team's effective capability is a factor of time commitment as well as size. For example, if a relatively small investment team is spending more than 25% of its time on non-investment issues then the structure of the hedge fund of funds management company must be questioned.
- What is the staff turnover of the team and why do you think people left? How long has the longest serving member of the investment team been in service? What succession planning is in place?
  - Turnover of staff can be very disruptive as it can take some time to find a suitably skilled replacement and for the replacement to get up to speed with processes, team ethos etc. Ideally you would be looking for an investment team with low turnover or at least one that has taken sizeable efforts to improve stability. NB not all staff turnover is due to resignation, some may be due to lesser skilled investment professionals being sacked! An effective succession plan is important as this should minimize the impact of a departure and, it could be argued, a company that has taken the time to think about succession planning should be proactive enough to survive any departures.

- What is the base salary and bonus structure and how does this ensure stability? Why would the best investment professionals come here and stay here over other hedge funds of funds?
  - The best hedge funds of funds treat their investment teams well and offer competitive base salaries and good performance based bonuses. Bonuses often consist of cash and equity or shadow equity in the company (or shares in the funds), which allows for deferred compensation and participation in the upside of the company. Usually, numerous benefits exist to ensure their investment team is happy and motivated – everything from good pension and health care provision to gym membership and free fruit! It is worth asking individual investment professionals within the investment team for their views on their remuneration package.

The above discussion should give you a good feeling for the level of experience and skill, and the level of motivation and the stability of the investment team. All these facets are equally important for continually good returns since staff turnover and instability can affect returns as much as lack of skill.

9.6   OPERATIONAL ASPECTS OF HEDGE FUNDS OF FUNDS

It is important to be sure that a favoured hedge fund of funds management company is operationally sound before its hedge fund of funds is invested with. Hedge funds of funds do not usually trade on a day-to-day basis and do not trade directly in markets other than to hedge. As a result, cases of fraud in hedge funds of funds are virtually non-existent but there is still potential for error and worse, so a full operational due diligence should be conducted. The questions below should help with this process.

Key questions:

- How is currency hedging done? What checks and balances are in place to guard against error?[*]
  - It is expected that a hedge fund of funds will be sure to currency hedge all hedge fund investments within the fund of funds back to the currency of the share class in question. That is, if a US dollar denominated share class of a hedge fund of funds invests in underlying hedge funds with euro denominated share classes,

this euro exposure is hedged back to US dollars. Otherwise you, as an investor, are exposed to currency risk through the hedge fund of funds. If currency hedging is not done then there must be a good excuse why. Currency hedging is probably the only time the hedge fund of funds trades directly in the markets and errors can be very costly. It must be checked thoroughly that there is someone within the team that understands what is being done and that there are detailed processes and proper checks in place.

- Is any other direct trading done? Has any been done historically?*
  - Sometimes a hedge fund of funds will place overlays to hedge other exposures although this is usually an irregular event. If this is the case then you must be 100% certain that you believe that the investment team has the skill to add this overlay and that they can be trusted with this responsibility.
- How were the administrator, custodian and auditor selected? Have any of these third parties been changed and if so why?
  - It needs to be checked that there has been a proper procedure in place to select these third parties so they are well suited to the job. Any changes in third parties should be looked at closely and be justified. If the third parties are not well known names in this area, there has to be a good excuse why.
- What communication lines exist between custodian, administrator and the fund of funds management company?*
  - There needs to be solid and ongoing lines of communication and also ability for independent communication between the third parties, excluding the fund of funds management company – this is a good anti-fraud measure.
- How are subscriptions and redemptions in underlying hedge funds effected?
  - There needs to be procedures in place to ensure that information is sent to the custodian and administrator in an accurate and timely manner. 'Missed trades' can be expensive.
- Explain the independent pricing process. Have net asset values (NAVs) ever been re-stated or suspended?*
  - This question is primarily to ensure that the administrator acts independently to price the portfolio using accurate prices received independently from the underlying hedge funds. NAVs are usually restated due to pricing error: as a result of error at the administrator or a mispriced/restated NAV of an underlying hedge fund.

Either case is unacceptable if a frequent occurrence. Restatement should be a once in a lifetime event for any hedge fund of funds. Suspension of NAVs is a more worrying event since it means that you would not be able to get your money back for a time whilst NAVs have been suspended and usually means there has been a serious issue.

- Can we approach all third parties for an independent reference?
  - Well worth doing although rarely an issue. If not allowed, you should be suspicious!
- Have audited financials ever been late or qualified? Please provide audited financials for the hedge fund of funds for the past three years (or since inception, if there is time to analyse this).
  - The audited financials are usually a good source of information on asset growth and will also highlight any issues with the hedge funds of funds in the past. Any qualifications from the auditors are something to be wary of as it sometimes indicates low level irregularities.
- Where are the funds domiciled and why?
  - The better known the domicile the more security there is. Dublin and Luxemburg are better, then Bermuda, Cayman and British Virgin Islands.
- Are all underlying funds priced independently on a monthly basis?
  - Another check on the valuation procedure and the presence of any self pricing funds in the portfolio. If this is the case, you should investigate further
- How soon after month end is the final hedge fund of funds price struck? Are prices published?
  - Hedge funds of funds take some time to price independently due to the complexity of some underlying hedge funds and the time they take to price. If the hedge fund of funds takes more than six weeks to price, you need to ask why as this is irregular. Expect the price to be published in the FT, IHT or some other well known source.
- Is there a separate compliance officer? Please provide a copy of the compliance manual.
  - Look either for a qualified compliance professional or reputable outsourced specialist. If the latter, there will still be an official compliance officer and this should not be a member of the investment team or a very junior member of staff. A well produced compliance manual is evidence that they are serious and rigorous in this area.

- Are there written procedures? Please provide.
  - Ideally all procedures will be written up in investment and operations.
- Please provide details of the experience and functions of all administration and IT staff and any outsourcing that is done. How long have they been here and what is the turnover?
  - Look for well experienced operations professionals that understand the hedge fund area. Ideally these professionals will be long serving and turnover low.
- What is the information back-up policy?
  - Look for automatic daily back-ups stored automatically offsite. Ideally this will be done by a third party.
- Please provide details of the disaster recovery plan.[*]
  - There should be a well thought out disaster recovery plan that allows the hedge fund of funds management company to continue its business irrespective of conditions.

Killer questions

- Have there ever been any errors in the hedging process?
  - Ideally the answer should be 'no' but honesty here should be respected and those that are honest about past errors and show clear evidence of why that error will not be repeated should be well rated in this area. A comparison of different share classes' excess returns over the local interest rate will highlight any undisclosed errors.
- Have there ever been any errors in the subscription or redemption processes with underlying hedge funds?
  - A check on the efficiency of the subscription and redemption processes.
- Is the hedge fund of funds ever priced on the back of estimates in any underlying funds?
  - This is usually the case in minority but be wary of hedge funds of funds that are priced in majority on estimates.
- Has the hedge fund of funds' gate ever been activated?
  - This will give indication of any sizeable withdrawals and such incidences should be further investigated.
- If the office burned down next Monday at 7 a.m. what would happen next? How would you contact staff, access information and continue operating?

○ The answer to this question should give confidence of the disaster recovery plan.

Finally, references from the local regulator (usually available online) should be taken to ensure the business and key individuals are registered appropriately.

Operational risk within a hedge fund of funds is usually overlooked but attention here will give that extra layer of confidence and ensure that the chances of operational loss are minimised.

9.7 SUMMARY

Above I have suggested some questions to ask a hedge fund of funds that should add some depth and understanding to what they tell you they do. I would expect such questions to follow a presentation on processes from any given fund of funds. When time is scarce and few questions can be asked, I would suggest using the questions marked with an asterisk*. In the final chapter of Part III, I give an example research report on a hedge fund of funds which should illustrate how this type of process can be used to assess such a hedge fund of funds. Before that, in the next chapter I suggest how an assessment process can be designed and in the penultimate chapter I give some information on investing and monitoring hedge fund of funds.

9.8 SUMMARY OF IDEAS FOR CHAPTER 9

- As well as listening to the process presentation for a hedge fund of funds, asking an array of carefully thought out questions can give a good insight to the strengths and weaknesses.
- More testing questions should also be asked to provide evidence that the process is real and implemented, not just cosmetic.
- The investment team is as important as the investment process.
- Operational due diligence should also be performed.

10

Designing the Investment Process

10.1 OVERVIEW

In this chapter I will suggest how to establish a selection process that allows you to home in on exactly what you want from a hedge fund of funds, establish a shortlist and then you use the questions in the previous chapter to find the most appropriate investment for you.

10.2 DESIGNING THE SELECTION AND INVESTMENT PROCESSES

It is important to have some structure to the way that you assess the hedge fund of funds universe before you choose one to invest with.

First of all you need to establish what kind of return stream you require, e.g. an involatile product with modest return aspirations or a 'shoot the lights out' product that could boost your returns but at a cost of volatility. Are you happy with equity exposure or must the portfolio be 'market independent', i.e. generate returns totally independent of market direction? Do you want to invest in an off the shelf product or would you rather a bespoke mandate? What is the minimum assets that a hedge fund or fund manager must have for you to invest?

All these questions should to be considered before you can even begin to look for a hedge fund of funds and I would recommend that as accurate as possible search criteria is established before the sourcing of hedge funds of funds begins. A suggestion of such search criteria is as follows:

Minimum necessary assets in fund	Minimum asset base of manager
Bespoke product or fund?	Do they have product in the area needed?

Is equity market exposure acceptable?	Is other market exposure acceptable?
Geographical base of manager	Are any strategies not acceptable?
Geographical coverage of manager	Minimum track record length
Minimum number of investment staff	Minimum people in manager as a whole
Worst acceptable historic loss	Minimum past performance
Expected return of fund	Expected risk/volatility of fund

The above criteria can be used to form a filter, which may be useful for you to establish what you want in a hedge fund of funds. It's best to be flexible if there are criteria where there is any doubt about what you need, e.g. ask yourself if everything else was brilliant with a hedge fund of funds, would I be flexible on its asset base – remember, we are establishing what would be broadly acceptable to you when the search begins and so you don't want to exclude a hedge fund of funds for arbitrary reasons.

Once the search criteria has been established you need to make sure that you have cast your net wide enough to consider a broad enough range of products and managers to find which one is best for you. For example, I would advise that you meet with a wide enough range of managers to give yourself exposure to the following: hedge funds of funds that vary in asset base (from the lowest asset base acceptable to you right up to the mega-sized $10 billion+ managers), hedge funds of funds that vary by geographical base, by product range and by research approach.

There are plenty of sources for finding hedge funds of funds, ranging from journals such as Investhedge, specialist databases, specialist conferences and AIMA (Alternative Investment Management Association) – the hedge fund industry body. In general, I would say that there's no need to pay significant amounts of money to attend conferences or buy databases as most of the information is out there for free or nominal amounts.

Once the sourcing and searching has been done, all hedge funds of funds that pass the criteria should then form a 'long list' and the next step is to make contact. Before doing so I would suggest a timetable for selection is established. Most of the information that you gather from now on will be time-sensitive and will need to be regathered if the selection process runs from weeks and months to over a year which often happens if unchecked. In recognition of this, I would suggest the following timetable.

Month 1:   Request marketing literature and presentations from the hedge funds of funds on the long list; read through and select several (5–10, I would recommend) of varying approaches and types to meet with. Hopefully the previous chapter in this section will have given you plenty of criteria to select which ones to keep and which ones to discard. 5–10 managers may sound a large number to meet but initial meetings can be kept short to say less than an hour and, in London at least, you will find that the hedge funds of funds are all located in roughly the same area of Mayfair – the hedge fund epicentre!

Month 2:   Perform the 5–10 meetings. These meetings in the first instance are generally with a member of the hedge fund of funds' sales team and possibly an introduction to someone from the investment team – the investment team usually get more involved should your interest grow. As I mentioned above, I would keep these meetings brief to save you time – the depth can come later. Before this meeting it's probably useful for you to read through the marketing presentation for the hedge fund of funds in order to formulate some questions but it is also useful to let the sales person run through the presentation themselves to get it 'straight from the horses mouth'. Prior to or at the start of the meeting, I would establish with the sales person the broad agenda for the meeting beforehand and tell her what you want to achieve. Let the sales person run through her pitch but remember – you are the customer and she has to give you the level of detail you want and keep to your timing. I would advise writing up these meetings straight after they happen as it is commonplace for different hedge funds of funds to give broadly the same pitch and it's easy for them to all merge in your mind!

Once these meetings have been established a shorter list needs to be formed. This should be based on your assessment of investment and

risk processes, infrastructure and operational strength, fund performance and product suitability criteria but also your general impressions
– if it doesn't feel right now, then this feeling may not go away!

Off The Record

*Don't be afraid to remove a hedge fund of funds from the process on gut feel
or instinct – remember, you are the customer and you are the one potentially
giving business to them; if it doesn't feel right to you then this is a valid reason not to go further with this fund of funds. Some hedge funds of funds can
be patronising, deliberately hide behind jargon and make you feel like you are
the one being selected. If you find this is the case, remember – you are the
customer!*

Month 3: Once a shorter list has been formed – of three or four say –
the next step is to meet with senior members of the investment, risk and
operations team; make sure that you get to see who you want to see, not
just a sales person again. This is a chance to build on the previous meeting and drill down deeper on how the hedge fund of funds is managed.
The other aims of this set of meetings are to make sure you are happy
with all aspects of the hedge funds of funds and the suitability of each
product for your investment. At this stage you are looking to make a
decision. Once a short list is established, it is also appropriate to discuss fees. At the most fees are around 1.5 % management fee and a
10 % performance fee at hedge fund of funds level and they should be
expected to fall in proportion with the size of assets you hope to invest.
Big institutional investors should expect fees to halve from these levels
(or sometimes fall even further).

Months 4–6: If, from the short list, there is no apparent final selection,
don't be afraid to use the sales representative to help you get any further information you need to help make that decision. It is reasonable,
also, to request a further meeting with senior investment, risk and
operations personnel and do another on-site visit. However, it is usually the case that the more assets you have to invest, the easier this is
to arrange. I would advise that the process be constructed so that there
is a decision needed within 6 months of starting the process. If not a
lot of the information may be out of date and the process may need to
be restarted.

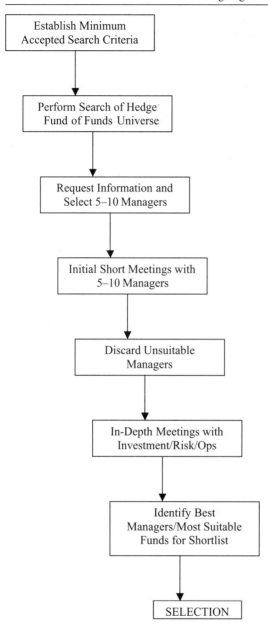

Figure 10.1   Outline of Selection Process.

10.3   SOME TIPS FOR MEETING WITH HEDGE FUNDS OF FUNDS

- Look through their marketing presentations, fund performance, website, etc. before the meeting and establish what questions you want to ask (although don't tell them beforehand – they have too much chance to prepare a smooth answer!).
- Always establish an agenda and the length of the meeting beforehand and inform the hedge fund of funds.
- Always meet them at their offices and make sure you ask for a tour.
- The more informed you are the more honest and detailed they will be.
- Don't be afraid to ask around about a hedge fund of funds and the individuals they employ.
- Don't be afraid to ask the same question again to different people – if they don't agree then ask why.
- Don't let the hedge funds of funds impress you with tales of investment success in the past – ask them about their shorter term outlook and follow up with this next time to see how they have done.
- Remember – you are the customer!

Off The Record

The role of Investment Consultant varies widely from firm to firm. Some consultancy teams have an excellent grasp of the hedge fund and hedge fund of funds world. They know the participants, are privy to timely information flows and truly understand the space. A considerable minority, however, are still catching up in this area. Most of what they know has been gleaned from hedge funds of funds and so they don't know the 'killer questions' to ask. As a result, never be afraid to challenge your consultant if you think they aren't up to speed in this relatively new area.

10.4   SUMMARY

Above, I have outlined a common sense approach for selecting a hedge fund of funds. The decisions on monitoring, mandate, fees, structure and product type are equally important and I address these in the next chapter.

10.5 SUMMARY OF IDEAS FOR CHAPTER 10

- When investing in hedge funds of funds, it is important to construct a timely process as information gathered in this area tends to be time sensitive.
- Before you invest, you should be happy with all aspects of the hedge fund of funds and have had a chance to meet the investment personnel and check out the offices.
- Asking around about the reputation and ability of a hedge fund of funds can be useful.
- As the customer, you should feel happy that you have had the access and information that you need to make the decision.

11

Investment and Monitoring

11.1 OVERVIEW

Selecting an appropriate product or mandate and benchmark can be as important as selecting the right hedge fund of funds manager and needs to have some thought given to it. Below, I run through the considerations that need to be taken when defining your needs within the hedge fund space and selecting an appropriate product or mandate and then constructing an appropriate monitoring methodology and benchmark.

11.2 INVESTING IN A HEDGE FUND OF FUNDS

Alongside the selection process for a hedge fund of funds manager you should also be thinking about product and mandate. If the type of hedge fund of funds/mandate that is needed is niche (i.e. not multi-strategy) then the search needs to be restricted to hedge funds of funds managers with that given skill set and, obviously, if you want to invest in an existing product rather than a bespoke portfolio then you will require that product to already be managed by the hedge funds of funds manager. For example, if you wanted a bespoke mandate that was market independent you would probably only want to focus on hedge fund of funds managers that run products or existing mandates in that area.

11.2.1 Deciding What Type of Return Stream You Need

Hedge funds can be used to produce a range of return streams from producing 'shoot the lights out' style big returns through to steady and involatile 'cash +' style returns. Some examples of this in practice can be seen as follows:

- A defined benefit scheme that is underwater picks the right type of hedge fund of funds portfolio for a steady and involatile return stream.

- A pension scheme selects a hedge fund of funds to add a source of return to a liability driven investment structure because the right type of hedge fund exposure will give a limited downside and is less likely to cause short and medium term loss.
- A family office wants equity exposure but sees that it is cost neutral, easier to evaluate and more effective to take portable alpha from a hedge fund of funds portfolio and equity exposure from an index.
- An individual seeking to increase expected return does so more effectively by adding a specialist Equity Long/Short hedge fund of funds rather than add to equity long only.
- A corporate treasury portfolio gains efficiency by adding to alternative investments but maintains good liquidity and takes less of a gamble on the economic cycle by choosing a hedge fund of funds over property or private equity.

As we can see from the examples above, hedge funds and hedge funds of funds can be used to generate return streams that act as solutions to many investment problems but if there is a specific problem to address then there must be a specific solution that is requested – otherwise you will end up with a multi-strategy hedge fund of funds that will probably fit fairly well but far from perfectly.

When specifying such a solution the first thing to do is consider how much direct market exposure you can take and how 'market independent' you need to be. Those portfolios that already have significant exposures to equities, government bonds or credit through traditional markets may wish to limit their exposure to directional hedge funds with exposures in these areas. Or, if the level of sophistication exists to measure it, you could limit the factor exposure to these factors at hedge fund of funds level.

Those seeking big returns should expect to have a high degree of directional strategy exposure in their portfolios, e.g. through Equity Long/Short strategies, as the directional strategies tend to generate the higher returns.

Those seeking to invest in hedge funds for their diversifying nature and involatile return stream should be sure that there is not too much exposure to directional strategies but also be wary of more complex strategies such as mortgage backed securities arbitrage or non-standard strategies such as asset based lending. These strategies are often very involatile and so smooth returns but can have a rare large and sharp downside since in these strategies volatility is a poorer indication of future downside. As a result, don't automatically pick the least volatile track records if downside control is essential without looking 'under the hood' first.

Remember, investing in hedge funds is not entirely a 'free lunch' as hedge fund risk isn't always reflected in volatility – in some more complex hedge funds the risk is 'bunched up' and yet to manifest itself. Think of hedge fund returns as different rather than necessarily better.

11.2.2   Bespoke vs Pooled

Once the type of product that is needed is decided, a decision needs to be made whether to invest in hedge funds through a standard hedge fund of funds (a pooled product) or through a bespoke product managed by the hedge fund of funds manager. NB, few hedge fund of funds managers will create a bespoke product for less than USD 20m of assets and so this choice is open to only bigger investors.

There are pros and cons to each approach, as outlined below:

The main positives of investing through a hedge fund of funds:

• Hedge funds of funds often tend to get more attention from the hedge fund of funds management team than bespoke products. This is because the hedge fund of funds should contain significantly more assets that yours alone, have many more investors and have a well publicised and ranked track record. As a result, to maintain existing fee revenue and win new business, hedge funds of funds tend to be flagship products which serve as an example of the skills of the fund of funds managers. As such, a bespoke product will probably have the remnants of best underlying hedge funds after the flagship fund of funds has had its fill.
• As there are many co-investors, a hedge fund of funds will have been open to greater scrutiny of its construction and risk than a one-off bespoke mandate.
• The hedge fund of funds will have pre-existing structure, documentation and governance and so be much quicker to invest in than through the construction of a bespoke product.
• There will already be a track record that can be used to give evidence of the level of skill in hedge fund selection, portfolio construction and the risk of the fund of funds.

The main negatives of investing through a hedge fund of funds:

- The objectives, restrictions, liquidity and risk parameters of the hedge fund of funds may be different to what you require.
- Co-investors may be more short-termist than you and pull their money on small downturns, resulting in you being left in a fund that is poorly structured due to the withdrawals and this also may be difficult to exit.
- Future growth of the hedge fund of funds due to inflows of new assets may dilute the capacity constrained hedge funds within it.

The positives of investing through a bespoke portfolio:

- You get to define the mandate, restrictions, objectives, liquidity and risk of the portfolio.
- You will be unaffected by co-investors exiting or diluting the portfolio as above.
- You own the shares in the underlying hedge funds. Thus, if you believe that the hedge fund of funds manager is doing a bad job sometime in the future, it is possible to sack them and appoint another one whilst still keeping ownership of the underlying funds, some of which may be rare commodities.

The negatives of investing through a bespoke portfolio:

- Requires more time, effort and cost to build a suitable structure.
- Need to ensure you get the right portfolio parameters in place.
- Need to ensure you get the appropriate level of top tier hedge funds that have scarce capacity and good access to the hedge funds that are highly rated by the hedge fund of funds manager – you should not be the 'trial run' for new hedge funds.
- Your portfolio may get less attention that the big, flagship hedge funds of funds.
- Liquidity may be disadvantageous compared to a hedge fund of funds.

Overall, my advice would be that if you have enough assets to ensure full diversification and you can get to an agreement with the hedge fund of funds manager that they will spend an appropriate amount of time and effort on your portfolio and give up capacity in the best hedge funds for you, then go for the bespoke mandate but otherwise, invest in the hedge fund of funds.

11.2.3   Picking a Hedge Fund of Funds

Should you decide to invest in a hedge fund of funds (a pooled product) rather than through a bespoke mandate then there are a number of questions you should ask to be sure you are investing with an appropriate fund. These are highlighted in the first chapter of this section. The answers to these questions should leave you happy with the following terms:

- Liquidity
- Fees
- Third Parties
- Governance
- Domicile
- Listing
- Regulation
- Past good conduct of the hedge funds of funds (e.g. no NAV suspension, etc.)

In addition, I would focus on fund assets and be sure that you represent no more than 10% of the assets in a hedge fund of funds. Thus, if you need to withdraw your assets at some point, this alone should not affect the performance of the hedge fund of funds for the month before you get your money back.

Finally, of course, the objectives of the fund of funds, the risk it takes and the funds it invests with has to fit in with your requirements.

11.2.4   Designing a Mandate

This section is really more relevant to those requiring a bespoke portfolio but may also be of use to those investing through a pooled fund. In the case of the latter, there will be little chance to specify details on return, risk and other limits beyond those that already exist for the hedge fund of funds. However, it is important to specify levels of communication and monitoring before any sizeable investment.

Once you have considered exactly the type of returns you need from your hedge fund of funds portfolio as outlined above, you need to formulate this as a set of restrictions and objectives.

First to note is that risk is interlinked with return and so any demands on return will have a certain level of associated risk involved and vice versa. It is reasonable to assume that a minimum Sharpe ratio (Return over cash rate/volatility of returns) of 0.7 is possible from a well run portfolio so if you want a LIBOR + 3.5% return p.a., the annualised volatility target should be no less than 5% and, ideally would lie at something like 7% if this can be weathered, not to overly constrain the hedge fund of funds in terms of returns in any one period. Note that it is more appropriate to measure returns in excess of LIBOR or some other appropriate cash rate since hedge fund returns are generally linked to the underlying cash rate.

When mandating risk, this could be done as a volatility measure (as above) or can be done through a Value at Risk measure on some mutually agreed risk measurement system, or as a maximum expected downside. Each way is viable although the latter is particularly appropriate for the hedge fund world given that risk is not necessarily expressed through volatility alone.

Another way to mandate risk and return is through a benchmark, which we will cover in the section below.

Once risk and return targets have been established, there are other criteria that should be established based on concentration and underlying hedge fund type. For example, for a multi-strategy portfolio it is sensible to have a limit of no more than 10% in any one hedge fund, no more than 20% in funds run by any one hedge fund manager and any investment into an underlying hedge fund should make up no more than 10% of that underlying hedge fund's assets, which are standard limits. You may also want to restrict the amount invested with new managers or managers under a certain asset level although this may affect performance. Also, the liquidity of the portfolio needs to be agreed.

Finally, the split between strategies needs to be established and any strategies that are not allowed need to be pre-agreed. Note, however, that the greater the restriction, the more difficult it is to generate outstanding performance.

Once the mandate has been designed, it should then be written up in the form of an agreement along with agreed fees and agreed levels of monitoring and access to the hedge fund of fund managers.

A typical mandate may look like this:

Target return: To beat three month LIBOR + 6% average annualised return over a 3-year rolling period.

Target risk: No more than 10% annualised volatility with no more than a −6% monthly loss.

Strategy: All hedge fund strategies; maximum strategy exposure of 50% to any one strategy other than mortgage backed securities; maximum 10% exposure to mortgage backed securities; minimum 4 strategies.

Liquidity: 50% of the portfolio six months liquidity or less; 90% of the portfolio 12 months liquidity or less; 100% of the portfolio 24 months liquidity or less.

Size: Minimum USD 30 million.

Reporting: Monthly reports consisting of returns compared to target, risk compared to target, strategy exposures compared to limits, liquidity analysis, summary of any fund redemption fees in the underlying fees, the hedge fund of funds portfolio itself, attribution analysis and commentary. Quarterly conference call with hedge fund of funds manager and twice yearly face-to-face meetings. Investor to be immediately informed of any significant changes to the hedge fund of funds management company or the fund.

Fees: 1% management fee; 5% performance fee over three month LIBOR hurdle rate with high water mark.

Above we can see that the investor has elected to invest in a multi-strategy portfolio (minimum four strategies) with a fair amount of freedom on strategy allocation – 50% max in any one strategy with the exception of mortgaged backed securities which is limited to 10%. Given the reasonably sized return target (for a multi-strategy mandate) with corresponding freedom on risk, I would imagine that this portfolio would contain a reasonable amount of directional strategies such as unconstrained equity long-short. Note that the return target is over a three year rolling period and so the portfolio is not too dependent on the underlying equity cycle. Note also that the investor has elected to have an absolute return target rather than a benchmark, which is a perfectly legitimate choice.

On a liquidity basis, 50% of the portfolio needs to be of 6 months liquidity or better but the rest needs to be mainly annual liquidity. This is a wise choice providing that the investor can handle this liquidity since it should lead to a wider universe of hedge funds to select from and so better returns. Most hedge funds nowadays have quarterly liquidity or less so this liquidity provision will accommodate that.

Reporting ensures transparency, and that the performance and risk are easy to track, that the limits are visible and that access to the hedge fund of funds manager is available to the investor; also, details of any significant changes at fund or group levels need to be relayed, as outlined in the section on Monitoring below. Finally, the fees ensure that the hedge fund of funds manager is incentivised to do a good job through the performance fees but note that performance fees are only charged on performance over a cash rate – this is known as a hurdle rate.

11.2.5   Fees

Fees are negotiable on both pooled hedge funds of funds and bespoke portfolios, and can be negotiated from their headline levels as a consequence of being a larger or more institutional investor. However, complexity of mandate may act against this as greater complexity will be more time intensive for the hedge fund of funds manager.

It may suit investors to pay a higher flat fee and no performance fee, or to negotiate down the flat fee to lower levels and pay an additional performance fee based on outperformance.

It is in everyone's interest that fees should incentivise risk control as well as outperformance, and that fees should be fair. It may seem clever to negotiate fees right down or to select the cheapest hedge fund of funds but generally you get what you pay for.

11.3   BENCHMARKING AND MONITORING

It is important to consider the process for monitoring and benchmarking the hedge fund of funds before investment, and incorporate this into the mandate.

11.3.1   Benchmarking

It is very difficult to properly benchmark a hedge fund of funds. This is particularly so given that the volatility of track record normally misestimates the true level of risk being taken in a hedge fund of funds or hedge fund index. As a result, direct comparison is very difficult. In the traditional world an investment manager can analyse a benchmark and then take underweights and overweights around it and thus scientifically measure risk. This is not the case with hedge fund indices given issues such as investability, liquidity and over diversification. As a result, we should not consider out and out benchmarks but instead look at return targets and comparative indices.

There are three main potential comparative indices or benchmarks that can be used:

- Cash +
  ○ E.g. LIBOR + 3.5%. Rather than stipulate an index to beat, many use a cash benchmark accompanied by an outperformance target or expectation.
- An underlying traditional index or mix thereof
  ○ Given that you will be taking money away from another part of the portfolio to put in a hedge fund of funds, one way of gauging the performance of the hedge fund investment is to analyse the impact of adding hedge funds to the portfolio. The best way to do this is to compare the hedge fund of funds performance to the performance of the remaining portfolio, or a simplification thereof. NB this would need to be on a risk adjusted basis as opposed to an outright return basis. For example, if the traditional part of the portfolio consists of a 60/40 mix of equities and bonds then a 60/40 split of equity and bond indices may be a suitable comparative index on a risk adjusted basis.
- A hedge fund index
  ○ There are a range of 'investable' hedge fund indices, e.g. HFRX that make good comparators. However, these indices can be quite concentrated and so unrepresentative and also, since hedge funds do not display risk entirely through volatility, it is not good for close comparison.

Whatever the benchmark or comparative index used, it is necessary to make sure comparisons are made over a long term basis, e.g. an economic cycle, three years, etc., as well as over a shorter term basis, to ensure a fair comparison is made.

11.3.2 Monitoring

It is important that the level of monitoring you practice is enough to alert you quickly to any potential problems with the hedge fund of funds or its management team.

With any sizeable investment I would initiate an agreement that ensures you are told straight away of any turnover of staff, large changes to infrastructure, strategy or policy, any issues with regulators, auditors, administrators or custodians and any significant changes to assets.

Furthermore, I would be keen to get a copy of the portfolio, some commentary, portfolio analysis and attribution analysis on a regular basis, ideally monthly if your level of investment permits this.

I would expect to get a conference call with an overview on a regular basis (quarterly if your level of investment permits) where changes to the portfolio are discussed and an outlook is presented.

Finally, I would expect an onsite visit once a year to get face-to-face access and to check for any changes to offices.

For big investors, it is also feasible to get access to investment reports for new constituent hedge funds as a check that an appropriate level of analysis is being performed.

11.4   SUMMARY

In this chapter I have given an outline of how to specify the type of returns you need and how to choose between a bespoke portfolio and a pooled hedge fund of funds. Once that has been done, the information above on mandate design and ongoing monitoring should also be of use. In the next chapter, I give an example of an appraisal report on a hedge fund of funds considered for investment, which should serve as a useful example of the points raised in Part III.

11.5   SUMMARY OF IDEAS FOR CHAPTER 11

- It is important to decide what return stream you need before selecting a hedge fund of funds.
- Accessing hedge funds through a hedge fund of funds is good for all bar enormous investors, who are better off investing through bespoke portfolios.
- Once a hedge fund of funds manager has been selected, it is important to implement a monitoring strategy and benchmark or return and risk target before investing.

A Sample Hedge Fund of Funds Investment Report

12.1 OVERVIEW

In this chapter I illustrate the points raised in the rest of this section through an example of an investment report on a hedge fund of funds. I have based the report on no particular hedge fund of funds although obviously, as Chief Investment Officer of Key Asset Management, some of the example comes from experience. Nonetheless, this is something of an amalgamation of hedge fund of funds I know and shouldn't be taken to be a factual representation of any one hedge fund of funds. All names of individuals and companies are imaginary where appropriate. As with the example in Part II, I add comments on answers in italics when I think it may be useful.

12.2 THE REPORT

Investment report on the K-Hedge Fund of Funds

12.2.1 Summary and Critical Analysis

Fund: K-Hedge

Manager: K Asset Management

Manager Contact: Jack F

Strategy: Multi-Strategy Fund of Funds

Geographical Focus: Global

Fund Inception: 1990

Manager Founded: 1989

Fund Overview

K-Hedge is a multi-strategy hedge fund of funds seeking to return 3 month LIBOR + 3–5% p.a. over a three year rolling period with risk of around 5% annualised volatility. The fund invests across all hedge fund strategies but there is an in-house bias away from CTAs, Structured Credit and ABL and mortgage backed securities arbitrage. The fund has been around for 16+ years without a losing year and has generally delivered on its return objectives.

In the case of companies with such a long track record it is worth talking to them about consistency of approach over time – a lot of things can change over the decades. It is also worth analysing performance and risk over the last five years as well as through the entire length of the track record to check that early strong returns are being used to boost the statistics.

Reputation of Fund and Manager

K Asset management has been around for some time and its reputation is sound, especially in Scandinavia. Despite its track record it has been slow to raise assets until recently. This was partially due to high staff turnover in the early 2000s which slowed asset growth. The problem is seemingly fixed by K taking the watershed move of distributing equity to key staff.

It is always worth asking around about any potential investment to gain the market's view of their reputation.

Company Overview

K Asset Management is an independently-owned asset management company which was founded in 1989 – an early player in the European fund of hedge funds industry. K launched its first hedge fund, K-Hedge – a multi-strategy hedge fund of funds, in April 1990. In addition to K-Hedge, K has developed a range of niche/strategy-focussed funds of hedge funds. This suite also includes:

K-Worldwide	(1992)	a global Equity Long/Short hedge fund of funds;
K-Asia	(1994)	an Asian-focused Equity Long/Short hedge fund of funds;
K-Europe	(1998)	a European Equity Long/Short hedge fund of funds;
K-Event	(2001)	an event driven focussed hedge fund of funds.

Although starting from a European family office asset base, today K's clients cover a broad variety of institutions, including banks, family offices and pension funds, located globally.

Edge/Reason for Level of Focus

Edge from longevity, risk management, skills of portfolio managers, thorough yet nimble process and active management ethos. Good ratio of capacity to assets.

Critical Analysis

K differentiates itself through its wide product range of core and niche hedge funds of funds, its approach based on concentrated portfolios (15 managers in single strategy funds of funds, 20–30 in multi-strategy) and its longevity. It is particularly strong in the area of risk management. Recent performance has also been strong.

Initially, staff turnover was a worry but since the distribution of equity, this problem seems to have been solved.

Remember, critical analysis is always very important. You should never take what you are told as your view, instead interpret the information and form your own opinion.

12.2.2   The Management Company

Management Company: K Asset Management

Address: #################

Founded: 1989

Group Assets: USD 2bn

Regulator: FSA, SEC; also see below in Ownership Structure.

In cases where registration with regulators is voluntary, if they are not registered find out why not.

Regulator Issues: None

Ownership Structure

The K Group consists of K Group Limited, a British Virgin Islands (BVI) incorporated company which owns 100% of the following subsidiaries:

1. K Asset Management (UK) Limited – incorporated in England and authorised and regulated by the FSA and SEC Registered. Member of AIMA.
2. K Asset Management (Norge) ASA – incorporated in Norway and regulated by Kredittilsynet.
3. K Asset Management (Sverige) AB – incorporated in Sweden and regulated by Finansinspektionen.
4. K Asset Management (USA) Inc. – incorporated in the USA.
5. K Asset Management (Switzerland) SARL – incorporated in Switzerland.
6. K Capital Management Inc. – incorporated in the BVI authorised by the BVI FSC.

Subsidiary 1 is the management company for all K funds.

The company's majority shareholder is a family Trust domiciled in the BVI. 30% is at present owned by staff directly or via the Employee Share Incentive Scheme.

For independently owned companies and companies that are part of a wider group, you should always analyse the stability of this situation.

Group Infrastructure and Notable Changes

See above. A share incentive scheme was constituted in 2002 and shares have been, and are expected to continue to be, allocated to the scheme for the benefit of employees.

In all areas find out if there have been any recent or planned changes, as this information isn't always volunteered.

Number of People in Total: 35

Other Offices

Norway, Sweden, USA and Switzerland (all sales offices).

Notes On Any Past Or Potential Legal Action

None

Company Asset and Staff Growth

Year	Assets (USD bn)	Staff
2000	0.35	15
2001	0.6	17
2002	0.7	21
2003	0.8	26
2004	1.0	34
2005	1.0	33
2006	1.8	35

Future Growth Strategy and Vision

They see growth in 2006 as exceptionally large since people were holding off investing in 04/05 to see how the new team fitted in. Generally expect asset growth of nearer 20–30% p.a. They say they are able to cope with new inflows until they reach USD 4–5bn assets under management (AUM) when they will have to increase the team.

Analysing assets growth and staff growth is important. Has the growth been rapid or too slow; has it been sustainable or are they at a point of serious flux?

12.2.3   Portfolio Management Team

Portfolio Managers

Investment team of nine consists of CIO (Craig J), three Portfolio Managers (Ivor P, Penny O, Emma P), three analysts and a Risk Manager (Terry G). It is a team effort with different PMs specialising in different strategies. Ivor P is the PM that covers market independent strategies (Fixed Income Relative Value, Arbitrage, etc) and also is responsible for the running of K-Hedge.

Who Else is Involved?

Alice H heads up the operations team and contributes to the Operational DD Process. Martin K is the founder and now the Non-Exec Chairman with around 25 years of hedge fund experience and his experience is on hand to consult also. Steven E, CEO and former COO has been with K for eight years and is also well experienced on the hedge fund operational side.

Time Commitment

Investment team focuses on investment full time.

Other Responsibilities

Typically 15% will be spent on client/potential client meetings.

A properly sized investment team is important but also you need to find out if any members of the investment team are doing any administrative or operational duties or are there just to bump up the numbers. Also, is there anybody else such as a CEO or operations person that also adds to the process?

Financial Participation, Remuneration and Lock-Ins

K's compensation scheme for employees includes:

* Market rate base salary
* Bonus scheme related to individual performance based on 50/50 cash/equities in K
* Participation in share incentive scheme
* Pension scheme
* Life assurance
* Health insurance
* Private gym membership

The base salary is around the market rate for a company of its size but bonus is on average 50% cash based with the rest coming in K shares to facilitate staff lock-in and participation in the upside. They are keen for employee ownership to rise.

Staff Turnover

When MK stood down as CIO to become Chairman and make way for a new incumbent and increase in investment team size, there was significant turnover as the new team did not fit in well and performance was mixed. The latest team was hired as a unit from a rival and have seemed to have bedded down in the two and a half years since they were hired, helped by the equity ownership. There has been no turnover in the core team that was brought in but all those that remained at K when the new team was brought in have now departed.

You need to check that people are appropriately paid, motivated and retained. If there has been high turnover then what has been done to stop it going forward?

Key Departures

See above.

Key People

CJ, IP, PO, EP, TG although the team could potentially weather a loss of any one of these as long as the rest of the team was intact.

You need to make a decision before investing, who is key to the generation of returns and management of risk – this allows more objective analysis should there be future departures. Also, if there have been recent departures then how much of the track record can be attributed to the current team?

12.2.4   Investment Process

Investment Universe

They invest across all hedge fund strategies but will not invest with funds dedicated to mortgage backed securities, asset based lending or structured credit.

Are there any areas they will not invest in? Hedge fund strategies are diverse and some are not appropriate for certain portfolios.

Investment Philosophy

K say that they seek to generate consistent positive returns with a highly controlled downside. In addition, they say that they hold the following investment beliefs:

- For consistent returns it is necessary to combine skilful fund selection and active strategy allocation.
- Risk management should be a primary focus and fully integrated with the investment process.

- In-depth face-to-face research and ongoing monitoring are essential.
- Difficult-to-measure risks and worst case scenarios should never be ignored.

It is good to get a feeling of investment ethos or philosophy. What are they all about and what are their beliefs?

Investment Process

The investment process can be broken down into the following layers:

- Strategy allocation
- Fund Selection
- Risk Analysis
- Portfolio Construction
- Decision Process

We deal with the penultimate two points in their own dedicated sections and look at Strategy Selection, Fund Selection and Decision Process below.

Strategy Allocation

On a monthly basis, a proprietary report based on drivers of risk and return, opportunity set and asset flows for each strategy is generated. The monthly strategy reports contain 35 pages of proprietary reports covering the drivers of risk, return and the opportunity set within each strategy and are generally portrayed in graphical form. For example, in the case of Convertible Bond Arbitrage, these factors would include implied volatility, new issuance and credit spread analysis.

In addition, the Head of Risk Management produces quantitative studies of the behaviour of these strategies within K's portfolios. This analysis and ongoing dialogue with a range of market participants, practitioners and academics, is discussed at the monthly Investment Committee meeting. This part of the meeting focuses on the evolution of strategies and the future opportunity sets rather than just where the strategies are at present. Each of the portfolio managers will play an active role in these discussions based on their individual strategy expertise.

K potentially has an edge in the strategy/style allocation process because:

- It has been developed over 17 years and has been tested through a range of market environments.

• It utilises the proprietary risk management system which is sensitive to style behaviour.
• Each portfolio manager has a particular strategy/style focus/ responsibility.

Hedge Fund Sourcing and Selection

Investment ideas are generated via K's industry connections and relationships, industry news flow as well as hedge fund databases and capital introduction meetings.

The selection process seeks to actively investigate all areas (investment, administration and operations, legal) of a fund and its management company. The process involves compiling information and then verifying, interpreting and analysing it. They say the process seeks to identify (a) stability and (b) edge and that they do not just rely on information provided by the fund manager but also seek to reference and verify all core information. For each fund under analysis, a portfolio manager has primary responsibility for the analysis, depending on his/her strategy expertise. The primary PM is supported by another manager and all information is verified by a member of the operations team.

Each year K meets >400 hedge fund managers face-to-face in the US, Europe and Asia (around five to 10 US trips and one to three Asia trips pa).

Before deciding to meet a hedge fund manager, preliminary quantitative analysis is carried out – not to pick the best performers but to filter out the worst. Hedge fund managers will also be asked to provide a copy of their marketing presentation and prospectus. During an initial meeting, fundamental details are collected: investment universe, investment process, risk management process, company background, key people and edge. This is documented in an initial report. The aim here is to find out the basic details of the fund but also test to see if the fund is investable and that there is possibly a definable edge.

If the hedge fund is then deemed to be a potential investment, further due diligence is carried into every part of the business from investment process and fund structure through to back office and corporate issues.

In terms of fund structure issues this will include terms, risk parameters, third parties and portfolio characteristics. The suitability of the reporting and transparency is also assessed. Transparency is determined on a fund/strategy specific basis to a level where the investment process can be independently analysed. They also consider the composition of the existing investor base, to avoid the potentially damaging effects of 'hot' money.

In addition, the viability of the management firm is considered, looking at such factors as ownership, longevity, product range, breakeven firm assets (including assessment of fixed cost to fixed fee ratios), staff turnover, remuneration and retention policies, time commitment of key people, suitability of infrastructure and disaster recovery procedures.

Finally, reference checks and investigation of all third parties are carried out. They say they speak not only to the referees that the hedge fund manager has supplied, but also relevant referees that they know. They also check the duties of the administrator and other service providers, and investigate the systems used and how they interact with the hedge fund manager – they have constructed bespoke due diligence questions for third parties to cover auditors, administrators, prime brokers and lawyers. They attempt to ascertain how information flows between the third parties, how the portfolio is priced and to verify the third parties' powers. They ask that the administrator confirms that they receive price and position information directly from the prime broker, and that they price the NAV independently of the hedge fund manager. They ask that the prime broker confirms margin agreements, instruments traded, AUM, etc. A questionnaire is also sent to the auditor to complete and this is often followed with a conference call. The fund's lawyers will be asked to confirm that there is no current or pending legal action against the fund. They also conduct on site visits with a range of third parties. They say that they would be very unlikely to invest in a fund where the service providers are small and unknown to them as the risk of fraud and mispricing would be too high.

All information collated during the investigation of a hedge fund is stored on K's proprietary, cross-sectional database which has 300+ fields. This is essentially a database that sections off different parts of the investigation process that allows comparative searches across the database on, e.g. instruments traded, third parties, etc. The database is updated every month when hedge fund characteristics change, e.g. assets.

This results in a 50+ page investment report consisting of a critical analysis of the hedge fund in question; this report seeks to define risk (including operational risk) and identify edge. If a fund/manager has not been eliminated by this stage, full quantitative analysis is performed, including quant risk analysis (implied risk distribution and scenario tests), track record analysis, strategy analysis (how the hedge fund performed in context of strategy) and attribution analysis (how the returns have been generated). As well as testing the fund on a stand-alone basis, the fund is subsequently examined in the context of the portfolio: combination analysis, correlation analysis, optimisations and worst-case scenarios.

They will not invest in a hedge fund before performing at least one on-site visit. Due diligence visits are not confined to the investment team of the hedge fund but can include middle and back office, lawyers, accountants and prime broking contacts. Additionally, regular on-site visits are conducted after investment.

The time spent with a hedge fund manager varies depending on the strategy and complexity of the investment and risk management processes and the number of issues that need to be revisited as the due diligence process progresses. The typical time to decision process once in-depth work has started is around four to eight weeks.

Risk Analysis/Portfolio Construction – see relevant sections below.

Decision Process

This compiled investment report on the given hedge fund is presented by the relevant portfolio manager at the monthly Investment Committee meeting. The Investment Committee concludes to allocate to the fund, place it on a watch list for further monitoring or take no further action.

The investment committee comprises of the full investment team including the risk manager along with a representative of the operations department. There is a 'challenge environment' but the Chief Investment Officer maintains the final veto on any decision.

The outcome for any hedge fund considered is one of the following:

- Invest
  ○ Place as an investment in one of more of the hedge fund of funds portfolios.
- More Work Needed
  ○ Answer the questions raised in the investment committee and then resubmit for consideration next time.
- Reserve List
  ○ Approved for investment but nowhere yet to place the fund. In this case, a further review by the Investment Committee is needed before an investment is placed.

- Observation List
  - Watch closely for a prescribed amount of months before resubmitting to the Investment Committee.
- Reject
  - Do not invest and do not reconsider.

Well thought out processes are good to see but remember, without a good process __and__ good people, it probably won't work. Also, is this process just for sales pitches or do they actually follow it – seek evidence!

Portfolio Construction

The portfolio construction is decided in the monthly Investment Committee meeting on the basis of input from the investment team, the strategy analysis and quantitative methods that have been outlined above and below. Strategy allocation will be determined taking into account this 'big picture' together with the portfolio's guidelines and investment objective. With regards to the allocation of individual managers within the portfolio, all funds must have passed the investment process detailed above, and the portfolio is constructed from suitable funds. K's risk systems are used to ensure that the portfolio is balanced in terms of risk both from individual hedge funds and from the factors that drive performance with no hedge fund or factor taking an excessive amount of the risk budget. The aim is to ensure that the portfolio is not just well diversified in normal conditions, but also in market shocks and 'worst case' scenarios.

On average there is around 20% turnover (adding and removing hedge funds) within the hedge fund of funds.

Be sure that there is a degree of science here as portfolio construction should be intimately related with risk management. Both processes should be forward looking and not overly reliant of past correlations or returns.

Monitoring and Portfolio Management

They estimate that they spend as much as 30% on monitoring and portfolio management. Each month they perform strategy, performance and portfolio and risk analysis on each fund. A questionnaire is sent to every constituent hedge fund covering simple but important things such as staff turnover, changes to infrastructure and processes, asset base, legal action, changes in third party suppliers etc. and the answers are used to keep the database information up-to-date and also to act as an early warning system for potential problems. In addition, the relevant portfolio manager will speak to each hedge fund manager on a monthly basis, aiming for a 'peer to peer' style conversation which will cover all the recent portfolio and operational changes in the fund, together with any anticipated future developments. They aim to meet every constituent hedge fund manager at least twice a year, one of which will be an onsite visit. Realistically, the more usual schedule is at least four times a year, two of which will be on-site.

Every month, the Investment Committee considers each hedge fund of funds portfolio afresh, justifying the investment in each fund. They say 'no change' is an active decision for them.

Reasons for deselecting a hedge fund include (but are not limited to):

- Significant changes to assets either up or down.
- Material changes to the investment process or team.
  - K identifies critical processes and people which provide the fund's 'edge'. If material changes occur, the fund is reassessed as a new entity. This includes middle/back office and third parties.
- Changes to fund terms.
- Style drift.
  - Both in an absolute context and relative to peer groups.
- Strategy rotation.
- Risk and Return.
  - Poor performance will trigger a review of the fund, but is in its own right not a reason for deselection until the source of the performance issue has been identified and critically assessed.

Without proper portfolio management and monitoring, you are buying static research rather than investment management; this is fine if it's what you want but don't pay the fees for the latter when you are getting the former.

Capacity

Capacity agreements have been made with underlying hedge fund managers; however these amounts may vary depending on market conditions.

K attempts to build close relationships with underlying hedge fund managers, both during the period of analysis prior to investment, and through the ongoing monitoring process, allowing them to be recognised as a rational and logical investor. Through this, their predominantly institutional asset base and as a result of their longevity and their relatively low-ish AUM, they seem to be able to get good capacity. Also, as an early investor in many hedge funds, they seem to be able to secure future capacity with new hedge funds.

Here I would keep revisiting the questions on capacity to check that there is not too much of an ongoing dilution effect to my investment.

Planned Changes to Processes Going Forward

Research is ongoing but no significant changes foreseen.

Again, always ask if there are any changes planned as investment managers in any area are rarely proactive in telling you about subtler changes.

12.2.5 Portfolio Risk Management

Named Risk Manager: Terry G
Monitoring Frequency by Portfolio Manager: Daily
Monitoring Frequency by Risk Manager: Monthly

Risk Management Policy and Processes

K place a high degree of emphasis on risk management, structuring the analysis such that it works hand in hand with the investment process They use a combination of quantitative and qualitative techniques to provide a realistic understanding of portfolio risk, especially with respect to the downside tail where the 'worst-case' scenarios reside. As little reliance as is practical is placed on pure historic return analysis and the assumption of 'normal' distributions, both of which they believe severely misestimates risk.

Instead they use a proprietary in-house risk model which they say combines both practitioner and academic knowledge to undertake rigorous risk analysis at both the constituent hedge fund and hedge fund of funds levels. The use of this proprietary risk system provides several benefits, namely full model transparency, adaptability and flexibility – they can improve the system when they want and also see its weaknesses.

The risk manager works closely with the investment team. Although he reports directly to the CIO, to avoid potential investment-related conflict he also has a reporting line into the CEO.

The following concepts are core to K's risk system:

- A bespoke model that uses a forward looking non-parametric approach that does not rely on normal distributions or historic returns alone. They believe both are big sources of risk underestimation.
- The model has a broad scope covering all hedge fund strategies, permitting a full overview of the hedge fund of funds portfolios. They believe that this is essential for monitoring style drift.
- The model generates implied risk distributions, a more accurate reflection of risk than historic returns. This provides the basis for other statistics such as Value at Risk, Expected Tail Loss, skew, kurtosis, etc.
- The risk model is dynamic and can adapt as new strategies come into favour.
- The employment of a factor based model allows a more accurate comparison of hedge funds employing different strategies.

Underlying transparency is treated pragmatically on a fund by fund basis, with no hard rules. Transparency and reporting schedules are covered pre-investment in the investment process. They say that if a fund can't meet their reporting requirements, they will not invest.

Risk Measurement

The primary risk measurement tool is through K's proprietary risk management system, which is a non-parametric (Monte Carlo) risk simulation. The model employs a factor-based modelling approach, where each underlying hedge fund and, at an aggregate level, each hedge fund of funds is described by its core drivers of risk and return. This technique offers a framework to model extra-historic risk, i.e. implied risk that is present but which has not yet materialised. Also, it provides a framework in which all hedge fund strategies can be considered directly on a level playing field without bias. Given the nature of the approach there is the ability to incorporate additional qualitative information to better describe the fund, for example when selecting descriptive factors.

The outputs are implied risk distributions for the given underlying hedge fund and hedge fund of funds, which permits full statistical generation capability as outlined above. They also employ stress test and scenario analysis techniques.

The risk engine is programmed in MatLab with a VB front-end and employs data feeds from both Bloomberg and Thomson Datastream. Full procedures are written for the system and the code is well commented and backed up daily. An analyst with full knowledge of the system acts as backup for the risk manager.

You need to check that there is a proper process in place that is appropriate to check the risk in the underlying hedge funds and also measure the risk in the hedge fund of funds i.e. more complex strategies require more complex risk measurement. There should also be a named risk manager and regular reporting in this area, as well as a back-up employee.

Portfolio Monitoring

The fund of funds portfolios are updated (with estimated and final NAVs for the underlying hedge funds) and monitored daily by the portfolio managers. Generally, there are estimated underlying hedge fund prices provided weekly but they arrive on different days. The portfolio managers use write-protected spreadsheets as monitoring tools. The operations team also monitor the portfolios to check for breaches, produce weekly estimates and monitor final prices in parallel with the independent administrator. They use bespoke software for this job.

Here you are looking for a regularly updated framework for monitoring the hedge fund of funds portfolio along with a second set of monitoring eyes for a check and balance. The portfolio should be monitored intra-month as weekly estimated prices from the underlying hedge funds are usually available.

Risk Limits

The only formal risk limits would be maximum 10% with any underlying hedge fund and 20% with any one hedge fund manager. Informally they aim for an implied risk level of 3.5% – 5% p.a. and say they would not invest more than 50% in any one strategy.

There may be internal risk limits as well as ones mentioned in the fund prospectus and these limits should be checked by investors on a monthly basis (ideally through the monthly report) to ensure that the process is disciplined and keeps within these limits.

Liquidity Analysis

Liquidity of each of the portfolios is monitored and controlled directly by the lead portfolio manager for each of the products using the manager cross sectional database. Changes to these criteria are discussed with risk management as part of the investment process. Liquidity is also monitored by the CEO and operations team to ensure that it is in line with investor liquidity.

You should check that the liquidity of the hedge fund of funds is monitored regularly and is appropriate for the product given the liquidity offered to investors. As an investor, I would be keen to check this analysis on a quarterly basis.

12.2.6 Qualitative Risk And Infrastructure

Infrastructure and Organisation

K Asset Management has a staff of 35 of which nine are investment, six are operations, 10 are client relationship/sales managers and the rest are administration and management. They outsource IT to an IT support company, MMMCo but have an in house compliance and legal function. All infrastructural and operational needs appear to be in order.

A solid and stable infrastructure is always a benefit and if the opposite is true then this should put you off from investing.

Improvements and Changes

The group has been steadily growing and there have been no significant infrastructural changes of late.

Again, any significant changes should be noted and assessed on a case-by-case basis.

Support

An operations team of six including four back office accounting staff, one legal/compliance and one COO. Each main office has a PA/Receptionist and several client relationship managers. IT support is outsourced but appears to work well.

There do not have to be hundreds of support staff at a hedge fund of funds management company but there should be several dedicated and experienced individuals in this area.

Systems Audit

Standard MS/Bloomberg systems with the addition of bespoke risk system, bespoke 'active' database, bespoke portfolio monitoring and reporting software (called FIT), all backed up offsite daily. Also they use Datastream as well as Bloomberg to get a broader level of data access. External log-in though Citrix.

Portfolio Management Systems

PMs use spreadsheets for day-to-day monitoring but operations have had bespoke software developed for monitoring, reporting and shadow-pricing. This software can create customised reports that can be web-accessed by investors.

Hedging

All share classes are currency hedged through rolling forwards (standard). Dealing is done through the custodian. Information on amounts to hedge is calculated automatically by FIT and double checked by hand by the COO and the custodian.

Here you are looking for a proper process and it is essential to have a double-check for correct calculation as hedging errors can be costly. This process is sometimes weak since this is often the only direct trading done by the hedge fund of funds, and so it is essential that you are satisfied it is done well; if done poorly, this should show up as a discrepancy in the returns of a given currency class compared to the base currency class.

Information Flow to Custodian and Administrator

CCC is used for both roles and they independently deal with subscriptions and redemptions, anti-money laundering and independent pricing in direct contact with the administrators of the underlying hedge funds so no room for pricing fraud.

NAV Calculation Process

Standard process, done independently by the administrator, with no unusual clauses.

All you are looking for here is total independence by the administrator.

Financing Agreements

Leverage versions of K-Hedge and K-Europe get leverage provision from BBB (a bank) but otherwise no financing or margining needed beyond hedging (see above).

Changes to Third Parties

Prior to September 2000, FFF Limited was the administrator for K's funds. K terminated this agreement and appointed CCC Limited as administrator as it was felt they offered superior transfer agency capabilities and provided a more comprehensive service at a more competitive rate. Both these factors were beneficial to K's funds and investors. CCC Limited is part CCC Group, which employs 2500 people worldwide, providing administration services to in excess of 1500 funds representing more than $500 billion. CCC Limited is regulated by IFSRA in Dublin.

Cash Management

Excess cash is placed with daily liquidity in the GGG Cash Fund which has a AAA rating.

It is good housekeeping to invest surplus cash in a cash fund as this will enhance returns slightly but make sure that it is very liquid and of a high credit quality.

Contingency Plans

The basic provisions are to ensure the business can operate fully within 24 hours.

K's systems are backed up on a daily basis by an independent, offsite data storage company that can be web accessed from any location. K has contingency offsite capability which can be accessed within 24 hours. Also, there are four other offices worldwide. Additionally, K uses back-up tapes on monthly basis and stored externally. In the event of failure of K's systems and offsite data storage, these back-up tapes can be restored externally ensuring continuity of business.

In the case of incapacitated investment decision makers, each portfolio manager has a secondary manager who can carry out the portfolio manager's work in the case of incapacity.

In the case of IT failure, they have external IT consultants who are on call when required. K's contract with them ensures a response time of within an hour.

Insurance: Director and Officers Liability, Professional Indemnity, Crime (Employee fidelity/third party fraud)

In the event of disaster call:

Craig J (London)	Terry G (London)	Martin K (Oslo)	Len B (Geneva)
Office: ########	Office: ########	Office: ########	Office: ########
Mobile: ########	Mobile: ########	Mobile: ########	Mobile: ########
Home: ########	Home: ########	Home: ########	Home: ########
Offsite: ########	Offsite: ########	Offsite: ########	Offsite: ########

A hedge fund of funds is less needy of instant disaster recovery than an actively trading hedge fund but all the same, offsite facility, contingency plans and good data back-up are all important failsafes and should be checked.

12.2.7   Qualitative Performance Analysis

Sources/Driving Factors of Returns

Some dependence on credit, equity markets and equity market volatility. Otherwise very diversified.

Estimated Value Added Due to Edge

Edge through strategy allocation, risk control and fund selection evident, but also through ongoing portfolio rebalancing.

Qualitative Return Analysis

Best Monthly Return: 6.17%   Date: 9/92   Correct as of 12/06
Worst Monthly Return: −5.7%   Date: 8/98   Correct as of 12/06

Explanation:

Total market shock environment of August 1998 when spreads widened based on Russian default, LTCM unwinding and equity market sell-off.

Worst Drawdown: −6.8%   Date: 5-9/98   Correct as of 12/06

Explanation:

As above. NB drawdown recovered within 7 months.

Worst Expected Monthly Return: −6%
Best Expected Monthly Return: 3%

Rationale for Expectations

Based on risk model and hedge fund of funds manager's feel for the portfolio. The worst expected monthly return would be based on an exogenous event large enough to cause panic and illiquidity resulting in spread widening. Such an even would also cause a massive equity sell-off and so the downside of the fund would be marginal by comparison. Note that the fund is less concentrated than in the early days of hedge funds of funds and hence the risk expectations do not reflect the volatility of the 1990s.

Actions in Event of Worst Expected Return

Would stay invested with or even add to the market independent part of the portfolio as these strategies tend to bounce back quickly after such an event.

Peer Group/Competition: *******, *****, *****, *****

This analysis is very worthwhile as it gives some attribution to extreme returns and also gives an insight to the way the hedge fund of funds manager thinks about extreme loss. For a fund with a very long track record, I would repeat the extreme return analysis and attribution for the last five-year period.

12.2.8   Fund Asset Growth And Investors

Assets

Fund Assets:	USD 220m	Last Updated December 06
Capacity Limit:	USD 500m+	Last Updated December 06

Investor Base

Number of Investors:	400	Last Updated December 06
3 Largest Investors:	14%	Last Updated December 06

Assets are important in as much as you do not want to be too sizeable investor in the fund – I would not wish to be more than 15–20% of assets for a hedge fund of funds unless there were exceptional circumstances; neither would you want to be exposed to the withdrawals of other sizeable investors. Also, it is useful to analyse the fund managers' growth estimated for the fund and find out how much capacity they think the hedge fund of funds has; this can then be reconciled with underlying hedge fund capacity to see whether certain holdings will be heavily diluted in the near future. Analysis of asset growth is also useful to check that the fund has neither recently gained nor lost a large percentage of asset base, which may impact on returns.

12.2.9   Fund Structure and Reporting

Fund Structure and Fees

Domicile	BVI
Currency	USD (GBP, EUR, NOK, SEK share classes)
Management Fee	1.5%
Performance Fee	5%
High Watermark	Yes
Minimum Investment	USD 100000
Minimum Top Up	USD 1000
Subscription Frequency	Monthly
Subscription Fee	None
Redemption Frequency	Monthly
Redemption Fee	None
Notice Period	35 Days
Lockups or Other Clauses	None
Changes to Fund Structure	None
Return of Funds	30 days
Initial %	100%
Possible Payment in specie?	No

Methodology for Manager's Collection of Fees

Monthly management fees, annual performance fees.

Side Letters, Fee Deals and Equity Stakes Held by Investors

No side letters. Some staff members that hold equities in K also have shares in K-Hedge. Fees vary based on investor type.

Independently looking through the fund prospectus for fund terms is always advisable if you have time. Either way, the terms should be analysed prior to investment.

Reporting

Final NAV Reporting	End of following month
Estimated Monthly NAV	8–12 calendar days after month end
Source	Manager
Intra-monthly estimates	Weekly
Source	Manager

Discrepancies, Restatements and Suspensions

None

Manager Reporting

On a weekly basis, internally calculated performance estimates are distributed. These are distributed on Monday afternoon and cover the period to the previous Friday.

On a monthly basis, final NAVs are calculated both internally and independently by CCC the independent administrator of all K funds. CCC is responsible for the production of the monthly NAV and processing of subscriptions and redemptions. CCC Global Custody act as custodian for the funds.

The core of the reporting function is called the Fund Information Tool (FIT). FIT is both a shadow accounting system and reporting tool. For segregated accounts it facilitates the reporting on a real time basis over a secure web based server. FIT removes the need for the use of multiple spreadsheet based systems, although the portfolio managers still utilise the spreadsheet tools for monitoring as a check and balance. FIT also facilitates the rapid calculation of a variety of performance figures, liquidity analysis and Foreign Exchange management. 'The system introduces straight through processing for hedge funds of funds.'

For segregated accounts K can offer full real time reporting over a secure web based server. This is a functionality that very few other hedge funds of funds can offer. For commingled investors the following regular reporting is available. Weekly estimated NAVs are sent out to clients every Monday (Tuesday if Monday is a bank holiday).

Monthly fact sheets are produced by the 20th of the month following the reporting period month end and distributed to clients. These contain information such as a market outlook, portfolio changes, review of underlying strategies, monthly performance history, annualised returns, top five holdings/sector breakdown and risk characteristics such as standard deviation, maximum drawdown and correlation to index. Both of these are available on the website (*www.#####.com*).

A check on the level of reporting you can expect is advisable before investing. If you are not happy with the detail, maybe further reporting can be arranged, but this would be more likely if negotiated before you make the decision to invest for obvious reasons.

Accounting

Date of Last Audit	6/06
On File?	Yes
Qualifications	None
Comments on Financials	Standard report and accounts with full transparency listing underlying hedge funds.

A check through the last year's financials is always worth doing, just in case there is something non-standard there which needs further investigation.

12.2.10   Contacts

Investment Manager Contacts

Samples:

Name	Jack F
Title	Client Relationship Manager
Telephone	#######
Fax	#######
E Mail	####@####.com

Has Left	No
Interviewed	Yes
Responsibilities	Oversees all risk management.
Principal of Company?	Equity holder
Key Person?	No

CV

Formerly similar role at MCMC Asset Management and prior to that, at BAR Asset Management. Been with K for four years.

Name	Terry G
Title	Head of Risk Management
Telephone	#######
Fax	#######
E Mail	####@####.com

Has Left	No
Interviewed	Yes
Responsibilities	Oversees all risk management.
Principal of Company?	Equity holder
Key Person?	Yes

CV

2004 – present	K Asset Management
2001 – 2004	O Asset Management
1998 – 2001	University of London Physics PhD
1994 – 1997	University of London Physics BSC (Class I)
Born	1977

Comment

Terry moved to O Asset Management in 2000 as an analyst in their quant department and quickly rose to be risk manager. When the team moved to K, he continued his role as risk manager.

Good reference on file.

A closer analysis of the CVs of the key people is also worth doing, as well as gathering some informal references to assess market reputation. Talking to an existing investor (at a similar level of investment to you) will give a good indication of what to expect once invested.

Other Contacts

Sample:

Name	Edgar Evans
Role	Account Manager
Company	CCC Limited
Company Type	Administrator
Telephone	#######
Fax	#######
E Mail	####@####.com

12.2.11   Meetings and Updates

Meeting with Jack F   1 Sept 2006 – 16:00

Initial run through of investment process and discussion on most appropriate strategies. Decided to home in on K-Hedge or a bespoke portfolio with similar properties and remit.

Meeting with Ivor P   2 Oct 2006 – 16:00

Ivor ran through the process again in his own words followed by Q&A. After discussion decided K-Hedge matches our requirements on mandate, risk and return and so no bespoke portfolio needed.

Meeting with Jack F, Craig J and Terry G   20 Oct 2006 – 16:00

Third and final meeting in process. Purely Q&A on risk and portfolio management side. All satisfactory.

Teleconference with Jack F   2 Nov 2006 – 16:00

Discussion on fees and reporting. Agreed 1%/5% for a GBP 10m investment into the GBP class. Also agreed on the reporting level and the creation of a live report that can be accessed online.

Teleconference with Ivor P and Jack F   10 Jan 2007 – 16:00

First teleconference post-investment. IP said that K-Hedge posted an estimated return of 1.6% in December, just beating the comparative index – HFRX Equal Weighted Strategies – and beyond our return target of 3 month LIBOR + 3%. Implied risk is currently running at 4% which is slightly lower than they would like longer term but falls well within our risk target of 7% volatility. All but one fund ended the month in positive territory. The most pronounced contributions to the return emanated from Equity Long/Short and Event Driven, while one Fixed Income Relative Value fund was the sole marginal detractor.

Writing up meetings is always advised as this is a good way of checking to see if what they say was about to happen in the space actually occurred!

END

12.3 SUMMARY

In this chapter I have provided an example of a basic investment report on a hedge fund of funds. This should illustrate some of the methodology discussed in earlier chapters in Part III and give a framework on which to build by asking some of the questions I suggested above. I will conclude the book with some examples of the more advanced uses of hedge funds of funds, and, being a closet academic, will take a look at some of the academic advances in this field.

12.4 SUMMARY OF IDEAS FOR CHAPTER 12

- Writing up a structured investment report as above on any hedge fund you are close to investing with is always advised.
- Analyse the information they tell you – don't just accept it at face value.

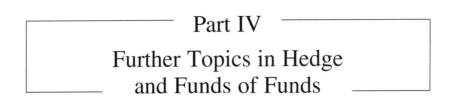

Part IV

Further Topics in Hedge and Funds of Funds

13

Structured Products, Portable Alpha and Liability Driven Investment

13.1 OVERVIEW OF PART IV

In this, the final part of the book, I address some of the more complex aspects of hedge funds of funds. In Chapter 13 we will take a look at structures that use hedge fund of funds to generate some kind of modified return stream, be it through a structure built around the hedge fund of funds or the addition of other external return streams. In Chapter 14 we will take a look at ways of getting hedge fund of funds style returns without actually investing in one, through hedge fund indices or through simulating such returns. In Chapter 15 we will take a brief look at the academic progress in the field which may benefit the investor in the future. Finally, in Chapter 16, we will take a look at the evolution of hedge fund of funds and also take a look at what investors can expect looking forward,

13.2 CHAPTER OVERVIEW

In Chapter 13 I introduce the different available methods that exist to modify the return stream of hedge funds of funds to create a solution to satisfy a specific demand. This could be through building a structured product out of a hedge fund of funds to provide a guarantee against loss, give potentially leveraged returns or modify returns to pay out in a specific way. Another potential modification would be to create what is known as a portable alpha solution. Here, the hedge fund of funds returns (the alpha) are added to the return stream of another asset class such as equities or bonds (the beta) to give a mix of hedge fund of funds and market returns. An extension of this area being liability driven investments which may use a hedge fund of funds to generate return above a duration based structure aimed at matching the liabilities of a pension plan.

I will split the above topics into three main areas:

- Structured products
- Portable alpha
- Liability driven investments

13.3 STRUCTURED PRODUCTS

Structured products are investment vehicles developed to modify hedge fund of funds returns. In the vast majority, such products offer leveraged and/or capital guaranteed access to hedge fund of funds. In the case of leveraged products, returns are amplified meaning that positive returns have potential to be greater but downside returns will be greater also. In capital guaranteed products, the original amount invested is guaranteed to be returned after a fixed period of time irrespective of underlying hedge fund performance, but this comes at a cost as I will discuss later. There are also modifications to the above where leverage may be varying over time or only a percentage of capital may be guaranteed. Also, structured products may have more complex objectives, e.g. where returns are paid out in a particular way for tax efficiency purposes, or where a certain maximum volatility is guaranteed.

13.3.1 Leveraged Hedge Fund of Funds

Leveraged products are usually the most straightforward structured products in as much as they involve a bank lending facility to generate leverage with no other whistles and bells. A typical leveraged hedge fund of funds will usually involve double or triple the exposure to the underlying fund ($2\times$ or $3\times$ exposure) with fees accordingly multiplied. The investment route is typically through a fund within which the leverage provider doubles or triples the invested capital and then invests in the hedge fund of funds in question.

The upsides are almost $2\times$ (or $3\times$ in the case of triple leverage) returns which, given that hedge funds of funds tend to have a well controlled downside and an involatile track record, can look impressive. Notice, however, that I say *almost* – the fees charged by the leverage provider and the cost of borrowing diminish both upside and add to downside. Thus, should there be a period of volatility where the upside returns are slightly diminished and downside returns slightly extended, there is potential for earning significantly less than $2\times$ (or $3\times$) returns.

Given that borrowing is necessary to effect leverage, the higher the cost of borrowing (i.e. base rates) the less effective a leveraged product will be and, should the returns of a hedge fund of funds be below the cost of borrowing then the leverage will add negative value. As a result it is sometimes not worth investing in a leverage product where the expected unleveraged returns are too close to base rates and projected base rates.

As well as fees and the cost of borrowing, there is one other potential negative with leveraged hedge funds of funds. Often the leverage provider will impose limits on concentration at underlying hedge fund level, underlying hedge fund manager level and underlying hedge fund strategy level, amongst other limits such as those based on liquidity. Although such limits are often similar to those which hedge funds of funds have anyway, it is worth checking this as the limits may be draconian enough to change the way in which the hedge fund of funds has been managed and the past track record may not now reflect the expected returns going forward.

Finally, just as with any underlying hedge fund or hedge fund of funds, past volatility may not reflect future downside and as a result one should not rely on 'worst case past loss $\times$ 2' to be the future worst case scenario in a twice levered product – it is likely to be greater.

All in all leveraged hedge fund of funds are a viable way of increasing the risk and return expectations within a hedge fund of funds but the above caveats should not be ignored.

13.3.2   Capital Guaranteed Hedge Funds of Funds

Capital guarantees on hedge funds of funds aim to give a good portion of the performance of a hedge fund of funds whilst giving insurance that the original amount invested cannot be lost. Thus if £100 were invested at the start of the product, if the investment was maintained to maturity then the minimum to be returned at the end would be £100. Typically, the duration of such a product is five years although they can be as short as three years and as long as 10 years. Also, there is generally a layer of fees for the structurer (as well as the hedge fund of funds and underlying hedge funds) so such products do not come cheap, but can be incredibly useful for an investor that needs such a structure.

Apart from the obvious benefits of the 'no lose' nature of these investments there are other positive characteristics. For example, such a product is generally structured as a bond and therefore has good tax efficiency under some regimes. Furthermore, some structurers make a weekly market in these bonds allowing beneficial liquidity for those who are happy to pay a spread. Note, however, that the capital guarantee only exists for those that keep their investments to maturity.

The main difference in capital guarantee products of a given maturity is the participation rate and the way in which it is constructed. That is, the level of exposure one has to the hedge fund of funds itself, and how this is achieved.

One methodology is to buy a zero coupon bond for your desired maturity and to get a product structurer to write you an at or in the money call option on a hedge fund of funds, i.e. a financial instrument that gives you exposure to only the profit on a hedge fund of funds. The maximum amount you can then afford on the call option is the current level the bond is trading at compared to its value at maturity. For example if you have £100 to invest and zero coupon bonds maturing at £100 in five years are priced at £85 now, you would buy the bond with £85 and buy as much exposure as you can through a call on the hedge fund of funds returns that expires in five years to match the maturity of the bond.

In other words, the process would be as follows for a 5 year maturity product:

Now: £100 = A 5 year zero coupon bond at £85 + £15 of
                call options

After 5 Years: £100 from maturing bond bought 5 years ago at £85 +
                any upside from call option

The problem is that it is unlikely that you can get full 100% exposure to the hedge fund of funds through the amount you can afford on the call and so you participate less in the hedge fund of funds. The amount you participate in the hedge fund of funds investment (i.e. the amount of exposure you have to it) is known as the participation rate and the participation rate for this strategy is typically less than 100% although this is dependent on the yield curve (how cheap you can buy a zero coupon bond to mature when you need it to) and how expensive the call option is. The investment banks that write such options are not thickies and as a result realise that the past volatility of a hedge funds of funds is a poor prediction of future volatility and so the call options are priced with greater volatility than history would lead you to expect.

Of course, if you do not want a full capital guarantee, there is nothing to force to buy as many bonds as you would otherwise need to and this approach may be valid for those who want downside protection but not a full capital guarantee, thereby permitting a higher participation level.

As well as flexibility, the other great benefit of investing through this approach is that you don't have to worry about the volatility of the hedge fund performance going forward – as long as it has made money by the end, you will benefit from the upside. In the other type of capital guarantee structure, you are very much exposed to the path the hedge fund of funds takes, although there are offsetting benefits from an increased participation rate (which can be greater than 100%); this approach is known as Constant Proportion Portfolio Insurance (CPPI).

The original capital guaranteed hedge fund products were based around managed accounts where only a small margin was required of the invested capital, leaving cash available to buy the zero coupon bond that made the guarantee. Even if the margin required on the portfolio increased, this could often be deposited as bonds rather than cash and so the process was incredibly straightforward. However, when hedge funds of funds rather than managed accounts were desired, another method was needed. The original solution was to make an initial investment of 100% in the hedge fund of funds and keep invested unless significant losses were made. 'Significant losses' means the invested amount dropped towards a predetermined level linked to the price of the zero coupon bond that would be needed to enforce the guarantee. In the latter case, the assets were pulled from the hedge fund of funds and invested straight into the zero coupon bond; as a result, the remaining years of the product was endured as a basic zero coupon bond fund.

In other words, the process could be as follows for a five year maturity product:

Now:	Investment = £100 = £100 invested in a hedge fund of funds
Scenario A:	Hedge fund of funds does not lose too much money and ends up in profit
Action:	Keep investment in the hedge fund of funds
After 5 Years:	Investment = £100 + return from hedge fund of funds

Now:	Investment = £100 = £100 invested in a hedge fund of funds
Scenario B:	Hedge fund of funds losses make invested capital fall to the price of the corresponding zero coupon bond, e.g. invested capital falls to £90 with four years to run/price of four year zero coupon bond is £90
Action:	Switch money from hedge fund of funds into corresponding zero coupon bond
After 5 Years:	Investment = £100 from maturing zero coupon bond

As can be seen above, the main problem is that if the hedge fund of funds incurs early losses then the investment is 'stopped out' and switched to bonds and any future upside from the hedge fund of funds is lost. However, this is favoured by some to the call option method because at least there is potential for a 100% participation rate. However, both of these issues have been addressed in more recent guaranteed products, where a constant proportion portfolio insurance (CPPI) model is used. Here, instead of an 'all or nothing' investment, the guarantor gives a larger participation rate (exposure) to the hedge fund of funds when it has done/is doing well and a smaller participation rate when it has done/is doing poorly. As the amount invested in a loss making hedge fund of funds would be less, and falling, and so the impact of following losses would be smaller and so the chance of being switched to bonds smaller than the above method. As a result, with a CPPI structure, there is a higher expected participation rate (and even potential for leverage) than the call option approach but with lesser risk of being stopped out than with the classic structure, above.

There is, however, an Achilles heal in CPPI structures. If the hedge fund of funds begins to incur losses very early on in the life of the product, guarantors may not have enough time to react and so the fund would get switched to bonds pretty much from the start. The other risk for CPPI and classic threshold structures is that the hedge fund of funds moves in a large and sharp move and the guarantor cannot rebalance in time. The maths behind these structures assumes continuous movement and corresponding rebalancing but in reality there can be some large losses in a matter of weeks. This is known as gap risk and sometimes it results in the guarantor having to cover losses and so it is important to assess the financial standing of the guarantor as well as the skill of a hedge fund of funds when selecting a guaranteed product. Recently, there have been solutions even to these issues based around options on CPPI.

The typical capital guaranteed hedge fund of funds will have the fund management done by the hedge fund of funds managers and the structure built by a separate guarantor – usually a large bank. Just as with leveraged hedge funds of funds, there are restrictions placed on the hedge fund of funds by the guarantor based on concentration but they may be also based on liquidity and the amount of new hedge funds in the portfolio. As a result, investors in the underlying hedge fund of funds as well as the guaranteed product need to check these restrictions to be satisfied that they don't overly constrain the hedge fund manager to the point where it negatively impacts returns. Also, investors need to consider the impact on the hedge fund of funds of CPPI-based guarantors rebalancing their holding in the fund, positively or negatively.

Structured products are a useful if sometimes expensive way to modify hedge fund of funds returns. Next I will discuss portable alpha products, which use hedge funds of funds to modify the returns of other, more standard asset classes.

13.4   PORTABLE ALPHA

Beta is the extent to which a portfolio moves in line with the underlying market and any residual returns (what's left) are called alpha. Hedge funds are broadly believed to be alpha generators, index funds as beta generators and traditional long-only (active) funds as a mix of alpha and beta.

The concept of portable alpha involves taking alpha from one source and transplanting it into another, usually market based, return series. For example, taking alpha from hedge funds and mixing it with beta from an equity index to give a desired return stream. Although this concept is called portable alpha, it is usually easier to import the beta into the alpha generating funds than import the alpha into the source of beta.

Portable alpha can be of use to those with existing portfolios that invest across one or more asset class (equities, bonds, etc.) that wish to restructure their portfolios to be more efficient, as well as those with liabilities that need to be matched.

There are a number of benefits to the portable alpha approach. First of all, investors are able to get the alpha of their return generated by experts in alpha production such as hedge funds rather than traditional fund managers that are mainly generators of a little alpha and a lot of beta. Also, attempts to get traditional fund managers to generate more alpha result in a mandate with an increased tracking error, allowing more off benchmark positions which in turn may result in less beta being delivered, and so investors cannot win in this zero sum game.

The portable alpha approach also allows alpha to be generated from a range of markets rather than just the market from which the beta is required. For example, a traditional equity fund can only invest in equities, which is fine for getting beta exposure but constrains the generation of alpha to that single market, whereas the portable alpha approach allows the alpha to be generated from wherever the investor chooses.

The other benefits of portable alpha are based around monitoring and cost. Having neatly compartmentalised and separated producers of alpha and beta means that exact contributions to return are easily measured and monitored, whereas the mixed up alpha and beta in traditional funds are more difficult to attribute. Similarly, this separation of return results in paying a very low amount for the cheap beta that is available, and a higher, usually performance driven amount for the difficult to produce alpha, which is both fair and suitably motivating.

As can be seen above, there are numerous benefits from taking the portable alpha approach; however, there are difficulties as well. The main difficulty is implementation. Although the concept of portable alpha sounds very simple, effecting such exposures can be more complex and the more precise the requirements for pure alpha, the more complexity there is.

The simplest portable alpha position would be a percentage invested in a source of alpha such as a hedge fund of funds and the remnant used to access an index fund in the market from which the beta is required. For example 20% in a hedge fund of funds and 80% in a FTSE 100 index tracker.

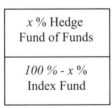

Figure 13.1   Portable Alpha: Simplest Route.

The problem here is that you only get part access to the beta – in our example you only get 80% participation when you may need 100% – and there is a trade off between beta and alpha. The solution to this under-participation is to access the underlying markets through a derivative product such as a swap or futures contract. The benefit of using a swap is that you can access the exact beta you require without exchanging principal, you just receive the profit or pay out the loss of the beta portfolio, along with regular fee. The downside is that swaps are OTC (over the counter) derivatives – bespoke derivatives where you deal with a counterparty rather than an exchange – and as such can be costly and less liquid. The benefit of using a futures contract is that they are a cheap, simple method of gaining access to the market but the main downside is that there may not always be a cheap and liquid contract available to access the market you require.

Either way, this is a viable solution to get 100% beta exposure although given that an initial outlay and/or ongoing payments are needed for either route, it would not be possible to get 100% alpha exposure as well. Also, using this route investors should be aware that they are using a degree of leverage and as such, have increased risk and run a notional risk of losing more that they invested, although this would require the underlying market to lose at least 100%-x% (80% in our example) and such risk can be removed through creating an appropriate investment structure.

If 100% alpha and 100% beta is required then this can be approximated by also investing in a leveraged hedge fund of funds in the above structure although few need to go this far.

In the above analysis we have assumed that hedge funds are 'pure alpha' strategies but this is rarely the case, even in the case of market neutral strategies where movements in correlations result in 'market neutrality' being no more than a transient state. Many investors are

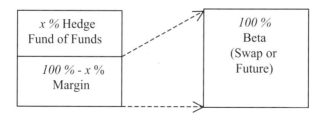

Figure 13.2   Portable Alpha: Derivative Route.

happy to invest in the most market independent of hedge funds (market neutral, arbitrage and relative value, etc) and assume that over time the returns will not display meaningful beta. Those with more stringent requirements can calculate the betas of the alpha driven investment at regular time periods and rebalance the beta part of the portfolio accordingly, although for many this is more of a check that betas lie within certain parameters rather than a constant rebalancing process.

Above we have looked at one of the more subtle benefits of portable alpha, namely the advantage of reaping alpha from a variety of sources and markets rather than just the market from which the beta is required. There is, however, an equally subtle counterpoint to this benefit which may be lost in a portable alpha approach; namely that there is a benefit of managing the bulk of a traditional mixed alpha and beta portfolio. In this case, a sizeable portfolio that is managed in an active manner may privilege its manager to information flows from the market where a 'beta driven' portfolio may not – from execution based information flow and research from brokers. In my own view, this does not counteract the benefits of portable alpha but it is an argument that should at least be considered.

Given the above, there are a few tips that can be derived for potential portable alpha investors:

- Understand exactly how much alpha and beta you are getting access to and remeasure this over time.
- Understand any increased level of risk involved and any leverage.
- Find out where the beta is coming from.
- Check that you can't lose more than you invest, even in a notional and almost impossible scenario.
- Complex structures attract more fees – understand all the fees involved at every level, including those charged by the structurers and get a total fee calculation; be aware of fixed structurers fees hidden as basis point charges where they look less innocuous.

In summary, the portable alpha approach is a sensible methodology for running a structured and diversified portfolio and despite having been conceptualised for at least 20 years it is not adopted by as many asset pools as one would expect for reasons purely based on inertia – things haven't been done this way in the past and so it takes a lot to get people to change. That being said, more and more pension plans are adopting this concept more from a liability driven approach. For example, a matching fund within a pension plan that has to generate a 'Gilts + ' return stream would use a portable alpha approach with beta from the Gilts markets and alpha from the hedge fund world rather than investing in a mix of government and corporate bonds as they would have done in the past. The further extension of this is where the matching fund matches liabilities with even greater precision – this is known as Liability Driven Investment and is discussed right below.

13.5   LIABILITY DRIVEN INVESTMENTS

A pension plan's liabilities are the expected outgoings that will need to be paid out in the future, e.g. payment of benefits to members on retirement, which can vary with salary growth, inflation, etc. These liabilities can be approximately matched with a variety of bonds and interest rate instruments although some form of investment to grow the plan's assets is needed to match factors that may force liabilities to increase.

In the past, such liabilities were covered by portfolios of assets such as bond portfolios that aimed to beat a market benchmark rather than match the liabilities. Nowadays, it is possible to use a derivative that will almost perfectly match the liability profile of a pension plan – usually through a bespoke swap. This way, although more complex, is a less cumbersome and better matched solution than using bonds. As a swap requires no exchange of principal, this approach also results in a cash balance that can then be used for growth-focussed investment. This concept of *liability driven investment* has grown as a result of the availability of such liability matching techniques and has been driven by the unsatisfactory nature of earlier liability management based around managed portfolios, where the portfolio manager's benchmark and the plan's liabilities were often poorly matched and hence a source of uncompensated risk. Formally, liability driven investment can be defined as an investment strategy that manages a plan's assets relative to its liabilities (implicitly, this means that it is not relative to a general benchmark).

Pension plans in deficit need to generate excess returns to redress this underfunding but even pension plans in surplus need to generate extra return as liabilities can always increase based on actuarial factors such as death rates and longevity. As a result, sources of alpha and risk premia are sought to generate returns above the liability matching level.

Hedge funds of funds are highly relevant to the area of liability driven investment as they are a good source of alpha to be imported into a pension plan. They are particularly useful, however, given the asymmetric nature of their returns, i.e. downside control. If a pension plan is liability matched using a swap then it could be disastrous should significant losses occur in the growth part of the portfolio as this would disrupt the entire structure that had been set in place. This would be especially so if negative returns occurred soon after the structure had started since there would be no cushion in place to soften the blow from losses and the matching structure may be fractured. A typical pension plan may then be forced to act defensively and dilute or shut down the growth portfolio, thus crystallising loss and missing any potential bounce back. As a result, the involatile, downside controlled and alpha-producing nature of hedge funds and funds of funds make them particularly useful as a source of portable alpha in liability driven investments.

When selecting a liability driven investment strategy there are many questions to ask including:

- What are the total fees being charged and how much premium is being added to the basic price of the swap and the cost of the alpha for 'structuring'?
- Do I fully understand the nature of swaps and hedge funds of funds?
- Is the manager of the source of alpha related to the structurer of the swap and is it being waived through due to this or do I get a choice of alpha source and manager?

In summary, liability driven investments can be thought of as the evolution of pension plan management that most efficiently matches liabilities and channels risk. Hedge funds of funds are one of the natural choices of imported alpha into such structures based on their 'pure alpha' objective and the structurally beneficial nature of their returns being downside controlled.

13.6 SUMMARY

It can be seen above that there is a multitude of ways to augment and modify hedge fund and hedge fund of funds returns to match a desired profile. Some methods involve changing the structure of returns through the use of leverage or capital guarantees, others involve adding hedge fund returns to another structure or asset class. Either way, the structure of hedge fund returns and their alpha-driven nature make a useful starting point for a range of augmentations that is continuously growing and evolving. Investors can pretty much get the return structure they need for an appropriate level of risk, albeit at a cost.

13.7 SUMMARY OF IDEAS FOR CHAPTER 13

- There are a variety of structures and augmentations based around hedge fund returns.
- Such structures can generate very useful return streams that can be tailor-made to fit most requirements, but at a cost.
- Structured hedge fund of funds can be used to augment traditional returns and can be particularly useful to enhance liability-based solutions.

14

Hedge Fund Indices and Replication

14.1 OVERVIEW

In recent years there has been a significant attempt to offer access to the hedge fund universe by indexation and replication. In the case of the former approach, an index compiler will calculate the overall return of a wide range of underlying hedge funds and reflect this in a hedge fund index, but also produce an investable version of this index as an investment vehicle where the returns can actually be accessed by an investor. In the case of replication, a more recent innovation, a provider will attempt to replicate hedge fund returns by taking exposure to factor based returns and/or other financial instruments with the aim of allowing investors to experience hedge fund-like returns without the cost, lack of transparency, operational risk or illiquidity. In this chapter I will discuss the benefits and downsides of investing through investable hedge fund indices and replication techniques.

14.2 HEDGE FUND INDICES

A hedge fund index is an entity that seeks to reflect the returns of the hedge fund universe. Such indices could be used as benchmarks or comparators for hedge fund and hedge fund of funds performance or just serve as a reflection of hedge fund returns. Most hedge fund indices are uninvestable, in as much as their returns could not be replicated on invested capital due to the fact that many of the constituent hedge funds are closed to new investment. Some uninvestable hedge fund indices do have investable versions that seek to offer well-diversified access to the hedge fund universe that tends to be cheaper and more liquid than many hedge funds of funds. As well as broader indices that seek to reflect the return of the entire hedge fund universe, there are also sub-indices that seek to reflect the return of various hedge fund strategies such as Equity Long/Short or Convertible Arbitrage.

Investable hedge fund indices aim to give diversified access to the hedge fund investment class by investing across a wide range of hedge funds. In most cases, investable hedge fund indices are based on uninvestable counterparts that are compiled by the same index providers. Investable indices are usually subsets of the headline indices but rarely, if ever, include all the funds in the uninvestable version; this is because some of the constituents in the uninvestable indices are 'closed' or not willing to take investment from such an index product. Investable hedge fund index providers include MSCI (in conjunction with Lyxor Asset Management – Société Générale's specialist hedge fund structuring subsidiary), CSFB (in conjunction with Tremont – the hedge fund of funds group) and HFR. Other classic index providers with hedge fund indices include Dow Jones, FTSE and S&P although the latter closed down a large part of this venture in 2006. It should be noted that there are many more hedge fund index providers that produce uninvestable indices with no investable spin-off, purely for benchmarking and comparative purposes (see Géhin and Vaissié, 2004).

The benefits of investing through an investable hedge fund index are based around access to hedge funds in a way that can be more diversified, more liquid and less expensive than accessing the hedge fund universe through a hedge fund of funds. For example, most hedge fund indices charge less than a hedge fund of funds (<1% management fees, no performance fees) and some offer higher liquidity, e.g. MSCI offers weekly trading. However, there are downsides with this approach.

One of the main downsides of hedge fund indices is when the index is not well diversified. Most of the major *un*investable indices are based on hundreds of hedge funds but sometimes even then do not give a diversified view of the hedge fund universe. Basic rules for eligibility for entry to an index are typically based on a minimum amount of assets under management, a minimum length of track record and provision of documentation but also, this requires the hedge funds to supply their performance data. Many hedge funds do not need to raise assets and due to this, or for other reasons, decide they have nothing to gain by supplying their performance to hedge fund data collectors and index providers and, as such, elect not to be in the index. As an illustration of this, only 12 of the 78 hedge funds we invest with across our full product range at Key Asset Management are represented within one of the broadest uninvestable indices provided by one of the biggest players in this field; in other words, over 80% of the hedge funds we invest with in our hedge funds of funds are not covered by the index even though they are notionally eligible and often well known, and so one must conclude that they have chosen not to supply their data for inclusion. This raises questions about the pertinence of the uninvestable hedge fund indices as benchmarks or comparative indices, given the potential for such a minimal overlap.

Furthermore, studies by EDHEC (2006), Géhin and Vaissié (2004) have shown the coverage by the different hedge fund index providers is more disparate than one would expect, leading to large discrepancies in performance, resulting in something of a conundrum when selecting a hedge fund index as a benchmark or comparator for gauging hedge fund of funds performance.

Given the above, further problems occur when uninvestable indices are pared down to allow them to become investable. To be eligible for an uninvestable hedge fund index, hedge funds need to have satisfied a range of criteria: they must be happy to be in the index, provide regular performance data, satisfy requirements based on length of track record, size of assets, provision of documentation and sometimes also need to go through a due diligence process as well. In addition, to be in the investable hedge fund index, hedge funds usually need to be in the uninvestable version index and be open for investments and sometimes need to provide certain levels of liquidity or even have to run a specific managed account. As a result of all this criteria, not only do uninvestable hedge fund indices seriously under represent the hedge fund universe as a whole, but in addition, the investable index sometimes seriously under represents the uninvestable index. For example, one of the bigger and better hedge fund indices has less than 30% of its constituent hedge funds from its uninvestable index in its investable version and this is typical.

The problem above is exacerbated when strategy focused sub-indices are considered. As well as a broader index, many hedge fund index providers also decompose this index into sub-indices that represent different strategies, e.g. Equity Long/Short, Convertible Arbitrage, etc. In certain sub-indices, the problems of under representation of the hedge fund universe in the investable indices are worsened. For example it is common for many investable sub-indices to have less than 10 constituents and a typical 60 constituent index can be reduced to 6 constituents in its investable form. In such low numbers and thus with such minimal diversification, investing with hedge funds that have had little analysis or operational due diligence performed on them can be dangerous, and a failure can potentially cause losses of 10–20% in a month.

To summarise, it can be seen that there are uninvestable hedge fund indices that seek to represent the returns of the hedge fund universe.

Some of these indices have investable versions that seek to offer liquid, low cost and diversified access to the hedge fund universe.

The uninvestable hedge fund indices have potential to be used as benchmarks or comparators for a hedge fund of funds' returns and so could be useful for hedge fund of funds investors seeking to gauge performance. However, there is an argument that the uninvestable hedge fund indices under represent the hedge fund universe as a whole and often do not cover some of the better hedge funds. Furthermore, different hedge fund indices appear to have less correlation with one another than one would hope. As a result, choosing a hedge fund index is not straight forward and subsequent relative performance of a hedge fund of funds may be spurious. Nonetheless, having such indices is better than nothing.

Investable hedge fund indices have even bigger issues with under representation of the hedge fund universe and in certain cases have sizeable concentration with respect to underlying hedge funds. In the worst case, some investable hedge fund indices have greater concentration than would be found in a hedge fund of funds, but with underlying hedge funds receiving much less scrutiny. As a result, investable hedge fund indices are not for everybody, as can be seen by their low take-up relative to hedge fund of funds.

14.3   HEDGE FUND REPLICATION

Hedge fund replication is a way of generating returns that may look like broad hedge fund index returns but without actually investing in hedge funds themselves (nor in hedge funds of funds or hedge fund indices). Instead, analysis of past hedge fund returns are used to create portfolios of underlying market positions with the aim of generating returns of similar structure to hedge fund returns. One such way is to estimate which underlying factors hedge funds are exposed to and, at the time of writing, this approach to creating hedge fund replication based investment vehicles has been pioneered by investment banks such as Goldman Sachs through their ART products and I will call this approach the IB approach. The other main method is based on generating a portfolio of underlying market instruments that aims to match the statistical properties of a hedge fund portfolio; this approach is based on the work and papers of Harry Kat, a City University professor, mainly with his PhD Student Helder Palaro and is available through a service called Fundcreator, so I term this the FC approach. Below, I take a look at each approach and also assess the benefits and downsides of replication.

The factor based (IB) approach to hedge fund replication is based on the observation that the universe of hedge funds often generates returns from a mixture of varying exposures (beta) to a range of market factors (such as credit, equity, etc) as well as potentially adding value due to skill (alpha). Thus, constructing appropriate exposures to these factors can replicate the beta exposures calculated to represent the universe of hedge funds. For example, if analysis of track record found that the returns of the universe of hedge fund returns were 30% linked to equities, 20% linked to bonds, 20% linked to equity volatility, 20% linked to commodities and 10% linked to interest rates, an investment vehicle of cost $100 could be constructed with a portfolio of $30 in equity index futures (S&P 500, FTSE 100, etc.), $20 in bonds (government bond futures, credit indices, etc), $20 exposure to volatility (VIX index, etc.) and $20 in commodities (e.g. commodity index futures, oil futures, etc) with $10 in cash or interest rate instruments. By investing in this vehicle, one could obtain the same exposures that have been calculated to exist in the universe of hedge funds. Of course, such exposures vary over time but the vehicle provider would test for such change with a certain frequency and change the allocation within the investment vehicle's portfolio accordingly. Similar products for specific hedge fund strategies are also on the horizon.

It is important to understand that such an approach isn't aiming to generate the return of a skilled hedge fund manager that outperforms due to a solid edge. Instead, the approach is based at replicating the entire universe of hedge funds, after all their fees, in which one would expect at least as many low skill and/or underperforming funds as skilled outperforming ones.

The benefits of such an approach is that one can gain the factor exposures of the hedge fund universe in a cheap (less than or equal to 1% total cost) and very liquid way (notionally daily liquidity) with low operational risk, but of course there are downsides. First of all, the way in such a product is constructed is based on extensive backward looking analysis and so this wholly quantitative approach will be vulnerable low accuracy through generalisation, and to spurious correlations and may be slow to pick up new exposures to existing factors or exposures to new factors. For example consider a simple case of a universe of one hedge fund that is long a reasonably deep in the money equity put and so would appear highly negatively correlated to underlying equity markets;

the replicator would allocate a short position to equities. However, should the equity markets experience a massive rally, the replicated hedge fund would lose a lot more than the actual hedge fund as the latter has an option with limited loss whilst the former has a naked short position with totally unlimited loss. A worse example would be where a correlation appeared significant even though underlying funds were not invested in the area – such as a spurious correlation to commodities when actually there was only interest rate exposure. Such an approach is also vulnerable to significant but quick changes to factor exposures such as what one would experience in a market meltdown or sizeable macro event that causes hedge funds to change exposures en masse.

Given these downsides, there is a certain vulnerability to misinterpretation of exposures, especially when there are significant short term movements in markets that may not be picked up by the quantitative analysis for a time. This leads to a propensity for such a replication process to underperform heavily in times of market difficulty although there is no evidence for this, just conjecture – we will just have to wait and see.

The FC approach is slightly different. First of all, this approach is based on a methodology which generates returns with given statistical properties, which could be of hedge funds or a range of other types of return. However, the FC approach can be used to replicate hedge funds in as much as the statistical properties of such funds can be replicated with the constraint of certain risk return trade-offs; namely you cannot get returns that are 'superior' to the underlying markets for any level of risk taken. The statistical properties that are replicated are the first four moments of a return distribution: mean standard deviation, skew and kurtosis – along with correlation (to some passive portfolio).

With this approach, rather than taking exposure to underlying factors in line with hedge funds, financial instruments are traded in a way that aim to generate the statistical qualities of hedge funds. Such returns are produced by maintaining exposures to given instruments, e.g. equity and bond futures, and trading them dynamically in line with basic algorithms in the same way that a dynamic hedging strategy can mimic owning an option. In other words, the IB approach aims to expose itself to the same factors as hedge funds but may not necessarily mimic the statistical properties whereas the FC approach mimics the statistical properties but may not be exposed to the same factors as the underlying hedge funds. Which one is better for you depends on what exactly you want.

The benefits of the FC approach are that the replication can be programmed to generate exactly the correlation and return profile you need, using the instruments of your choice, both within reason. As such, the approach can be thought of more as a bespoke return generator or completion fund creator rather than a hedge fund replicator.

Like the IB approach, the downsides are also in need of consideration. First of all, the approach cannot be used to replicate hedge funds with superior risk adjusted returns to the underlying market so there is no chance of replicating a fund with great alpha generation that can produce market-beating returns with half the risk, for example, which can be possible when investing in the hedge fund space. Secondly, this approach does not aim to match hedge fund returns on a month-by-month basis, just returns with the similar statistical properties to the past returns of a given hedge fund over time. As a result, improved returns from the underlying hedge fund in question will not be experienced in the FC model, and also, it may not be possible to test to see if the statistical structure is being successfully simulated, with any degree of significance, until a few years later, when it is too late. Finally, the FC approach is based on a model that assumes perfect or complete markets, where as in real life this is not the case. For example, trading the instruments used in this approach is subject to slippage (the impact of turning theory into reality) which may be significant, especially in fast moving markets.

Overall, the main upsides of both the above approaches is that they have potential to give hedge fund style returns without entering this arcane world directly and so avoiding the operational risk, illiquidity and higher fees. However, the only way to access outperforming, skilled hedge fund managers remains through direct investment or through a hedge fund of funds.

There are, however, other benefits to hedge fund replication for those that are willing to run the 'tracking error' risk – the risk of significance variance in relative performance. This will be especially so for the IB approach, on a shorter term basis, when the strategy replication vehicles are launched (by this I mean replication of, say, Convertible Arbitrage or Equity Long/Short, for example), since this approach better replicates the strategies on a shorter term basis. Those with shorter term strategy views may be able to add to, reduce or hedge out exposure to a given hedge fund strategy since the vehicles (at least notionally) are shortable as well as liquid. For example, a hedge fund of funds manager that wishes to sack a Fixed

Income Arbitrage hedge fund that has six-monthly liquidity, and will place money with an Equity Long/Short hedge fund in its place will be able to instantly short a Fixed Income Arbitrage replication vehicle and go long the Equity Long/Short replication vehicle (or, indeed, the new fund) until the Fixed Income Arbitrage fund leaves the hedge fund of funds in six months time, at which point the replication vehicles are removed. Similarly, an investor needing a given return stream may invest with a hedge fund of funds and modify the returns to exactly what is required through addition of a vehicle using the FC approach. Finally, the replication vehicles, especially those that take the IB approach, will make good benchmarks for hedge fund performance since, prior to this, there has been no transparent, investable and cheap underlying entity that sought to resemble hedge funds in a passive form – all necessary requirements for a passive benchmark.

The downside is that there will be no alpha delivered through replication (one of the main reasons many invest in hedge funds) and the replication is based on what hedge funds have done looking back, not what they are doing now and tomorrow. For those who believe that there are hedge funds out there that will generate superior risk adjusted returns after all fees are paid, and that these funds can be detected, selected and invested with before such returns are generated, they would be better off sticking with investing in hedge funds instead of their replicants.

To summarise, if you require a liquid investment that will approximate average hedge fund returns on a monthly basis at a reasonable price with lower operational risk and higher transparency, then the IB approach is probably for you; but beware, approximation error may be significant under certain conditions, especially times of market stress and the long term results may differ greatly from average hedge fund performance. If you require a product that can statistically replicate the average values of average performing hedge funds and are not to worried about the short term performance, again with liquidity, transparency and lower cost but also with nice simple instruments, then probably the FC approach is for you; but beware, there may be long periods of time where the returns look nothing like that of hedge funds and you may find out after a time that market slippage may act to diminish returns. Also you must beware that you are investing with a dynamic trading strategy that may look like a very basic CTA strategy, an approach with its own risks.

Off The Record

The area of replication is in its infancy. Given that it is a useful commodity and set of algorithms being provided rather than any ongoing skill, expect something of a war in this area based on price, flexibility and innovation. Also, it should be possible to constrain the FC approach to access the factors in the IB approach, so hybridisation may also ensue.

14.4   SUMMARY

In this chapter we have looked at ways of accessing hedge fund returns in a diversified manner but avoiding the fees of hedge funds of funds. It has been seen that hedge fund indices are useful in their uninvestable form but that the investable versions often do not have enough coverage to provide a true reflection of hedge fund returns, especially at hedge fund strategy levels – they miss the closed funds that are often important contributors to returns. The replication route has also been discussed, where it has been suggested that due to their backward looking nature and lack of alpha generation, this may offer an alternative only to those that seek to capture the returns of lesser skilled hedge funds. Nonetheless, both these approaches are useful to those seeking to capture average hedge fund returns and the endeavours of both indexers and replicators have been beneficial to the hedge fund world.

In the next chapter, I will take a look at other applications for factor modelling in this area along with other recent innovations in the hedge fund of funds world.

14.5   SUMMARY OF IDEAS FOR CHAPTER 14

- There are a range of hedge fund indices compiled to reflect the returns of the hedge fund universe.
- Such indices have investible counterparts which are not ideal since they greatly under represent the hedge fund universe as a whole.
- Recent innovations have allowed the construction of hedge fund replication vehicles.
- It is too soon to tell if such approaches will be successful.

15

The Leading Edge: Recent Innovations in the Hedge Fund of Funds World

15.1 OVERVIEW

In this chapter, we will take a look at some work in the hedge fund space from academics, and some recent innovations from practitioners in the field. Given that the research of the former often provides product ideas for the latter, it is beneficial to look at both parties. For example, the Goldman Sachs research paper issued in 2004 (Goldman Sachs, 2004) resulted in the Goldman Sachs ART hedge fund replication vehicles launched in December 2006. As a result, I will present new work by topic, irrespective of academic or practitioner origin. Specifically, I will look at the academic and practitioner work one each of the following areas:

- Hedge fund returns
- Hedge fund indexation and replication
- Hedge fund structures and structured products
- Hedge fund risk
- Other hedge fund work

I will cover ongoing work and working papers as well as peer-reviewed publications in journals in order to fully represent current areas of research, as it can take a considerable amount of time to get work published. Wherever possible, I have included the latest work on the subject area (i.e. since 2005) but have also referenced older 'classic' papers when their relevance is still strong.

15.2 HEDGE FUND RETURNS

Some of the first published academic work on hedge funds was based around analysis of track records through databases and indices, and has shown that basic results imply that hedge funds are capable of superior performance to underlying markets for any given level of risk (e.g. Fung and Hsieh, 1997, Liang, 1999, Brown, Goetzmann and Ibbotson, 1999, Agarwal and Naik, 2000a, 2000b, Caglayan and Edwards, 2001, Capocci and Hübner, 2004 and Naik, Kosowski and Do, 2007). More recently, however, some work has been done that suggests that this outperformance at a broad level may have been overestimated as a result of survivor bias in indices and databases (i.e. due to the fact that losing funds are less well covered, see Fung and Hsieh, 2000, Malkiel and Saha, 2005) or just due to the very nature of hedge fund returns that make them appear to have lower risk than they actually take, e.g. Amin and Kat (2003), Fung *et al.* (2007). Specifically, Kat and Miffre (2006) deal with the potential for risk mis-estimation given the non-normality of hedge fund returns.

Also, some recent work has found that there has been deterioration in recent hedge fund returns, possibly linked to asset inflows, e.g. Kat and Palaro (2006b, 2007), Fung *et al.* (2007).

The latest work questions what portion of hedge fund returns can be replicated by basic strategies such as taking static exposure to a range of factors, or to straightforward trading strategies that can be easily put into practice, e.g. Kat and Palaro (2006a, 2006b).

The one thing that none of the workers in the field deny is that there are a portion of hedge funds that generate unreplicable returns – alpha – due to skill and edge. Kat (Kat and Palaro, 2007) estimates that over 20% of the 2000 or so hedge funds he tested fall into this category (although, of course, this implies that over three quarters of the hedge funds he tested are better off ignored than invested with). Similarly, Fung *et al.* (2007) have shown that there is a range of hedge fund of funds capable of steady alpha generation, which is a relief!

Although a lot of the analysis in this area has been backward looking and so does not necessarily present conclusions that would hold going forward, this work has been of benefit to investors' understanding of how hedge funds returns decompose to factor-based returns ('alternative beta') and what true alpha is left, thereafter. As a direct result of this analysis, the field of hedge fund replication has grown to the point where investable products are now available.

Over the last few years, academic work has emerged that presents analysis – factor-based and otherwise – of specific hedge fund strategies. This is a fundamentally important evolution given that there is often very little in common between the different strategies that make up the hedge fund universe, a fact that renders broader based analysis somewhat superficial. For example, Duarte *et al.* (2006) apply factor based analysis to the Fixed Income hedge fund space, Mitchell and Pulvino (2001) to Merger Arbitrage, Fung and Hsieh (2004c) to Equity Long/Short and Aggarwal, Fung *et al.* (2006) use an active style factor approach to analyse the Convertible Bond Arbitrage world.[1] Such work can be harnessed for the purposes of risk measurement, benchmarking and general understanding of the skills needed for a practitioner in a given strategy, and is extremely useful to practitioners.

15.3 HEDGE FUND INDEXATION AND REPLICATION

As we have seen above and in the previous chapter, there are currently two main bodies of work on hedge fund replication. One is a factor based approach based on work pioneered by Sharpe (1992), as extended by Agarwal and Naik (2000a, 2000b), that seeks to replicate the factor exposures taken by hedge funds on a month-by-month basis and hence generate returns that look something like hedge fund returns. The other approach, pioneered by Kat and Palaro (2005), based on work by Dybvig (1988a, 1988b), seeks to generate overall returns that look like hedge funds' returns with no attempt to match the returns on a monthly basis. Despite criticism from the 'other camp', Hasanhodzic and Lo (2006) have found that there is merit in the factor-based approach although some strategies are better replicated than others.

There is recent work that could progress both approaches. For example, Kat (2007) notes that his approach to fund replication need not be based around set distributions, thus rendering his approach able to replicate hedge funds returns that do not resemble formal distributions. Furthermore, I would be surprised if a hybrid approach did not develop between the two schools by using hedge fund factors with exposure constraints to generate hedge fund return distributions using the Kat methodology.

Another advanced factor approach that utilises dynamic trading strategies is based on the work of Fung and Hsieh (2002, and most recently 2007 with Naik and Romadorai). Here, simple active trading strategies that replicate the very basis of what a given hedge fund strategy does are

---

[1]In fact, Convertible Bond Arbitrage is one of the more academically studied hedge fund strategies, with further work on the area by Choi *et al.* (2006), Loncarski *et al.* (2007) and Ammann *et al.* (2006).

used as factors themselves. For example, a basic Convertible Arbitrage active factor may buy all tradable convertible bonds and delta hedge using stock – the basis of what a Convertible Arbitrage manager does. The logical conclusion to this approach is that one day we may see core returns from hedge fund strategies generated through a mix of static and basic active factors, with hedge fund specialists mandated to generate just pure 'alternative alpha'. However, if Kat and Palaro (2007) are to be believed, only 20% of hedge fund managers are capable of doing this, and so I can't imagine this happening for some time yet as the capable hedge fund managers themselves will be in no rush given the over demand for their skills.

There has also been academic work on hedge fund indices that has resulted in innovation in the practitioner world. Academics at EDHEC (EDHEC, 2006) have developed uninvestable hedge fund indices with the potential to be the most representative in the field, i.e. best reflect the performance of the true underlying hedge fund universe. This is because the EDHEC indices use combinations of all the main hedge fund indices along with additional funds not found in any other indices. These underlying indices are combined in a way that results in the best summary of the indices in total (using a mathematical technique called Principal Component Analysis) and hence should be more representative of any one underlying hedge fund index alone. However, such techniques are difficult to extend to investable hedge fund indices. Nonetheless, the spirit of the approach is applied to underlying hedge funds on the Lyxor platform although the resulting investable indices, as with competing approaches, actually cover very few hedge funds.

15.4 HEDGE FUND STRUCTURES AND STRUCTURED PRODUCTS

15.4.1 Listed Products

Both hedge funds and hedge funds of funds are starting to list shares linked to their portfolios on recognised stock exchanges. Instead of owning a share in the fund that you sell back to the fund itself when you want to free-up capital, here you would own a share that you would trade with others when you want to sell, just like any other common stock. The benefits of this for the underlying funds is permanent capital, i.e. when an investor wants out he will sell the share on to another investor so there will be no change to the capital base of the fund; the benefits for the investor would be much better liquidity – provided there would be a liquid market in the shares, it would be possible to add and lessen exposure to the fund on even an intra-day basis. The downsides would be mainly for the investor – market forces may result in shares trading at excessive premia or deep discounts to net asset value, which is not beneficial for those looking to buy or sell, respectively. Often, to protect the discount from disadvantaging investors, there will be a policy in place to protect this happening for long periods such as a promised share buy-back at NAV.

Over the past few years, a range of hedge funds of funds have introduced listed products in this way with varying success but in the last few months several hedge funds have also raised capital this way and it is expected that many more hedge funds will follow this route.

15.4.2   Collateralised Fund Obligations (CFOs)

One the more recent innovations in structuring is called a Collateralised Fund Obligations (CFO). Just as in a standard hedge fund of funds, investors gain exposure to a diverse range of hedge funds but in this instance, the hedge fund of funds portfolio is structured into tranches, as in a collateralised debt obligation. In other words, the hedge fund of funds is split into a range of capital structure instruments from rated debt securities through to equities, thus proving another access route to hedge funds of funds for investors. Another way to think of this is that the shareholders of the fund issue debt to leverage their exposure, which must be paid off before the profits trickle down to the shareholders themselves. As a result, investors can access leveraged equity in a hedge fund as well as rated asset-backed bonds (where the asset is the hedge fund of funds portfolio), allowing more flexibility and access to a range of risk profiles and instruments.

15.5   HEDGE FUND RISK

Measuring and monitoring hedge fund risk is notoriously difficult for a range of reasons:

- Limited transparency
  - Many hedge funds will only disclose partial information on their underlying portfolio.

- Liquidity and pricing risk
  - Even when an investor gets full transparency, the portfolio risk is often difficult to measure as a result of the instruments within; for example the portfolio may contain OTC instruments with only indicative prices or difficult-to-price derivatives.
- Model risk
  - Traditional VaR-style risk measures will often misestimate the risk in a hedge fund portfolio. Many such portfolios will be constructed by their managers to have carefully matched long and short positions in pairs or baskets as a hedge, and so will have low VaR. However, this may not reflect the risk in the future since often such positions are event driven with a severe covariance structure altering event yet to come. Similarly, a manager may invest in such a position straight after the event, giving 'higher VaR, lower risk'.
- Complexity
  - Hedge fund portfolios can be vast and complex meaning there is just not enough time to accurately measure the risk of many hedge fund portfolios over a month.

As can be seen from above, and more generally in Lo (2001), using traditional techniques to measure the risks associated with a hedge fund portfolio can be difficult and inaccurate. Also, Fung and Hsieh (1999) and Agarwal and Naik (2004) have shown that normal mean-variance risk measurement techniques do not work for hedge funds due to the dominance of non-normal returns. As a result, there is a challenge to both academics and practitioners alike to develop methods to accurately measure hedge fund risk.

One method of understanding hedge fund risk is to take a factor-based approach. Based on Sharpe's (1992) style analysis, Fung and Hsieh (1997) and more recently Agarwal and Naik (2000a, 2000b) have used a factor based approach to help understand how hedge funds generate returns, with Brealey and Kaplanis (2001) applying this approach specifically to understand hedge fund risk. Fung and Hsieh (2002), amongst others, have extended the factors used in such analysis to 'Asset Based Style' factors, which are better descriptors of what hedge fund managers do but, given the active nature of such hypothetical factors, are inappropriate for risk measurement in this context. As a result, a working paper by Fung and Hsieh (2004a, 2004b) looking at hedge fund risk using asset based style factors is of interest but not extendable for this style of risk measurement. Finally, the most pragmatic and active use to date of style factor analysis in hedge funds is by Amenc *et al.* (2003), where this analysis is applied to tactical asset allocation for hedge funds.

An example of how the challenges of measuring hedge fund risk can be met by hedge fund investors can be found in the work I have done with Toby Goodworth (Goodworth and Jones, 2004, 2007). In this work, we have sought to avoid distribution-based pitfalls such as under-estimation of tail risk by making the framework non-parametric and forward-looking wherever possible. Furthermore, to avoid the problem of portfolio transparency, we have assumed zero transparency and instead built a factor-based model, which has been enhanced by our qualitative choice of factors based on knowledge of the drivers of hedge fund returns for each strategy. Such a factor-based approach is also useful for hedge fund of funds risk measurement and portfolio construction. The resulting approach was one of the first attempts to extend factor-based analysis of hedge fund returns to form a pragmatic hedge fund risk evaluation framework that, given the non-parametric forward looking nature, should better estimate tail risk.

Other innovations in hedge fund risk management include Riskmetrics' HedgePlatform which gets hedge funds to sign up to give transparency to them on the grounds that the data will only be presented in an amalgamated form. Although useful in solving the problem in hedge fund transparency, the problems of hedge fund complexity and tail mis-estimation are still not dealt with. Also, the choice of hedge funds to invest with is limited to those that have signed up with this effort.

Other academic work on hedge fund risk includes some good general discussions in L'habitant (2005) and Vaissié (2005) along with studies of hedge fund tail risk and tail risk appraisal in Liang and Park (2006) and Giamouridis and Ntoula (2006), a study of the relationship between hedge fund risk and value at risk analysis in Liang, Bali and Gokcan (2006), a study of hedge fund capital adequacy through value at risk analysis in Gupta and Liang (2004) and an analysis of contagion between hedge fund strategies (for which there is good evidence) in Boyson *et al.* (2006).

15.6   OTHER HEDGE FUND WORK

There has been a range of other useful work on hedge funds that doesn't directly fit into any one category above. For example, Agarwal *et al.* (2007) have produced an interesting study of hedge fund terms and performance, Naik *et al.* (2006) and Vaissié (2006) have studied hedge fund capacity constraints with Liang *et al.* (2006) considering the effect of investor flows; Martinelli and Zieman (2005) have developed work on the role of hedge funds in asset liability management and Agarwal, Naik and Naveen (2006) have studied the 'December effect' of outsized hedge fund returns at year end. All in all, the current academic research on hedge funds is broadening in scope, which is brilliant news for hedge fund and fund of funds managers and investors as well.

At the time of writing, the academic study of hedge funds seems to be in the process of grabbing the attention of some heavy hitting academics, on a very broad basis. For example, a search for those that proclaim a research interest in hedge funds at Harvard University results in a show of interest from not only an eminent economist, but also an eminent modern historian.

15.7 SUMMARY

The hedge fund world is in a maturing state where there is now an active body of academic work on the area and such work is being used by practitioners to inspire and develop new approaches. Similarly, practitioner developments continue to feed back to inspire academic work. Looking forward it seems that many generalist financial researchers and economists of high esteem are beginning to tackle problems within the hedge fund world, which can only be beneficial for the area. Furthermore, practitioner/academic collaborations at, e.g London Business School ensure that that future research will remain relevant and useful.

15.8 SUMMARY OF IDEAS FOR CHAPTER 15

- Academic work in hedge funds has evolved to be more widespread, more relevant and more useful for practitioners.
- Areas inspired by academic research include hedge fund replication and hedge fund of funds risk management.
- There is an exciting range of new products and structures driven by both practitioners and academics that will broaden and enhance the way we access hedge funds and hedge fund of funds.

16
Conclusion

It's an oft quoted fact that hedge funds began in 1949, the first one being managed by an economist and journalist called Alfred W. Jones. However, hedge funds before the 1990s were something of a cottage industry and so were the hedge funds of funds that invested in them. Even back in the early 1990s, there was such a high barrier to raising assets and becoming a hedge fund manager that those who managed to do so invariably had amazing skill and edge. That made hedge fund selection a lot more straight forward than it is today. Furthermore, problems associated with hedge funds taking in too much money too quickly, and the detrimental effects on the hedge fund world of vast amounts inflows or outflows in a given strategy were just not issues. Since then there has been a dramatic growth in the sophistication, complexity, number, assets and impact of hedge funds in the world, resulting in a corresponding evolution of hedge funds of funds. Nowadays, hedge funds are viewed more as an asset class than just a bunch of clever investment techniques (although I would suggest that 'asset class' is a misnomer). With such demand has come increased supply, but the growth has resulted in a greater variability in edge, investment skill and returns; there are many 'me too' hedge funds where the existence of edge and experience is highly debateable that manage to raise capital purely on the basis of current hedge fund popularity. This forces hedge fund of funds managers to look a lot harder to find the best.

In the early 1990s, the investor base for hedge fund of funds consisted of smart, wealthy individuals who wanted steady growth for their assets – the rich that wanted to stay rich. They were generally driven to hedge fund of funds following the shock market crash of '87. However, the benefits of this uncorrelated, involatile return stream were also being noted by investment consultants and pension plan managers. Hedge fund returns could be used to lower the risk and downside of pension plan portfolios without sacrificing too much return and as a result the growth of pension plan, endowment and other institutional investment into hedge funds began, once again spurred by tough equity markets, this time the popping of the tech bubble.

Currently, there is very strong asset growth in the hedge fund investment class based on inflows of institutional assets investing in hedge funds of funds. As a result of this growth coupled with the evolution of the hedge fund world and associated techniques, we are seeing a number of distinct progressions in hedge funds of funds:

- *Improved Risk Management*

  The underlying mathematics of risk measurement is developing to allow risk to be more appropriately appraised within hedge funds and hedge funds of funds. Hedge fund returns do not usually follow a normal distribution and implied risk distributions can sometimes take strange shapes that reflect the esoteric nature of instruments traded by some types of hedge fund. Newer mathematical techniques can be used to assess such distributions, especially in the *left hand tail* – the place where extreme loss is reflected. The left hand tail of a distribution measures the propensity for very bad things to happen and improved modelling and estimation of this part of the distribution allows much better analysis and appraisal of worst case events in both operational and portfolio driven instances. As a result, it will be possible to construct hedge fund of funds portfolios with much better estimation and control of downside, albeit at the expense of some upside, should investors wish for such portfolios.

- *Growth Of Niche Hedge Funds Of Funds*

  Those that have already invested in hedge funds have usually done so through multi-strategy hedge funds of funds. Going forward, we are seeing a desire by such investors to augment the returns of their existing hedge fund investment by adding hedge funds of funds with more specific mandates e.g. geographically focussed hedge funds of funds and strategy focussed hedge funds of funds. This is a reaction to the decreasing volatility (and often corresponding returns) from multi-strategy hedge funds of funds and the realisation of investors that they can stomach more volatility from the area than they originally anticipated. This core/satellite approach will lead to growing specialisation in hedge funds of funds and fits well with the bifurcation in the development of this area between mega-sized funds of funds that offer broad exposure to the hedge funds universe and the more targeted, smaller funds of funds.

- *Growth Of Sophisticated And Hybrid Structured Products*

  Hedge funds of funds are being seen less as a mystical source of steady returns and more as alpha-generators that form useful and flexible building blocks in the broader scheme of things. Here I think that we are only at the tip of the iceberg in terms of structured solutions that can be built using hedge funds of funds. Innovative structures have already been built importing beta into hedge funds of funds yielding equity or bond index and hedge fund alpha style returns. Future products will include the mixing and netting of long only and long/short portfolios (why be long in one product and short the same thing in another) and also increase use of hedge fund alpha in liability driven investment structures.

- *Growth In Bespoke Solutions*

  The current structure of pension plans using investment consultants to advise on which product to invest in is now evolving. Increasingly in the hedge fund of funds world, pension plans have the assets to demand a bespoke fit rather than the best available off-the-peg product, resulting in hedge fund of funds managers and consultants working together to gauge what is the ideal portfolio for the pension plan and constructing the resulting perfect fit. If that sounds like hedge fund acting as consultants then equally so, some consultants have began investigating single manager hedge funds (although generally only in the Equity Long/Short area). Going forward, I see hedge funds of funds becoming much more solutions based businesses, working more in partnership with investment consultants.

Above I have sketched out how hedge funds of funds have developed in terms of sophistication and product, in line with the underlying hedge fund world but also with the growth in sophisticated institutional investors in this area. This evolution has much more to offer and the future for hedge funds of funds is set to be an exiting and innovative time.

In this book I have tried to produce an honest, objective and pragmatic introduction to the world of hedge funds of funds. I have tried to 'tell it like it is', even when it hurt. I hope that it has been of some use.

References

Agarwal, V. and Naik, N. (2000a) On Taking the Alternative Route: Risks, Rewards, and Performance Persistence of Hedge Funds. *Journal of Alternative Investments,* **2**(4), 6–23.

Agarwal, V. and Naik, N. (2000b) Generalised Style Analysis of Hedge Funds. *Journal of Asset Management,* **1**(1), 93–109.

Agarwal, V. and Naik, N. (2004) Risks and Portfolio Decisions Involving Hedge Funds. *Review of Financial Studies,* **17**, 63–98.

Agarwal, V., Fung, B., Loon, Y. & Naik, N. (2006) Risk and Return in Convertible Arbitrage: Evidence from the Convertible Bond Market. *EFA 2006 Zurich Meetings.*

Agarwal, V., Naik, N. and Naveen D. (2006) Why is Santa So Kind to Hedge Funds? The December Return Puzzle! *Purdue University,* Working Paper.

Agarwal, V., Daniel, N. and Naik, N. (2007) Role of Managerial Incentives and Discretion in Hedge Fund Performance. *BNP Paribas Hedge Fund Centre Working Paper Series LBS.*

Ammann, M., Kind, A. and Seiz, R. (2006) What Drives the Performance of US Convertible Bond Funds. *University of St. Gallen,* Working Paper.

Amenc, N., El Bied, S. and Martinelli, L. (2003) Predictability in Hedge Fund Returns. *Financial Analysts Journal* Sept/Oct 2003, 32–46.

Amin, G. and Kat, H. (2003) Hedge Fund Performance 1990–2000: Do the Money Machines Really Add Value? *Journal of Financial and Quantitative Analysis,* **38** June, 1–24.

Boyson, N., Stahel, C. and Stulz, R. (2006) Is There Hedge Fund Contagion? *NBER, Working Paper Series* WP 12090.

Brealey, R. and Kaplanis, E. (2001) Changes in the Factor Exposures of Hedge Funds. *BNP Paribas Hedge Fund Centre Working Paper Series, LBS,* Working Paper HF-004.

Brown, S., Goetzmann, W. and Ibbotson, R. (1999) Offshore Hedge Funds: Survival and Performance 1989–1995. *Journal of Business,* **72**, 91–117.

Caglayan, M. and Edwards, F. (2001) Hedge Fund Performance and Manager Skill. *Journal of Futures Markets*, **21**, 1003–28.

Capocci, D. and Hübner, G. (2004) An Analysis of Hedge Fund Performance. *Journal of Empirical Finance*, **11**, 55–89.

Choi, D., Getmansky, M. and Tookes, H. (2006) Convertible Bond Arbitrage, Liquidity Externalities and Stock Prices. *Yale ICF*, Working Paper No. 06–16.

Duarte, J., Longstaff, F. and Yu, F. (2005) Risk and Return in Fixed Income Arbitrage: Nickels in Front of a Steamroller? *Revue of Financial Studies*, **20**(3), 769–811.

Dybvig, P. (1988a) Distributional Analysis of Portfolio Choice. *Journal of Business*, **61**, 369–393.

Dybvig, P. (1988b) Inefficient Dynamic Portfolio Strategies or How to Throw Away a Million Dollars in the Stock Market. *Review of Financial Studies*, **1**, 67–88.

EDHEC (2006) EDHEC Investable Hedge Fund Indices: Construction Methodology & Management Principles. www.edhec-risk.com.

Fung, W. and Hsieh, D. (1997) Empirical Characteristics of Dynamic Trading Strategies: The Case of Hedge Funds. *Review of Financial Studies*, **10**, 275–302.

Fung, W. and Hsieh, D. (1999) Is Mean-Variance Analysis Applicable to Hedge Funds? *Economics Letters*, **62**, 53–8.

Fung, W. and Hsieh, D. (2000) Performance Characteristics of Hedge Funds and Commodity Funds: Natural vs. Spurious Biases. *Journal of Financial and Quantitative Analysis*, **35**(3), 291–307.

Fung, W. and Hsieh, D. (2002) Asset Based Style Factors for Hedge Funds. *Financial Analysts Journal*, **57**, 16–33.

Fung, W. and Hsieh, D. (2004a) Hedge Fund Benchmarks: A Risk Based Approach. *Financial Analyst Journal*, **60**, 65–80.

Fung, W. and Hsieh, D. (2004b) The Risk in Hedge Fund Strategies: Alternative Alphas and Alternative Betas. *BNP Paribas Hedge Fund Centre Working Paper Series, LBS*, Working Paper HF-013.

Fung, W. and Hsieh, D. (2004c) Extracting Portable Alphas from Equity Long/Short Hedge Funds. *Journal of Investment Management*, **2**(4), 1–19.

Fung, W., Hsieh, D., Naik, N. and Ramadorai, T. (2007) Hedge Funds: Performance, Risk and Capital Formation. *BNP Paribas Hedge Fund Centre, Working Paper Series, LBS*.

Géhin, W. and Vaissié, M. (2004) Hedge Fund Indices: Investable, Non-Investable and Strategy Benchmarks. *EDHEC*, Working Paper.

Giamouridis, D. and Ntoula, I. (2006) A Comparison of Alternative Approaches for Determining the Downside Risk of Hedge Fund Strategies. *Cass Business School*, Research Paper.

Goldman Sachs (2004). The "Secret Sauce" of Hedge Fund Investing – Trading Risk Dynamically. *Goldman Sachs Quantitative Insights,* November 2004.

Goodworth, T. and Jones, C. (2004) Building a Risk Measurement Framework for Hedge Funds and Funds of Funds. *Judge Business School, University of Cambridge,* Working Paper WP08/2004.

Goodworth, T. and Jones, C. (2004) Factor-Based, Non-Parametric Risk Measurement Framework for Hedge Funds and Fund-of-Funds. *European Journal of Finance,* forthcoming.

Gupta, A. and Liang, B. (2005) Do Hedge Funds Have Enough Capital? A Value-at-Risk Approach. *Journal of Financial Economics,* **77,** July, 219–53.

Hasanhodzic, J. and Lo, A. (2006) Can Hedge Fund Returns Be Replicated? The Linear Case. *Working Paper MIT Laboratory for Financial Engineering.*

Kat, H. and Palaro, H. (2005) Who Needs Hedge Funds? A Copula-Based Approach to Hedge Fund Return Replication. *Alternative Investment Research Centre, Cass Business School, City University London,* Working Paper No. 27.

Kat, H. and Miffre, J. (2006) The Impact of Non-Normality Risks and Tactical Trading on Hedge Fund Alphas. *Alternative Investment Research Centre, Cass Business School, City University London,* Working Paper 26.

Kat, H. and Palaro, H. (2006a) Replication and Evaluation of Fund of Hedge Funds Returns. *Alternative Investment Research Centre, Cass Business School, City University London,* Working Paper No. 28.

Kat, H. and Palaro, H. (2006b) Superstars or Average Joes? A Replication-Based Performance Evaluation of 1917 Individual Hedge Funds. *Alternative Investment Research Centre, Cass Business School, City University London,* Working Paper No. 30.

Kat, H. and Palaro, H. (2007) Replication-Based Evaluation of Hedge Fund Performance. *Alternative Investment Research Centre, Cass Business School, City University London,* Working Paper No. 40.

Kat, H. (2007) Alternative Routes to Hedge Fund Return Replication: A Note. *Alternative Investment Research Centre, Cass Business School, City University London,* Working Paper No. 37.

L'habitant, F.-S. (2005) The Methods for Analysing the Risks of Hedge Funds and Funds of Hedge Funds. *EDHEC,* Working Paper.

Liang, B. (1999) On the Performance of Hedge Funds. *Financial Analysts Journal,* July–August, 72–84.

Liang, B., Bali, T. and Gokcan, S. (2006) Value at Risk and the Cross-Section of Hedge Fund Returns. *EFA 2005 Moscow Meetings.*

Liang, B., Wermers, R., Ding, B. and Getmansky, M. (2006) Market Volatility, Investor Flows, and the Structure of Hedge Fund Markets. *Isenberg School of Management University of Massachusetts Amherst,* Working Paper.

Liang, B. and Park, H. (2007) Risk Measures for Hedge Funds: A Cross-Sectional Approach. *European Financial Management Journal*, **13**(2), 333–70.

Lo, A. (2001) Risk Management for Hedge funds: Introduction and Overview. *Financial Analysts Journal*, **57**, 16–33.

Loncarski, I., Horst, J. and Veld, C. (2007) The Rise and Demise of the Convertible Arbitrage Strategy. *Tilburg University – Center for Economic Research*, Working Paper.

Malkiel, B. and Saha, A. (2005) Hedge Fund: Risk and Return. *Financial Analysts Journal*, November/December, 80–88.

Martellini, L. and Ziemann, V. (2005) The Benefits of Hedge Funds in Asset-Liability Management. *EDHEC*, Working Paper.

Mitchell, M. and Pulvino, T. (2001) Characteristics of Risk and Return in Risk Arbitrage. *Journal of Finance*, **56**(6), 2135–75.

Naik, N., Ramadorai, T. and Stromqvist, M. (2006) Capacity Constraints and Hedge Fund Strategy Returns. *European Financial Management*, **13**(2), 239–56.

Naik N., Kosowski, R. and Do, T. (2007) Can Hedge Funds Deliver Alpha? A Baysian and Bootstrap Analysis of Hedge Funds. *Journal of Financial Economics*, **84**, 229–64.

Rajan, A., Martin, B., Brown, T. and Johnson, M. (2006) Hedge Funds: A Catalyst Reshaping Global Investment. *KPMG Report*.

Ridley, M. (2006) *How to Invest in Hedge Funds*. Kogan Page, London.

Sharpe, W.F. (1992) Asset Allocation, Management Style and Performance Measurement. *Journal of Portfolio Management*, **18**, 7–19.

Vaissié, M. (2005) Let's Talk Risk. *EDHEC*, Working Paper.

Vaissié, M. (2006) The 'Capacity Effect' Conundrum: Confronting Academic Evidence and Practitioners' Opinions. *EDHEC*, Working Paper.

Glossary

Absolute Return

A fund manager seeks to generate absolute returns if he aims to generate positive returns irrespective of the movements of underlying markets or benchmarks.

Alpha

Return generated through skill rather than just passive market exposure.

Arbitrage

A risk free instantaneous profit from financial markets; nowadays taken to mean a low risk market independent profit.

Beta

The reliance of any return or portfolio on passive underlying market exposure.

Beta Neutral

A portfolio is beta neutral if its long and short positions are matched to leave no residual market exposure.

Capacity

The maximum amount of assets that can be managed in a given hedge fund, as decided by the hedge fund manager. A hedge fund manager may search for *capacity* in a hedge fund when it looks soon to close but they want to get in. A hedge fund that has enough assets under management to close to new investment is said to be at *capacity*.

Closed

A fund that is closed will not take in any new investors or investments.

Convertible Bond

A corporate bond that can be converted into an equity from the same issuer.

Convertible Bond Arbitrage

A hedge fund strategy based on misevaluations and arbitrage opportunities in the convertible bond market.

Credit Derivatives

Options, swaps and other derivatives based on the credit rating of an underlying company or index.

Credit Spreads

The difference in yield between corporate and government bonds.

Crystallised Loss

A loss that cannot be regained from a given position (unlike a mark to market loss).

CTA

A hedge fund that uses systematic trading strategies to trade a broad range of markets (usually based on futures trading).

Delta Hedge

Hedging out the equity exposure of an option using an equity position.

Distressed Investing

A hedge fund strategy based around generating returns from companies that are in a state of stress or default.

Double Alpha

Generating alpha independently from both the long and short portfolios of a hedge fund.

Equity Long/Short

A hedge fund strategy based around buying underpriced stocks and shorting overpriced stocks.

Equity Market Neutral

An equity long/short strategy where long and short positions are matched to eradicate market exposure, either with respect to beta or just invested capital on long and short sides.

Event Driven

A hedge fund strategy based on generating returns from corporate events.

Exchange Traded

Traded on a financial exchange such as a stock exchange as opposed to traded privately.

Fixed Income Arbitrage & Relative Value

A hedge fund strategy that seeks to generate low risk, hedged returns from anomalies in the fixed income markets.

Fundamental Valuation

The value of an equity or bond based on analysis of balance sheet and profitability.

Fund of Hedge Funds

Another name for a hedge fund of funds.

Gate

A gate on a hedge fund limits the amount of withdrawals in any one trading period.

Gamma Trading

The trading involved in delta hedging when the delta moves around and the hedge needs to be rebalanced.

Global Macro

A broad based trading strategy with a broad geographical and asset class remit, usually based on top-down analysis.

Hedge Fund

Funds that are flexible and incentivised enough to generate absolute returns.

Hedge Fund of Funds

A fund that invests solely in a number of hedge funds.

Hedge Fund Manager

An individual or company that manages a hedge fund.

Hedge Fund Strategy

A given methodology applied to given markets that describes the approach of a hedge fund, e.g. an equity long/short hedge fund seeks to invest in equity markets with both long and short positions.

Hurdle Rate

A pre-agreed level over which a performance fee is charged, e.g. 5% performance fee over a LIBOR hurdle means that performance fee will only be charged on performance over LIBOR.

Long-Biased

A portfolio is long-biased if its exposure to long positions has a tendency to be greater than its exposure to short positions.

Long-Only Fund

A fund that only holds long positions (as opposed to long and short).

Long

A position in a portfolio that has been bought and is being held, e.g. long 1 equity in ABC means the portfolio holds an equity in company ABC.

Management Fee

A fixed percentage of assets that is paid to a fund for management of assets.

Mandate

A set of rules governing or restricting the management of assets issued to a fund and its manager by investors.

Mark to Market Loss

A temporary loss based on short term adverse valuation; such a position has potential to become profitable again, unlike one with a crystallised loss.

Market Independent

Hedge fund strategies with returns that are notably unlinked with underlying equity and bond markets.

Multi-strategy Hedge Fund

A hedge fund that utilises a range of hedge fund strategies.

Negative Exposure

Having a position in a market that moves in the opposite direction to that market.

Net Long

A portfolio is net long if it has a greater percentage of long positions than short positions within it.

Net Short

A portfolio is net short if it has a greater percentage of short positions than long positions within it.

Neutral

Having no exposure to a given market (usually whilst holding positions in that market that are hedged or offset).

Operational Due Diligence

Analysis and assessment of internal or third party processes, people and systems.

Operational Risk

The risk of loss resulting from inadequate or failed internal or third party processes, people and systems.

OTC

Stands for 'over the counter'. Traded directly with a counterparty rather than through an exchange.

Performance Fee

A fixed percentage of positive returns that is paid to a fund for management of assets.

Portfolio Efficiency

The amount of return generated given the risk that is taken, e.g. portfolio efficiency is improved if more return is generated for the risk taken or, conversely, if risk is lowered whilst maintaining return.

Positive Exposure

Having a position in a market that moves in line with that market.

Prime Broker

The main broker for a hedge fund.

Relative Value

A hedge fund approach based on exploiting a temporary differential in price between similar securities by taking a long position in one and a short in the other.

Risk Adjusted Returns

Returns generated scaled (divided) by the risk taken to generate them.

Short Position

Holding a position in a security that moves in the opposite direction to that security, i.e. a position that has been borrowed and sold in the market so that when the security falls, the short position rises and vice versa.

Side Letter

Agreements with particular investors that soften the investment terms in the fund prospectus in some way, e.g. offering better liquidity.

Spread

The difference in price between two similar securities; usually the potential profit to be made in an arbitrage or relative value trade.

Statistical Arbitrage

A form of equity market neutral investing that seeks to capture small and short term moves in stocks.

Third Party

In the contents of hedge funds, this term usually refers to a provider of services to the hedge fund (of funds) and/or hedge fund manager such as broker, lawyer, administrator and auditor.

Traditional Fund

Another name for a long-only fund.

VaR

The VaR (Value at Risk) for a portfolio is the percentage return that one would expect to perform better than with a given probability over a given time period. For example, a 95% 1-day VaR of -3.5% means that there is a 95% chance that the portfolio will generate a one-day return of greater than -3.5%.

Index

Note: Page references in *italics* refer to Figures; numbers in **bold** refer to end of chapter and Glossary definitions

Index compiled by Annette Musker